THE SAVOY OPERAS

VOLUME ONE

ST MARTIN'S LIBRARY

THE SAVOY OPERAS

BEING THE COMPLETE TEXT OF THE
GILBERT AND SULLIVAN OPERAS
AS ORIGINALLY PRODUCED IN THE
YEARS 1875–1896

BY

SIR W. S. GILBERT

VOLUME ONE

THE MIKADO
H.M.S. PINAFORE
THE GONDOLIERS
PATIENCE
PRINCESS IDA
THE GRAND DUKE

LONDON
MACMILLAN & CO LTD
1957

MACMILLAN AND COMPANY LIMITED
London Bombay Calcutta Madras Melbourne

THE MACMILLAN COMPANY OF CANADA LIMITED
Toronto

ST MARTIN'S PRESS INC
New York

*First published 1926
First issued in St Martin's Library 1957*

PRINTED IN GREAT BRITAIN

CONTENTS

VOLUME ONE

THE MIKADO

OR

THE TOWN OF TITIPU

DRAMATIS PERSONÆ

THE MIKADO OF JAPAN

NANKI-POO (*his Son, disguised as a wandering minstrel, and in love with* YUM-YUM)

KO-KO (*Lord High Executioner of Titipu*)

POOH-BAH (*Lord High Everything Else*)

PISH-TUSH (*a Noble Lord*)

YUM-YUM ⎫
PITTI-SING ⎬ *Three Sisters — Wards of* KO-KO
PEEP-BO ⎭

KATISHA (*an elderly Lady, in love with* NANKI-POO)

Chorus of School-girls, Nobles, Guards, and Coolies.

———————

ACT I. — Courtyard of Ko-Ko's Official Residence.

ACT II. — Ko-Ko's Garden.

First produced at the Savoy Theatre on March 14, 1885.

THE MIKADO

OR

THE TOWN OF TITIPU

ACT I

SCENE. — *Courtyard of* KO-KO's *Palace in Titipu. Japanese nobles discovered standing and sitting in attitudes suggested by native drawings.*

CHORUS OF NOBLES.

If you want to know who we are,
　　We are gentlemen of Japan:
On many a vase and jar —
　　On many a screen and fan,
　　　We figure in lively paint:
　　　Our attitude's queer and quaint —
　　　You're wrong if you think it ain't, oh!

If you think we are worked by strings,
　　Like a Japanese marionette,
You don't understand these things:
　　It is simply Court etiquette.
　　　Perhaps you suppose this throng
　　　Can't keep it up all day long?
　　　If that's your idea, you're wrong, oh!

Enter NANKI-POO *in great excitement. He carries a native guitar on his back and a bundle of ballads in his hand.*

RECIT. — NANKI-POO.

Gentlemen, I pray you tell me
Where a gentle maiden dwelleth,

3

Named Yum-Yum, the ward of Ko-Ko ?
In pity speak — oh, speak, I pray you !

A Noble. Why, who are you who ask this question ?
Nank.   Come gather round me, and I'll tell you.

SONG AND CHORUS — Nanki-Poo.

A wandering minstrel I —
　　A thing of shreds and patches,
　　Of ballads, songs and snatches,
And dreamy lullaby !

My catalogue is long,
　　Through every passion ranging,
　　And to your humours changing
I tune my supple song !

　　　Are you in sentimental mood ?
　　　　I'll sigh with you,
　　　　　Oh, sorrow, sorrow !
　　　On maiden's coldness do you brood ?
　　　　I'll do so, too —
　　　　　Oh, sorrow, sorrow !
　　　I'll charm your willing ears
　　　With songs of lovers' fears,
　　　While sympathetic tears
　　　　My cheeks bedew —
　　　　　Oh, sorrow, sorrow !

But if patriotic sentiment is wanted,
　I've patriotic ballads cut and dried ;
For where'er our country's banner may be planted,
　All other local banners are defied !
Our warriors, in serried ranks assembled,
　Never quail — or they conceal it if they do —
And I shouldn't be surprised if nations trembled
　Before the mighty troops of Titipu !

CHORUS. We shouldn't be surprised, etc.

NANK. And if you call for a song of the sea,
     We'll heave the capstan round,
    With a yeo heave ho, for the wind is free,
    Her anchor's a-trip and her helm's a-lee,
     Hurrah for the homeward bound !

CHORUS.   Yeo-ho — heave-ho —
     Hurrah for the homeward bound !

    To lay aloft in a howling breeze
     May tickle a landsman's taste,
    But the happiest hour a sailor sees
     Is when he's down
     At an inland town,
    With his Nancy on his knees, yeo-ho !
    And his arm around her waist !

CHORUS.   Then man the capstan — off we go,
     As the fiddler swings us round,
    With a yeo heave ho,
    And a rumbelow,
     Hurrah for the homeward bound !

    A wandering minstrel I, etc.

Enter PISH-TUSH.

PISH. And what may be your business with Yum-Yum ?

NANK. I'll tell you. A year ago I was a member of the Titipu town band. It was my duty to take the cap round for contributions. While discharging this delicate office, I saw Yum-Yum. We loved each other at once, but she was betrothed to her guardian Ko-Ko, a cheap tailor, and I saw that my suit was hopeless. Overwhelmed with despair, I quitted the town. Judge of my delight when I heard, a month ago, that Ko-Ko had been condemned to death for flirting ! I hurried back at once, in the hope of finding Yum-Yum at liberty to listen to my protestations.

PISH. It is true that Ko-Ko was condemned to death for flirting, but he was reprieved at the last moment, and raised to the exalted rank of Lord High Executioner under the following remarkable circumstances :

SONG — PISH-TUSH *and* CHORUS.

Our great Mikado, virtuous man,
When he to rule our land began,
     Resolved to try
     A plan whereby
Young men might best be steadied.
So he decreed, in words succinct,
That all who flirted, leered or winked
(Unless connubially linked),
     Should forthwith be beheaded.

     And I expect you'll all agree
     That he was right to so decree.
          And I am right,
          And you are right,
     And all is right as right can be !

CHORUS.   And you are right,
            And we are right, etc.

This stern decree, you'll understand,
Caused great dismay throughout the land !
     For young and old
     And shy and bold
Were equally affected.
The youth who winked a roving eye,
Or breathed a non-connubial sigh,
Was thereupon condemned to die —
     He usually objected.

     And you'll allow, as I expect,
     That he was right to so object.

And I am right,
And you are right,
And everything is quite correct !

CHORUS.   And you are right,
And we are right, etc.

And so we straight let out on bail
A convict from the county jail,
Whose head was next
On some pretext
Condemnĕd to be mown off,
And made *him* Headsman, for we said,
'Who's next to be decapited
Cannot cut off another's head
Until he's cut his own off.'

And we are right, I think you'll say,
To argue in this kind of way;
And I am right,
And you are right,
And all is right — too-looral-lay !

CHORUS.   And you are right,
And we are right, etc.

[*Exeunt* CHORUS.

Enter POOH-BAH.

NANK. Ko-Ko, the cheap tailor, Lord High Executioner of Titipu ! Why, that's the highest rank a citizen can attain !

POOH. It is. Our logical Mikado, seeing no moral difference between the dignified judge who condemns a criminal to die, and the industrious mechanic who carries out the sentence, has rolled the two offices into one, and every judge is now his own executioner.

NANK. But how good of you (for I see that you are a nobleman of the highest rank) to condescend to tell all this to me, a mere strolling minstrel !

POOH. Don't mention it. I am, in point of fact, a particularly haughty and exclusive person, of pre-Adamite ancestral descent.

You will understand this when I tell you that I can trace my ancestry back to a protoplasmal primordial atomic globule. Consequently, my family pride is something inconceivable. I can't help it. I was born sneering. But I struggle hard to overcome this defect. I mortify my pride continually. When all the great officers of State resigned in a body, because they were too proud to serve under an ex-tailor, did I not unhesitatingly accept all their posts at once?

PISH. And the salaries attached to them? You did.

POOH. It is consequently my degrading duty to serve this upstart as First Lord of the Treasury, Lord Chief Justice, Commander-in-Chief, Lord High Admiral, Master of the Buckhounds, Groom of the Back Stairs, Archbishop of Titipu, and Lord Mayor, both acting and elect, all rolled into one. And at a salary! A Pooh-Bah paid for his services! I a salaried minion! But I do it! It revolts me, but I do it!

NANK. And it does you credit.

POOH. But I don't stop at that. I go and dine with middle-class people on reasonable terms. I dance at cheap suburban parties for a moderate fee. I accept refreshment at any hands, however lowly. I also retail State secrets at a very low figure. For instance, any further information about Yum-Yum would come under the head of a State secret. (NANKI-POO *takes the hint, and gives him money.*) (*Aside.*) Another insult, and, I think, a light one!

SONG — POOH-BAH *with* NANKI-POO *and* PISH-TUSH.

Young man, despair,
    Likewise go to,
Yum-Yum the fair
    You must not woo.
    It will not do:
    I'm sorry for you,
You very imperfect ablutioner!
    This very day
    From school Yum-Yum
Will wend her way,
    And homeward come,
    With beat of drum
    And a rum-tum-tum,

> To wed the Lord High Executioner !
> And the brass will crash,
>> And the trumpets bray,
> And they'll cut a dash
>> On their wedding day.
> She'll toddle away, as all aver,
> With the Lord High Executioner !

NANK. *and* POOH. And the brass will crash, etc.

> It's a hopeless case,
>> As you may see,
> And in your place
>> Away I'd flee;
> But don't blame me —
>> I'm sorry to be
> Of your pleasure a diminutioner.
>> They'll vow their pact
>> Extremely soon,
>> In point of fact
>> This afternoon.
>> Her honeymoon
>> With that buffoon
> At seven commences, so *you* shun her !

ALL.   And the brass will crash, etc.

                      [*Exit* PISH-TUSH.

     RECIT. — NANKI-POO *and* POOH-BAH.

NANK.   And I have journeyed for a month, or nearly,
            To learn that Yum-Yum, whom I love so dearly,
            This day to Ko-Ko is to be united !
POOH.   The fact appears to be as you've recited:
            But here he comes, equipped as suits his station;
            He'll give you any further information.

                 [*Exeunt* POOH-BAH *and* NANKI-POO.

     Enter CHORUS OF NOBLES.

Behold the Lord High Executioner !
　A personage of noble rank and title —
A dignified and potent officer,
　Whose functions are particularly vital !
　　Defer, defer,
　To the Lord High Executioner !

Enter Ko-Ko *attended.*

SOLO — Ko-Ko.

Taken from the county jail
　By a set of curious chances;
Liberated then on bail,
　On my own recognizances;
Wafted by a favouring gale
　As one sometimes is in trances,
To a height that few can scale,
　Save by long and weary dances;
Surely, never had a male
　Under such-like circumstances
So adventurous a tale,
　Which may rank with most romances.

CHORUS. 　　　　　　Defer, defer,
　　　　　To the Lord High Executioner, etc.

Ko. Gentlemen, I'm much touched by this reception. I can only trust that by strict attention to duty I shall ensure a continuance of those favours which it will ever be my study to deserve. If I should ever be called upon to act professionally, I am happy to think that there will be no difficulty in finding plenty of people whose loss will be a distinct gain to society at large.

SONG — Ko-Ko *with* Chorus of Men.

As some day it may happen that a victim must be found,
　I've got a little list — I've got a little list

Of society offenders who might well be underground,
   And who never would be missed — who never would be missed!
There's the pestilential nuisances who write for autographs —
All people who have flabby hands and irritating laughs —
All children who are up in dates, and floor you with 'em flat —
All persons who in shaking hands, shake hands with you like
   that —
And all third persons who on spoiling *tête-à-têtes* insist —
   They'd none of 'em be missed — they'd none of 'em be missed !

CHORUS. He's got 'em on the list — he's got 'em on the list;
             And they'll none of 'em be missed — they'll none of
             'em be missed.

There's the banjo serenader, and the others of his race,
   And the piano-organist — I've got him on the list !
And the people who eat peppermint and puff it in your face,
   They never would be missed — they never would be missed !
Then the idiot who praises, with enthusiastic tone,
All centuries but this, and every country but his own;
And the lady from the provinces, who dresses like a guy,
And who 'doesn't think she waltzes, but would rather like to try';
And that singular anomaly, the lady novelist —
   I don't think she'd be missed — I'm *sure* she'd not be missed !

CHORUS. He's got her on the list — he's got her on the list;
             And I don't think she'll be missed — I'm *sure* she'll not
             be missed !

And that *Nisi Prius* nuisance, who just now is rather rife,
   The Judicial humorist — I've got *him* on the list !
All funny fellows, comic men, and clowns of private life —
   They'd none of 'em be missed — they'd none of 'em be missed.
And apologetic statesmen of a compromising kind,
Such as — What d'ye call him — Thing'em-bob, and likewise —
   Never-mind,
And 'St — 'st — 'st — and What's-his-name, and also You-know-
   who —
The task of filling up the blanks I'd rather leave to *you*.

But it really doesn't matter whom you put upon the list,
  For they'd none of 'em be missed — they'd none of 'em be missed !

CHORUS. You may put 'em on the list — you may put 'em on the list;
        And they'll none of 'em be missed — they'll none of 'em be missed !

Enter POOH-BAH.

KO. Pooh-Bah, it seems that the festivities in connection with my approaching marriage must last a week. I should like to do it handsomely, and I want to consult you as to the amount I ought to spend upon them.

POOH. Certainly. In which of my capacities ? As First Lord of the Treasury, Lord Chamberlain, Attorney-General, Chancellor of the Exchequer, Privy Purse, or Private Secretary ?

KO. Suppose we say as Private Secretary.

POOH. Speaking as your Private Secretary, I should say that, as the city will have to pay for it, don't stint yourself, do it well.

KO. Exactly — as the city will have to pay for it. That is your advice.

POOH. As Private Secretary. Of course you will understand that, as Chancellor of the Exchequer, I am bound to see that due economy is observed.

KO. Oh ! But you said just now 'Don't stint yourself, do it well'.

POOH. As Private Secretary.

KO. And now you say that due economy must be observed.

POOH. As Chancellor of the Exchequer.

KO. I see. Come over here, where the Chancellor can't hear us. (*They cross the stage.*) Now, as my Solicitor, how do you advise me to deal with this difficulty ?

POOH. Oh, as your Solicitor, I should have no hesitation in saying 'Chance it——'

KO. Thank you. (*Shaking his hand.*) I will.

POOH. If it were not that, as Lord Chief Justice, I am bound to see that the law isn't violated.

KO. I see. Come over here where the Chief Justice can't hear us (*They cross the stage.*) Now, then, as First Lord of the Treasury ?

Pooh. Of course, as First Lord of the Treasury, I could propose a special vote that would cover all expenses, if it were not that, as Leader of the Opposition, it would be my duty to resist it, tooth and nail. Or, as Paymaster-General, I could so cook the accounts that, as Lord High Auditor, I should never discover the fraud. But then, as Archbishop of Titipu, it would be my duty to denounce my dishonesty and give myself into my own custody as First Commissioner of Police.

Ko. That's extremely awkward.

Pooh. I don't say that all these distinguished people couldn't be squared; but it is right to tell you that they wouldn't be sufficiently degraded in their own estimation unless they were insulted with a very considerable bribe.

Ko. The matter shall have my careful consideration. But my bride and her sisters approach, and any little compliment on your part, such as an abject grovel in a characteristic Japanese attitude, would be esteemed a favour.

[*Exeunt together.*

Enter procession of Yum-Yum's *schoolfellows, heralding* Yum-Yum, Peep-Bo, *and* Pitti-Sing.

CHORUS OF GIRLS.

Comes a train of little ladies
    From scholastic trammels free,
Each a little bit afraid is,
    Wondering what the world can be !

Is it but a world of trouble —
    Sadness set to song ?
Is its beauty but a bubble
    Bound to break ere long ?

Are its palaces and pleasures
    Fantasies that fade ?
And the glory of its treasures
    Shadow of a shade ?

Schoolgirls we, eighteen and under,
From scholastic trammels free,
And we wonder — how we wonder ! —
What on earth the world can be !

TRIO.

YUM-YUM, PEEP-BO, *and* PITTI-SING, *with* CHORUS OF GIRLS.

THE THREE.	Three little maids from school are we,
	Pert as a school-girl well can be,
	Filled to the brim with girlish glee,
	Three little maids from school !
YUM-YUM.	Everything is a source of fun. (*Chuckle.*)
PEEP-BO.	Nobody's safe, for we care for none ! (*Chuckle.*)
PITTI-SING.	Life is a joke that's just begun ! (*Chuckle.*)
THE THREE.	Three little maids from school !
ALL (*dancing*).	Three little maids who, all unwary,
	Come from a ladies' seminary,
	Freed from its genius tutelary —
THE THREE (*suddenly demure*).	Three little maids from school !

YUM-YUM.	One little maid is a bride, Yum-Yum —
PEEP-BO.	Two little maids in attendance come —
PITTI-SING.	Three little maids is the total sum.
THE THREE.	Three little maids from school !
YUM-YUM.	From three little maids take one away.
PEEP-BO.	Two little maids remain, and they —
PITTI-SING.	Won't have to wait very long, they say —
THE THREE.	Three little maids from school !
ALL (*dancing*).	Three little maids who, all unwary,
	Come from a ladies' seminary,
	Freed from its genius tutelary —
THE THREE (*suddenly demure*).	Three little maids from school !

Enter KO-KO *and* POOH-BAH.

KO. At last, my bride that is to be ! (*About to embrace her.*)
YUM. You're not going to kiss me before all these people ?

KO. Well, that was the idea.

YUM (*aside to* PEEP-BO). It seems odd, doesn't it ?

PEEP. It's rather peculiar.

PITTI. Oh, I expect it's all right. Must have a beginning, you know.

YUM. Well, of course I know nothing about these things; but I've no objection if it's usual.

KO. Oh, it's quite usual, I think. Eh, Lord Chamberlain ? (*Appealing to* POOH-BAH.)

POOH. I have known it done. (KO-KO *embraces her.*)

YUM. Thank goodness that's over ! (*Sees* NANKI-POO, *and rushes to him.*) Why, that's never you ? (*The Three Girls rush to him and shake his hands, all speaking at once.*)

    YUM. Oh, I'm so glad ! I haven't seen you for ever so long, and I'm right at the top of the school, and I've got three prizes, and I've come home for good, and I'm not going back any more !

    PEEP. And have you got an engagement ? — Yum-Yum's got one, but she doesn't like it, and she'd ever so much rather it was you ! I've come home for good, and I'm not going back any more !

    PITTI. Now tell us all the news, because you go about everywhere, and we've been at school, but, thank goodness, that's all over now, and we've come home for good, and we're not going back any more !

(*These three speeches are spoken together in one breath.*)

KO. I beg your pardon. Will you present me ?

YUM.   ⎧ Oh, this is the musician who used —

PEEP.   ⎨ Oh, this is the gentleman who used —

PITTI. ⎩ Oh, it is only Nanki-Poo who used —

KO. One at a time, if you please.

YUM. Oh, if you please he's the gentleman who used to play so beautifully on the — on the——

PITTI. On the Marine Parade.

YUM. Yes, I think that was the name of the instrument.

NANK. Sir, I have the misfortune to love your ward, Yum-Yum — oh, I know I deserve your anger !

KO. Anger ! not a bit, my boy. Why, I love her myself. Charming little girl, isn't she ? Pretty eyes, nice hair. Taking little thing, altogether. Very glad to hear my opinion backed by a competent authority. Thank you very much. Good-bye. (*To* Pish-Tush.) Take him away. (Pish-Tush *removes him*.)

Pitti (*who has been examining* Pooh-Bah). I beg your pardon, but what is this ? Customer come to try on ?

Ko. That is a Tremendous Swell.

Pitti. Oh, it's alive. (*She starts back in alarm*.)

Pooh. Go away, little girls. Can't talk to little girls like you. Go away, there's dears.

Ko. Allow me to present you, Pooh-Bah. These are my three wards. The one in the middle is my bride elect.

Pooh. What do you want me to do to them ? Mind, I *will not* kiss them.

Ko. No, no, you shan't kiss them; a little bow — a mere nothing — you needn't mean it, you know.

Pooh. It goes against the grain. They are not young ladies, they are young persons.

Ko. Come, come, make an effort, there's a good nobleman.

Pooh. (*aside to* Ko-Ko). Well, I shan't mean it. (*With a great effort*.) How de do, little girls, how de do ? (*Aside*.) Oh, my protoplasmal ancestor !

Ko. That's very good. (*Girls indulge in suppressed laughter*.)

Pooh. I see nothing to laugh at. It is very painful to me to have to say 'How de do, little girls, how de do ?' to young persons. I'm not in the habit of saying 'How de do, little girls, how de do ?' to anybody under the rank of a Stockbroker.

Ko. (*aside to girls*). Don't laugh at him, he can't help it — he's under treatment for it. (*Aside to* Pooh-Bah.) Never mind them, they don't understand the delicacy of your position.

Pooh. We know how delicate it is, don't we ?

Ko. I should think we did ! How a nobleman of your importance can do it at all is a thing I never can, never shall understand.

[Ko-Ko *retires up and goes off*.

QUARTET and Chorus of Girls.

Yum-Yum, Peep-Bo, Pitti-Sing, *and* Pooh-Bah.

Yum., Peep. So please you, sir, we much regret
and Pitti.   If we have failed in etiquette

| | Towards a man of rank so high — |
| | We shall know better by and by. |

YUM. But youth, of course, must have its fling,
So pardon us,
So pardon us,

PITTI. And don't, in girlhood's happy spring,
Be hard on us,
Be hard on us,
If we're inclined to dance and sing.
Tra la la, etc. (*Dancing.*)

CHORUS OF GIRLS. But youth, of course, etc.

POOH. I think you ought to recollect
You cannot show too much respect
Towards the highly titled few;
But nobody does, and why should you?
That youth at us should have its fling,
Is hard on us,
Is hard on us;
To our prerogative we cling —
So pardon us,
So pardon us,
If we decline to dance and sing.
Tra la la, etc. (*Dancing.*)

CHORUS OF GIRLS. But youth, of course, must have its fling, etc.

[*Exeunt all but* YUM-YUM.

Enter NANKI-POO.

NANK. Yum-Yum, at last we are alone! I have sought you night and day for three weeks, in the belief that your guardian was beheaded, and I find that you are about to be married to him this afternoon!

YUM. Alas, yes!

NANK. But you do not love him?

YUM. Alas, no!

NANK. Modified rapture! But why do you not refuse him?

YUM. What good would that do? He's my guardian, and he wouldn't let me marry you!

NANK. But I would wait until you were of age !

YUM. You forget that in Japan girls do not arrive at years of discretion until they are fifty.

NANK. True; from seventeen to forty-nine are considered years of indiscretion.

YUM. Besides — a wandering minstrel, who plays a wind instrument outside tea-houses, is hardly a fitting husband for the ward of a Lord High Executioner.

NANK. But—— (*Aside.*) Shall I tell her ? Yes ! She will not betray me ! (*Aloud.*) What if it should prove that, after all, I am no musician ?

YUM. There ! I was certain of it, directly I heard you play !

NANK. What if it should prove that I am no other than the son of his Majesty the Mikado ?

YUM. The son of the Mikado ! But why is your Highness disguised ? And what has your Highness done ? And will your Highness promise never to do it again ?

NANK. Some years ago I had the misfortune to captivate Katisha, an elderly lady of my father's Court. She misconstrued my customary affability into expressions of affection, and claimed me in marriage, under my father's law. My father, the Lucius Junius Brutus of his race, ordered me to marry her within a week, or perish ignominiously on the scaffold. That night I fled his Court, and, assuming the disguise of a Second Trombone, I joined the band in which you found me when I had the happiness of seeing you ! (*Approaching her.*)

YUM (*retreating*). If you please, I think your Highness had better not come too near. The laws against flirting are excessively severe.

NANK. But we are quite alone, and nobody can see us.

YUM. Still, that doesn't make it right. To flirt is capital.

NANK. It *is* capital !

YUM. And we must obey the law.

NANK. Deuce take the law !

YUM. I wish it would, but it won't !

NANK. If it were not for that, how happy we might be !

YUM. Happy indeed !

NANK. If it were not for the law, we should now be sitting side by side, like that. (*Sits by her.*)

YUM. Instead of being obliged to sit half a mile off, like that. (*Crosses and sits at other side of stage.*)

NANK. We should be gazing into each other's eyes, like that. (*Gazing at her sentimentally.*)

YUM. Breathing sighs of unutterable love — like that. (*Sighing and gazing lovingly at him.*)

NANK. With our arms round each other's waists, like that. (*Embracing her.*)

YUM. Yes, if it wasn't for the law.

NANK. If it wasn't for the law.

YUM. As it is, of course we couldn't do anything of the kind.

NANK. Not for worlds !

YUM. Being engaged to Ko-Ko, you know !

NANK. Being engaged to Ko-Ko !

DUET — YUM-YUM *and* NANKI-POO.

NANK.
Were you not to Ko-Ko plighted,
    I would say in tender tone,
'Loved one, let us be united —
    Let us be each other's own !'
I would merge all rank and station,
    Worldly sneers are nought to us,
And, to mark my admiration,
    I would kiss you fondly thus — (*Kisses her.*)

BOTH.
$\left.{I \atop He}\right\}$ would kiss $\left\{{you \atop me}\right\}$ fondly thus —   (*Kiss.*)

YUM.
But as I'm engaged to Ko-Ko,
    To embrace you thus, *con fuoco*,
Would distinctly be no *giuoco*,
    And for yam I should get toko —

BOTH.
    Toko, toko, toko, toko !

NANK.
So, in spite of all temptation,
    Such a theme I'll not discuss,
And on no consideration
    Will I kiss you fondly thus —   (*Kissing her.*)
Let me make it clear to you,
This is what I'll never do !
    This, oh, this, oh, this, oh, this — (*Kissing her.*)

TOGETHER.   This, oh, this, etc.

[*Exeunt in opposite directions.*

Enter KO-KO.

KO. (*looking after* YUM-YUM). There she goes ! To think how entirely my future happiness is wrapped up in that little parcel ! Really, it hardly seems worth while ! Oh, matrimony ! — (*Enter* POOH-BAH *and* PISH-TUSH.) Now then, what is it ? Can't you see I'm soliloquizing ? You have interrupted an apostrophe, sir !

PISH. I am the bearer of a letter from his Majesty the Mikado.

KO. (*taking it from him reverentially*.) A letter from the Mikado ! What in the world can he have to say to me ? (*Reads letter.*) Ah, here it is at last ! I thought it would come sooner or later ! The Mikado is struck by the fact that no executions have taken place in Titipu for a year, and decrees that unless somebody is beheaded within one month the post of Lord High Executioner shall be abolished, and the city reduced to the rank of a village !

PISH. But that will involve us all in irretrievable ruin !

KO. Yes. There is no help for it, I shall have to execute somebody at once. The only question is, who shall it be ?

POOH. Well, it seems unkind to say so, but as you're already under sentence of death for flirting, everything seems to point to *you*.

KO. To me ? What are you talking about ? I can't execute myself.

POOH. Why not ?

KO. Why not ? Because, in the first place, self-decapitation is an extremely difficult, not to say dangerous, thing to attempt; and, in the second, it's suicide, and suicide is a capital offence.

POOH. That is so, no doubt.

PISH. We might reserve that point.

POOH. True, it could be argued six months hence, before the full Court.

KO. Besides, I don't see how a man *can* cut off his own head.

POOH. A man might try.

PISH. Even if you only succeeded in cutting it half off, that would be something.

POOH. It would be taken as an earnest of your desire to comply with the Imperial will.

Ko. No. Pardon me, but there I am adamant. As official Heads-man, my reputation is at stake, and I can't consent to embark on a professional operation unless I see my way to a successful result.

Pooh. This professional conscientiousness is highly creditable to *you*, but it places us in a very awkward position.

Ko. My good sir, the awkwardness of your position is grace itself compared with that of a man engaged in the act of cutting off his own head.

Pish. I am afraid that, unless you can obtain a substitute——

Ko. A substitute? Oh, certainly — nothing easier. (*To* Pooh-Bah.) Pooh-Bah, I appoint you Lord High Substitute.

Pooh. I should be delighted. Such an appointment would realize my fondest dreams. But no, at any sacrifice, I must set bounds to my insatiable ambition !

TRIO.

Ko-Ko.	Pooh-Bah.	Pish-Tush.
My brain it teems	I am so proud,	I heard one day
With endless schemes	If I allowed	A gentleman say
Both good and new	My family pride	That criminals who
For Titipu;	To be my guide,	Are cut in two
But if I flit,	I'd volunteer	Can hardly feel
The benefit	To quit this sphere	The fatal steel,
That I'd diffuse	Instead of you,	And so are slain
The town would lose!	In a minute or two.	Without much pain.
Now every man	But family pride	If this is true,
To aid his clan	Must be denied,	It's jolly for you;
Should plot and plan	And set aside,	Your courage screw
As best he can,	And mortified.	To bid us adieu,
And so,	And so,	And go
Although	Although	And show
I'm ready to go,	I wish to go,	Both friend and foe
Yet recollect	And greatly pine	How much you dare.
'Twere disrespect	To brightly shine,	I'm quite aware
Did I neglect	And take the line	It's your affair,
To thus effect	Of a hero fine,	Yet I declare
This aim direct,	With grief condign	I'd take your share,
So I object —	I must decline —	But I don't much care —
So I object —	I must decline —	I don't much care —
So I object —	I must decline —	I don't much care —

ALL. To sit in solemn silence in a dull, dark dock,
        In a pestilential prison, with a life-long lock,
        Awaiting the sensation of a short, sharp shock,
        From a cheap and chippy chopper on a big black block !

[*Exeunt* Pooh. *and* Pish.

Ko. This is simply appalling! I, who allowed myself to be respited at the last moment, simply in order to benefit my native town, am now required to die within a month, and that by a man whom I have loaded with honours! Is this public gratitude? Is this—— (*Enter* NANKI-POO, *with a rope in his hands.*) Go away, sir! How dare you? Am I never to be permitted to soliloquize?

NANK. Oh, go on — don't mind me.

Ko. What are you going to do with that rope?

NANK. I am about to terminate an unendurable existence.

Ko. Terminate your existence? Oh, nonsense! What for?

NANK. Because you are going to marry the girl I adore.

Ko. Nonsense, sir. I won't permit it. I am a humane man, and if you attempt anything of the kind I shall order your instant arrest. Come, sir, desist at once, or I summon my guard.

NANK. That's absurd. If you attempt to raise an alarm, I instantly perform the Happy Despatch with this dagger.

Ko. No, no, don't do that. This is horrible! (*Suddenly.*) Why, you cold-blooded scoundrel, are you aware that, in taking your life, you are committing a crime which — which — which is—— Oh! (*Struck by an idea.*) Substitute!

NANK. What's the matter?

Ko. Is it *absolutely certain* that you are resolved to die?

NANK. Absolutely!

Ko. Will *nothing* shake your resolution?

NANK. Nothing.

Ko. Threats, entreaties, prayers — all useless?

NANK. All! My mind is made up.

Ko. Then, if you really mean what you say, and if you are absolutely resolved to die, and if nothing whatever will shake your determination — don't spoil yourself by committing suicide, but be beheaded handsomely at the hands of the Public Executioner!

NANK. I don't see how that would benefit me.

Ko. You don't? Observe: you'll have a month to live, and you'll live like a fighting-cock at my expense. When the day comes there'll be a grand public ceremonial — you'll be the central figure — no one will attempt to deprive you of that distinction. There'll be a procession — bands — dead march — bells tolling — all the girls in tears — Yum-Yum distracted — then, when it's all over, general rejoicings, and a display of fireworks in the evening. *You* won't see them, but they'll be there all the same.

NANK. Do you think Yum-Yum would really be distracted at my death ?

KO. I am convinced of it. Bless you, she's the most tender-hearted little creature alive.

NANK. I should be sorry to cause her pain. Perhaps, after all, if I were to withdraw from Japan, and travel in Europe for a couple of years, I might contrive to forget her.

KO. Oh, I don't think you could forget Yum-Yum so easily ; and, after all, what is more miserable than a love-blighted life ?

NANK. True.

KO. Life without Yum-Yum — why, it seems absurd !

NANK. And yet there are a good many people in the world who have to endure it.

KO. Poor devils, yes ! You are quite right not to be of their number.

NANK. (*suddenly*). I *won't* be of their number !

KO. Noble fellow !

NANK. I'll tell you how we'll manage it. Let me marry Yum-Yum to-morrow, and in a month you may behead me.

KO. No, no. I draw the line at Yum-Yum.

NANK. Very good. If you can draw the line, so can I. (*Preparing rope.*)

KO. Stop, stop — listen one moment — be reasonable. How can I consent to your marrying Yum-Yum if I'm going to marry her myself ?

NANK. My good friend, she'll be a widow in a month, and you can marry her then.

KO. That's true, of course. I quite see that. But, dear me ! my position during the next month will be most unpleasant — most unpleasant.

NANK. Not half so unpleasant as my position at the end of it.

KO. But — dear me ! — well — I agree — after all, it's only putting off my wedding for a month. But you won't prejudice her against me, will you ? You see, I've educated her to be my wife ; she's been taught to regard me as a wise and good man. Now I shouldn't like her views on that point disturbed.

NANK. Trust me, she shall never learn the truth from me.

FINALE.

Enter CHORUS, POOH-BAH, *and* PISH-TUSH.

CHORUS.

With aspect stern
    And gloomy stride,
We come to learn
    How you decide.

Don't hesitate
    Your choice to name,
A dreadful fate
    You'll suffer all the same.

POOH. To ask you what you mean to do we punctually appear.
KO.   Congratulate me, gentlemen, I've found a Volunteer !
ALL.   The Japanese equivalent for Hear, Hear, Hear !
KO. (*presenting him*).   'Tis Nanki-Poo !
ALL.   Hail, Nanki-Poo !
KO.   I think he'll do ?
ALL.   Yes, yes, he'll do !

KO.   He yields his life if I'll Yum-Yum surrender.
        Now I adore that girl with passion tender,
        And could not yield her with a ready will,
            Or her allot,
            If I did not
        Adore myself with passion tenderer still !

Enter YUM-YUM, PEEP-BO, *and* PITTI-SING.

ALL.   Ah, yes !
    He loves himself with passion tenderer still !
KO. (*to* NANKI-POO). Take her — she's yours !

                            [*Exit* KO-KO.

ENSEMBLE.

NANKI-POO.   The threatened cloud has passed away,
YUM-YUM.   And brightly shines the dawning day;
NANKI-POO.   What though the night may come too soon,
YUM-YUM.   There's yet a month of afternoon !

NANKI-POO, POOH-BAH, YUM-YUM, PITTI-SING, *and* PEEP-BO.

> Then let the throng
> Our joy advance,
> With laughing song
> And merry dance,

CHORUS.	With joyous shout and ringing cheer,
	Inaugurate our brief career !
PITTI-SING.	A day, a week, a month, a year——
YUM.	Or far or near, or far or near,
POOH.	Life's eventime comes much too soon,
PITTI-SING.	You'll live at least a honeymoon !
ALL.	Then let the throng, etc.
CHORUS.	With joyous shout, etc.

SOLO — POOH-BAH.

> As in a month you've got to die,
> If Ko-Ko tells us true,
> 'Twere empty compliment to cry
> 'Long life to Nanki-Poo !'
> But as one month you have to live
> As fellow-citizen,
> This toast with three times three we'll give —
> 'Long life to you — till then !'

[*Exit* POOH-BAH.

CHORUS.	May all good fortune prosper you,
	May you have health and riches too,
	May you succeed in all you do !
	Long life to you — till then !

(*Dance.*)

Enter KATISHA *melodramatically.*

KAT.	Your revels cease ! Assist me, all of you !
CHORUS.	Why, who is this whose evil eyes
	Rain blight on our festivities ?
KAT.	I claim my perjured lover, Nanki-Poo !
	Oh, fool ! to shun delights that never cloy !
CHORUS.	Go, leave thy deadly work undone !
KAT.	Come back, oh, shallow fool ! come back to joy !

CHORUS. Away, away ! ill-favoured one !
NANK. (*aside to* YUM-YUM). Ah !
          'Tis Katisha !
          The maid of whom I told you.   (*About to go.*)
KAT. (*detaining him*). No !
          You shall not go,
          These arms shall thus enfold you !

SONG — KATISHA.

KAT. (*addressing* NANKI-POO).
          Oh fool, that fleest
            My hallowed joys !
          Oh blind, that seest
            No equipoise !
          Oh rash, that judgest
            From half, the whole !
          Oh base, that grudgest
            Love's lightest dole !
               Thy heart unbind,
               Oh fool, oh blind !
               Give me my place,
               Oh rash, oh base !

CHORUS.   If she's thy bride, restore her place,
              Oh fool, oh blind, oh rash, oh base !

KAT. (*addressing* YUM-YUM).
          Pink cheek, that rulest
            Where wisdom serves !
          Bright eye, that foolest
            Heroic nerves !
          Rose lip, that scornest
            Lore-laden years !
          Smooth tongue, that warnest
            Who rightly hears !
               Thy doom is nigh,
               Pink cheek, bright eye !
               Thy knell is rung,
               Rose lip, smooth tongue !

CHORUS.   If true her tale, thy knell is rung,
      Pink cheek, bright eye, rose lip, smooth tongue !

PITTI-SING. Away, nor prosecute your quest —
      From our intention, well expressed,
        You cannot turn us !
      The state of your connubial views
      Towards the person you accuse
        Does not concern us !
      For he's going to marry Yum-Yum —
ALL.   Yum-Yum !
PITTI.   Your anger pray bury,
       For all will be merry,
      I think you had better succumb —
ALL.   Cumb — cumb !
PITTI.   And join our expressions of glee.
      On this subject I pray you be dumb —
ALL.   Dumb — dumb.
PITTI.   You'll find there are many
       Who'll wed for a penny —
      The word for your guidance is 'Mum' —
ALL.   Mum — mum !
PITTI.   There's lots of good fish in the sea !
ALL.   On this subject we pray you be dumb, etc.

SOLO — KATISHA.

The hour of gladness
  Is dead and gone;
In silent sadness
  I live alone !
The hope I cherished
  All lifeless lies,
And all has perished
  Save love, which never dies !
Oh, faithless one, this insult you shall rue !
In vain for mercy on your knees you'll sue.
  I'll tear the mask from your disguising !

B

NANK. (*aside*).   Now comes the blow !
KAT.   Prepare yourselves for news surprising !
NANK. (*aside*).   How foil my foe ?
KAT.   No minstrel he, despite bravado !
YUM. (*aside, struck by an idea*). Ha ! ha ! I know !
KAT.   He is the son of your——

> (NANKI-POO, YUM-YUM, *and* CHORUS, *interrupting*, *sing Japanese words, to drown her voice.*)

                    O ni ! bikkuri shakkuri to !
KAT.   In vain you interrupt with this tornado !
            He is the only son of your——
ALL.   O ni ! bikkuri shakkuri to !
KAT.   I'll spoil——
ALL.   O ni ! bikkuri shakkuri to !
KAT.   Your gay gambado !
            He is the son ——
ALL.   O ni ! bikkuri shakkuri to !
KAT.   Of your——
ALL.   O ni ! bikkuri shakkuri to !
KAT.   The son of your——
ALL.   O ni ! bikkuri shakkuri to ! oya ! oya !

ENSEMBLE.

KATISHA.	THE OTHERS.
Ye torrents roar !	We'll hear no more,
Ye tempests howl !	Ill-omened owl,
Your wrath outpour	To joy we soar,
With angry growl !	Despite your scowl !
Do ye your worst, my vengeance call	The echoes of our festival
Shall rise triumphant over all !	Shall rise triumphant over all !
Prepare for woe,	Away you go,
Ye haughty lords,	Collect your hordes;
At once I go	Proclaim your woe
Mikado-wards,	In dismal chords;
My wrongs with vengeance shall be crowned !	We do not heed their dismal sound,
My wrongs with vengeance shall be crowned !	For joy reigns everywhere around.

(KATISHA *rushes furiously up stage, clearing the crowd away right and left, finishing on steps at the back of stage.*)

END OF ACT I.

ACT II

SCENE. — KO-KO's *Garden.*

YUM-YUM *discovered seated at her bridal toilet, surrounded by maidens, who are dressing her hair and painting her face and lips, as she judges of the effect in a mirror.*

SOLO — PITTI-SING *and* CHORUS OF GIRLS.

CHORUS.
Braid the raven hair —
   Weave the supple tress —
Deck the maiden fair
   In her loveliness —
Paint the pretty face —
   Dye the coral lip —
Emphasize the grace
   Of her ladyship !
Art and nature, thus allied,
Go to make a pretty bride.

SOLO — PITTI-SING.

Sit with downcast eye —
   Let it brim with dew —
Try if you can cry —
   We will do so, too.
When you're summoned, start
   Like a frightened roe —
Flutter, little heart,
   Colour, come and go !
Modesty at marriage-tide
Well becomes a pretty bride !

29

CHORUS.

Braid the raven hair, etc.

[*Exeunt* PITTI-SING, PEEP-BO, *and* CHORUS.

YUM. Yes, I am indeed beautiful ! Sometimes I sit and wonder, in my artless Japanese way, why it is that I am so much more attractive than anybody else in the whole world. Can this be vanity ? No ! Nature is lovely and rejoices in her loveliness. I am a child of Nature, and take after my mother.

SONG — YUM-YUM.

The sun, whose rays
Are all ablaze
   With ever-living glory,
Does not deny
His majesty —
   He scorns to tell a story !
He don't exclaim,
   'I blush for shame,
   So kindly be indulgent.'
But, fierce and bold,
In fiery gold,
   He glories all effulgent !

   I mean to rule the earth,
     As he the sky —
   We really know our worth,
     The sun and I !

Observe his flame,
That placid dame,
   The moon's Celestial Highness ;
There's not a trace
Upon her face
   Of diffidence or shyness :
She borrows light
That, through the night,

Mankind may all acclaim her !
And, truth to tell,
She lights up well,
So I, for one, don't blame her !

Ah, pray make no mistake,
We are not shy ;
We're very wide awake,
The moon and I !

Enter PITTI-SING *and* PEEP-BO.

YUM. Yes, everything seems to smile upon me. I am to be married to-day to the man I love best, and I believe I am the very happiest girl in Japan !

PEEP. The happiest girl indeed, for she is indeed to be envied who has attained happiness in all but perfection.

YUM. In 'all but' perfection ?

PEEP. Well, dear, it can't be denied that the fact that your husband is to be beheaded in a month is, in its way, a drawback. It does seem to take the top off it, you know.

PITTI. I don't know about that. It all depends !

PEEP. At all events, *he* will find it a drawback.

PITTI. Not necessarily. Bless you, it all depends !

YUM. (*in tears*). I think it very indelicate of you to refer to such a subject on such a day. If my married happiness *is* to be — to be——

PEEP. Cut short.

YUM. Well, cut short — in a month, can't you let me forget it ? (*Weeping.*)

Enter NANKI-POO, *followed by* PISH-TUSH.

NANK. Yum-Yum in tears — and on her wedding morn !

YUM. (*sobbing*). They've been reminding me that in a month you're to be beheaded ! (*Bursts into tears.*)

PITTI. Yes, we've been reminding her that you're to be beheaded. (*Bursts into tears.*)

PEEP. It's quite true, you know, you *are* to be beheaded ! (*Bursts into tears.*)

NANK. (*aside*). Humph ! Now, some bridegrooms would be

depressed by this sort of thing ! (*Aloud.*) A month ? Well, what's a month ? Bah ! These divisions of time are purely arbitrary. Who says twenty-four hours make a day ?

PITTI. There's a popular impression to that effect.

NANK. Then we'll efface it. We'll call each second a minute — each minute an hour — each hour a day — and each day a year. At that rate we've about thirty years of married happiness before us !

PEEP. And, at that rate, this interview has already lasted four hours and three-quarters !

[*Exit* PEEP-BO.

YUM. (*still sobbing*). Yes. How time flies when one is thoroughly enjoying oneself !

NANK. That's the way to look at it ! Don't let's be downhearted ! There's a silver lining to every cloud.

YUM. Certainly. Let's — let's be perfectly happy ! (*Almost in tears.*)

PISH. By all means. Let's — let's thoroughly enjoy ourselves.

PITTI. It's — it's absurd to cry ! (*Trying to force a laugh.*)

YUM. Quite ridiculous ! (*Trying to laugh.*)

(*All break into a forced and melancholy laugh.*)

MADRIGAL.

YUM-YUM, PITTI-SING, NANKI-POO, *and* PISH-TUSH.

> Brightly dawns our wedding day;
> > Joyous hour, we give thee greeting !
> > Whither, whither art thou fleeting ?
> Fickle moment, prithee stay !
> > What though mortal joys be hollow ?
> > Pleasures come, if sorrows follow :
> Though the tocsin sound, ere long,
> > Ding dong ! Ding dong !
> Yet until the shadows fall
> Over one and over all,
> Sing a merry madrigal —
> > > A madrigal !
>
> Fal-la — fal-la ! etc. (*Ending in tears.*)

Let us dry the ready tear,
　　Though the hours are surely creeping
　　Little need for woeful weeping,
Till the sad sundown is near.
　　All must sip the cup of sorrow —
　　I to-day and thou to-morrow;
This the close of every song —
　　Ding dong ! Ding dong !
What, though solemn shadows fall,
Sooner, later, over all ?
Sing a merry madrigal —
　　　　　A madrigal !

Fal-la — fal-la ! etc. (*Ending in tears.*)

[*Exeunt* PITTI-SING *and* PISH-TUSH.

(NANKI-POO *embraces* YUM-YUM. *Enter* KO-KO. NANKI-
POO *releases* YUM-YUM.)

KO. Go on — don't mind me.

NANK. I'm afraid we're distressing you.

KO. Never mind, I must get used to it. Only please do it by degrees.
Begin by putting your arm round her waist. (NANKI-POO *does so.*)
There; let me get used to that first.

YUM. Oh, wouldn't you like to retire ? It must pain you to see
us so affectionate together !

KO. No, I must learn to bear it ! Now oblige me by allowing her
head to rest on your shoulder.

NANK. Like that ? (*He does so.* KO-KO *much affected.*)

KO. I am much obliged to you. Now — kiss her ! (*He does so.*
KO-KO *writhes with anguish.*) Thank you — it's simple torture !

YUM. Come, come, bear up. After all, it's only for a month.

KO. No. It's no use deluding oneself with false hopes.

NANK. ⎱
YUM. ⎰ What do you mean ?

KO. (*to* YUM-YUM). My child — my poor child ! (*Aside.*) How
shall I break it to her ? (*Aloud.*) My little bride that was to have
been——

YUM. (*delighted*). *Was* to have been ?

Ko. Yes, you never can be mine !

Nank. } *(in ecstasy).* { What !
Yum. } { I'm so glad !

Ko. I've just ascertained that, by the Mikado's law, when a married man is beheaded his wife is buried alive.

Nank. } Buried alive !
Yum. }

Ko. Buried alive. It's a most unpleasant death.

Nank. But whom did you get that from ?

Ko. Oh, from Pooh-Bah. He's my Solicitor.

Yum. But he may be mistaken !

Ko. So I thought; so I consulted the Attorney-General, the Lord Chief Justice, the Master of the Rolls, the Judge Ordinary, and the Lord Chancellor. They're all of the same opinion. Never knew such unanimity on a point of law in my life !

Nank. But stop a bit ! This law has never been put in force.

Ko. Not yet. You see, flirting is the only crime punishable with decapitation, and married men never flirt.

Nank. Of course they don't. I quite forgot that ! Well, I suppose I may take it that my dream of happiness is at an end !

Yum. Darling — I don't want to appear selfish, and I love you with all my heart — I don't suppose I shall ever love anybody else half as much — but when I agreed to marry you — my own — I had no idea — pet — that I should have to be buried alive in a month !

Nank. Nor I ! It's the very first I've heard of it !

Yum. It — it makes a difference, doesn't it ?

Nank. It *does* make a difference, of course.

Yum. You see — burial alive — it's such a stuffy death !

Nank. I call it a beast of a death.

Yum. You see my difficulty, don't you ?

Nank. Yes, and I see my own. If I insist on your carrying out your promise, I doom you to a hideous death; if I release you, you marry Ko-Ko at once !

TRIO. — Yum-Yum, Nanki-Poo, *and* Ko-Ko.

Yum.   Here's a how-de-do !
                         If I marry you,

When your time has come to perish,
Then the maiden whom you cherish
          Must be slaughtered, too !
          Here's a how-de-do !

NANK.   Here's a pretty mess !
          In a month, or less,
I must die without a wedding !
Let the bitter tears I'm shedding
          Witness my distress,
          Here's a pretty mess !

KO.   Here's a state of things !
          To her life she clings !
Matrimonial devotion
Doesn't seem to suit her notion —
          Burial it brings !
          Here's a state of things !

ENSEMBLE.

YUM-YUM *and* NANKI-POO.
With a passion that's intense
  I worship and adore,
But the laws of common sense
  We oughtn't to ignore
If what he says is true,
  'Tis death to marry you!
Here's a pretty state of things !
Here's a pretty how-de-do!

KO-KO.
With a passion that's intense
  You worship and adore,
But the laws of common sense
  You oughtn't to ignore.
If what I say is true,
  'Tis death to marry you!
Here's a pretty state of things!
Here's a pretty how-de-do!

[*Exit* YUM-YUM.

KO. (*going up to* NANKI-POO). My poor boy, I'm really very sorry for you.

NANK. Thanks, old fellow. I'm sure you are.

KO. You see I'm quite helpless.

NANK. I quite see that.

KO. I can't conceive anything more distressing than to have one's marriage broken off at the last moment. But you shan't be disappointed of a wedding — you shall come to mine.

NANK. It's awfully kind of you, but that's impossible.

KO. Why so ?

NANK. To-day I die.

Ko. What do you mean ?

NANK. I can't live without Yum-Yum. This afternoon I perform the Happy Despatch.

Ko. No, no — pardon me — I can't allow that.

NANK. Why not ?

Ko. Why, hang it all, you're under contract to die by the hand of the Public Executioner in a month's time ! If you kill yourself, what's to become of me ? Why, I shall have to be executed in your place !

NANK. It would certainly seem so !

Enter POOH-BAH.

Ko. Now then, Lord Mayor, what is it ?

POOH. The Mikado and his suite are approaching the city, and will be here in ten minutes.

Ko. The Mikado ! He's coming to see whether his orders have been carried out ! (*To* NANKI-POO.) Now look here, you know — this is getting serious — a bargain's a bargain, and you really mustn't frustrate the ends of justice by committing suicide. As a man of honour and a gentleman, you are bound to die ignominiously by the hands of the Public Executioner.

NANK. Very well, then — behead me.

Ko. What, now ?

NANK. Certainly; at once.

POOH. Chop it off ! Chop it off !

Ko. My good sir, I don't go about prepared to execute gentlemen at a moment's notice. Why, I never even killed a blue-bottle !

POOH. Still, as Lord High Executioner——

Ko. My good sir, as Lord High Executioner, I've got to behead him in a month. I'm not ready yet. I don't know how it's done. I'm going to take lessons. I mean to begin with a guinea pig, and work my way through the animal kingdom till I come to a Second Trombone. Why, you don't suppose that, as a humane man, I'd have accepted the post of Lord High Executioner if I hadn't thought the duties were purely nominal ? I *can't* kill you — I can't kill anything ! I can't kill anybody ! (*Weeps.*)

NANK. Come, my poor fellow, we all have unpleasant duties to discharge at times; after all, what is it ? If I don't mind, why should you ? Remember, sooner or later it must be done.

Ko. (*springing up suddenly*). *Must it ?* I'm not so sure about that !

NANK. What do you mean ?

Ko. Why should I kill you when making an affidavit that you've been executed will do just as well ? Here are plenty of witnesses — the Lord Chief Justice, Lord High Admiral, Commander-in-Chief, Secretary of State for the Home Department, First Lord of the Treasury, and Chief Commissioner of Police.

NANK. But where are they ?

Ko. There they are. They'll all swear to it — won't you ? (*To* POOH-BAH.)

POOH. Am I to understand that all of us high Officers of State are required to perjure ourselves to ensure your safety ?

Ko. Why not ? You'll be grossly insulted, as usual.

POOH. Will the insult be cash down, or at a date ?

Ko. It will be a ready-money transaction.

POOH. (*Aside.*) Well, it will be a useful discipline. (*Aloud.*) Very good. Choose your fiction, and I'll endorse it ! (*Aside.*) Ha ! ha ! Family Pride, how do you like *that*, my buck ?

NANK. But I tell you that life without Yum-Yum——

Ko. Oh, Yum-Yum, Yum-Yum ! Bother Yum-Yum ! Here, Commissionaire (*to* POOH-BAH), go and fetch Yum-Yum. (*Exit* POOH-BAH.) Take Yum-Yum and marry Yum-Yum, only go away and never come back again. (*Enter* POOH-BAH *with* YUM-YUM.) Here she is. Yum-Yum, are you particularly busy ?

YUM. Not particularly.

Ko. You've five minutes to spare ?

YUM. Yes.

Ko. Then go along with his Grace the Archbishop of Titipu; he'll marry you at once.

YUM. But if I'm to be buried alive ?

Ko. Now, don't ask any questions, but do as I tell you, and Nanki-Poo will explain all.

NANK. But one moment——

Ko. Not for worlds. Here comes the Mikado, no doubt to ascertain whether I've obeyed his decree, and if he finds you alive I shall have the greatest difficulty in persuading him that I've be-headed you. (*Exeunt* NANKI-POO *and* YUM-YUM, *followed by* POOH-BAH.) Close thing that, for here he comes !

[*Exit* KO-KO.

March. — Enter procession, heralding MIKADO, *with* KATISHA.

Entrance of MIKADO *and* KATISHA.
('*March of the Mikado's troops.*')

CHORUS.
Miya sama, miya sama,
On n'm-ma no mayé ni
Pira-Pira suru no wa
Nan gia na
Toko tonyaré tonyaré na ?

DUET — MIKADO *and* KATISHA.

MIK.
From every kind of man
Obedience I expect ;
I'm the Emperor of Japan —

KAT.
And I'm his daughter-in-law elect !
He'll marry his son
(He's only got one)
To his daughter-in-law elect !

MIK.
My morals have been declared
Particularly correct ;

KAT.
But they're nothing at all, compared
With those of his daughter-in-law elect !
Bow — Bow —
To his daughter-in-law elect !

ALL.
Bow — Bow —
To his daughter-in-law elect.

MIK.
In a fatherly kind of way
I govern each tribe and sect,
All cheerfully own my sway —

KAT.
Except his daughter-in-law elect !
As tough as a bone,
With a will of her own,
Is his daughter-in-law elect !

MIK.   My nature is love and light —
                     My freedom from all defect —

KAT.   Is insignificant quite,
                     Compared with his daughter-in-law elect !
                         Bow — Bow —
                     To his daughter-in-law elect !

ALL.   Bow — Bow —
                       To his daughter-in-law elect !

SONG — MIKADO *and* CHORUS.

A more humane Mikado never
    Did in Japan exist,
       To nobody second,
       I'm certainly reckoned
    A true philanthropist.
It is my very humane endeavour
    To make, to some extent,
       Each evil liver
       A running river
Of harmless merriment.

       My object all sublime
       I shall achieve in time —
To let the punishment fit the crime —
       The punishment fit the crime;
    And make each prisoner pent
    Unwillingly represent
A source of innocent merriment !
    Of innocent merriment !

All prosy dull society sinners,
    Who chatter and bleat and bore,
       Are sent to hear sermons
       From mystical Germans
Who preach from ten till four.
The amateur tenor, whose vocal villainies

All desire to shirk,
   Shall, during off-hours,
   Exhibit his powers
To Madame Tussaud's waxwork.

The lady who dyes a chemical yellow
   Or stains her grey hair puce,
     Or pinches her figger,
     Is painted with vigour
And permanent walnut juice.
The idiot who, in railway carriages,
   Scribbles on window-panes,
     We only suffer
     To ride on a buffer
In Parliamentary trains.

       My object all sublime, etc.

CHORUS.   His object all sublime, etc.

The advertising quack who wearies
   With tales of countless cures,
     His teeth, I've enacted,
     Shall all be extracted
By terrified amateurs.
The music-hall singer attends a series
   Of masses and fugues and 'ops'
     By Bach, interwoven
     With Spohr and Beethoven,
At classical Monday Pops.

The billiard sharp whom any one catches,
   His doom's extremely hard —
     He's made to dwell —
     In a dungeon cell
On a spot that's always barred.
And there he plays extravagant matches

> In fitless finger-stalls
> On a cloth untrue,
> With a twisted cue
> And elliptical billiard balls !

> My object all sublime, etc.

CHORUS.   His object all sublime, etc.

Enter POOH-BAH, KO-KO, *and* PITTI-SING. *All kneel.*

(POOH-BAH *hands a paper to* KO-KO.)

KO. I am honoured in being permitted to welcome your Majesty. I guess the object of your Majesty's visit — your wishes have been attended to. The execution has taken place.

MIK. Oh, you've had an execution, have you ?

KO. Yes. The Coroner has just handed me his certificate.

POOH. I am the Coroner. (KO-KO *hands certificate to* MIKADO.)

MIK. And this is the certificate of his death. (*Reads.*) 'At Titipu, in the presence of the Lord Chancellor, Lord Chief Justice, Attorney-General, Secretary of State for the Home Department, Lord Mayor, and Groom of the Second Floor Front——'

POOH. They were all present, your Majesty. I counted them myself.

MIK. Very good house. I wish I'd been in time for the performance.

KO. A tough fellow he was, too — a man of gigantic strength. His struggles were terrific. It was really a remarkable scene.

MIK. Describe it.

TRIO AND CHORUS.

KO-KO, PITTI-SING, POOH-BAH *and* CHORUS.

KO.   The criminal cried, as he dropped him down,
> In a state of wild alarm —
> With a frightful, frantic, fearful frown,
> I bared my big right arm.

I seized him by his little pig-tail,
    And on his knees fell he,
        As he squirmed and struggled,
        And gurgled and guggled,
    I drew my snickersnee !
        Oh, never shall I
        Forget the cry,
    Or the shriek that shriekèd he,
        As I gnashed my teeth,
        When from its sheath
    I drew my snickersnee !

CHORUS.

        We know him well,
        He cannot tell
    Untrue or groundless tales —
        He always tries
        To utter lies,
    And every time he fails.

PITTI. He shivered and shook as he gave the sign
        For the stroke he didn't deserve;
    When all of a sudden his eye met mine,
        And it seemed to brace his nerve;
    For he nodded his head and kissed his hand,
        And he whistled an air, did he,
            As the sabre true
            Cut cleanly through
        His cervical vertebræ !
            When a man's afraid,
            A beautiful maid
        Is a cheering sight to see;
            And it's oh, I'm glad
            That moment sad
        Was soothed by sight of me !

CHORUS.

        Her terrible tale
        You can't assail,

With truth it quite agrees:
  Her taste exact
  For faultless fact
Amounts to a disease.

POOH.   Now though you'd have said that head was dead
      (For its owner dead was he),
    It stood on its neck, with a smile well-bred,
      And bowed three times to me !
    It was none of your impudent off-hand nods,
      But as humble as could be;
        For it clearly knew
        The deference due
      To a man of pedigree !
        And it's oh, I vow,
        This deathly bow
      Was a touching sight to see;
        Though trunkless, yet
        It couldn't forget
      The deference due to me !

CHORUS.
  This haughty youth,
  He speaks the truth
Whenever he finds it pays :
    And in this case
    It all took place
Exactly as he says !   [*Exeunt* CHORUS.

MIK. All this is very interesting, and I should like to have seen it. But we came about a totally different matter. A year ago my son, the heir to the throne of Japan, bolted from our Imperial Court.

KO. Indeed ! Had he any reason to be dissatisfied with his position !

KAT. None whatever. On the contrary, I was going to marry him — yet he fled !

POOH. I am surprised that he should have fled from one so lovely !

KAT. That's not true.

POOH. No !

KAT. You hold that I am not beautiful because my face is plain. But you know nothing; you are still unenlightened. Learn, then, that it is not in the face alone that beauty is to be sought. My face is unattractive !

POOH. It is.

KAT. But I have a left shoulder-blade that is a miracle of loveliness. People come miles to see it. My right elbow has a fascination that few can resist.

POOH. Allow me !

KAT. It is on view Tuesdays and Fridays, on presentation of visiting card. As for my circulation, it is the largest in the world.

KO. And yet he fled !

MIK. And is now masquerading in this town, disguised as a Second Trombone.

KO. ⎱
POOH. ⎬ A Second Trombone !
PITTI. ⎰

MIK. Yes; would it be troubling you too much if I asked you to produce him ? He goes by the name of——

KAT. Nanki-Poo.

MIK. Nanki-Poo.

KO. It's quite easy. That is, it's rather difficult. In point of fact, he's gone abroad !

MIK. Gone abroad ! His address.

KO. Knightsbridge !

KAT. (*who is reading certificate of death*). Ha !

MIK. What's the matter ?

KAT. See here — his name — Nanki-Poo — beheaded this morning. Oh, where shall I find another ? Where shall I find another ?

(KO-KO, POOH-BAH *and* PITTI-SING *fall on their knees.*)

MIK. (*looking at paper*). Dear, dear, dear ! this is very tiresome. (*To* KO-KO.) My poor fellow, in your anxiety to carry out my wishes you have beheaded the heir to the throne of Japan !

KO. I beg to offer an unqualified apology.

POOH. I desire to associate myself with that expression of regret.

PITTI. We really hadn't the least notion——

MIK. Of course you hadn't. How could you? Come, come, my good fellow, don't distress yourself — it was no fault of yours. If a man of exalted rank chooses to disguise himself as a Second Trombone, he must take the consequences. It really distresses me to see you take on so. I've no doubt he thoroughly deserved all he got. (*They rise.*)

KO. We are infinitely obliged to your Majesty——

PITTI. Much obliged, your Majesty.

POOH. Very much obliged, your Majesty.

MIK. Obliged? not a bit. Don't mention it. How *could* you tell?

POOH. No, of course we couldn't tell who the gentleman really was.

PITTI. It wasn't written on his forehead, you know.

KO. It might have been on his pocket-handkerchief, but Japanese don't use pocket-handkerchiefs! Ha! ha! ha!

MIK. Ha! ha! ha! (*To* KATISHA.) I forget the punishment for compassing the death of the Heir Apparent.

KO. ⎫
POOH. ⎬ Punishment. (*They drop down on their knees again.*)
PITTI. ⎭

MIK. Yes. Something lingering, with boiling oil in it, I fancy. Something of that sort. I think boiling oil occurs in it, but I'm not sure. I know it's something humorous, but lingering, with either boiling oil or melted lead. Come, come, don't fret — I'm not a bit angry.

KO. (*in abject terror*). If your Majesty will accept our assurance, we had no idea——

MIK. Of course——

PITTI. I knew nothing about it.

POOH. I wasn't there.

MIK. That's the pathetic part of it. Unfortunately, the fool of an Act says 'compassing the death of the Heir Apparent.' There's not a word about a mistake——

KO., PITTI., *and* POOH. No!

MIK. Or not knowing——

KO. No!

MIK. Or having no notion——

PITTI. No!

MIK. Or not being there——

POOH. No!

MIK. There should be, of course——

KO., PITTI., *and* POOH. Yes !

MIK. But there isn't.

KO., PITTI., *and* POOH. Oh !

MIK. That's the slovenly way in which these Acts are always drawn. However, cheer up, it'll be all right. I'll have it altered next session. Now, let's see about your execution — will after luncheon suit you ? Can you wait till then ?

KO., PITTI., *and* POOH. Oh, yes — we can wait till then !

MIK. Then we'll make it after luncheon.

POOH. I don't want any lunch.

MIK. I'm really very sorry for you all, but it's an unjust world, and virtue is triumphant only in theatrical performances.

GLEE.

PITTI-SING, KATISHA, KO-KO, POOH-BAH, *and* MIKADO.

MIK.   See how the Fates their gifts allot,
          For A is happy — B is not.
          Yet B is worthy, I dare say,
          Of more prosperity than A !

KO., POOH., *and* PITTI. *Is* B more worthy ?

KAT.   I should say
          He's worth a great deal more than A.

ENSEMBLE.   Yet A is happy !
              Oh, so happy !
              Laughing, Ha ! ha !
              Chaffing, Ha ! ha !
              Nectar quaffing, Ha ! ha ! ha !
              Ever joyous, ever gay,
              Happy, undeserving A !

KO., POOH., *and* PITTI.
          If I were Fortune — which I'm not —
          B should enjoy A's happy lot,
          And A should die in miserie —
          That is, assuming I am B.

MIK. *and* KAT. But *should* A perish ?

KO., POOH., *and* PITTI.   That should he
          (Of course, assuming I am B).

B should be happy !
Oh, so happy !
Laughing, Ha ! ha !
Chaffing, Ha ! ha !
Nectar quaffing, Ha ! ha ! ha !
But condemned to die is he,
Wretched meritorious B !

[*Exeunt* MIKADO *and* KATISHA.

Ko. Well, a nice mess you've got us into, with your nodding head and the deference due to a man of pedigree !

Pooh. Merely corroborative detail, intended to give artistic verisimilitude to an otherwise bald and unconvincing narrative.

Pitti. Corroborative detail indeed ! Corroborative fiddlestick !

Ko. And you're just as bad as he is with your cock-and-a-bull stories about catching his eye and his whistling an air. But that's so like you ! You must put in your oar !

Pooh. But how about your big right arm ?

Pitti. Yes, and your snickersnee !

Ko. Well, well, never mind that now. There's only one thing to be done. Nanki-Poo hasn't started yet — he must come to life again at once. (*Enter* NANKI-POO *and* YUM-YUM *prepared for journey.*) Here he comes. Here, Nanki-Poo, I've good news for you — you're reprieved.

Nank. Oh, but it's too late. I'm a dead man, and I'm off for my honeymoon.

Ko. Nonsense ! A terrible thing has just happened. It seems you're the son of the Mikado.

Nank. Yes, but that happened some time ago.

Ko. Is this a time for airy persiflage ? Your father is here, and with Katisha !

Nank. My father ! And with Katisha !

Ko. Yes, he wants you particularly.

Pooh. So does she.

Yum. Oh, but he's married now.

Ko. But, bless my heart ! what has that to do with it ?

Nank. Katisha claims me in marriage, but I can't marry her because I'm married already — consequently she will insist on my execution, and if I'm executed, my wife will have to be buried alive.

Yum. You see our difficulty.

Ko. Yes. I don't know what's to be done.

Nank. There's one chance for you. If you could persuade Katisha to marry you, she would have no further claim on me, and in that case I could come to life without any fear of being put to death.

Ko. I marry Katisha!

Yum. I really think it's the only course.

Ko. But, my good girl, have you seen her? She's something appalling!

Pitti. Ah! that's only her face. She has a left elbow which people come miles to see!

Pooh. I am told that her right heel is much admired by connoisseurs.

Ko. My good sir, I decline to pin my heart upon any lady's right heel.

Nank. It comes to this: While Katisha is single, I prefer to be a disembodied spirit. When Katisha is married, existence will be as welcome as the flowers in spring.

DUET — Nanki-Poo *and* Ko-Ko.

(*With* Yum-Yum, Pitti-Sing, *and* Pooh-Bah.)

Nank.   The flowers that bloom in the spring,
                  Tra la,
        Breathe promise of merry sunshine —
      As we merrily dance and we sing,
                  Tra la,
      We welcome the hope that they bring,
                  Tra la,
        Of a summer of roses and wine.
          And that's what we mean when we say that a thing
        Is welcome as flowers that bloom in the spring.
                Tra la la la la la la, etc.

All.   Tra la la la la, etc.

Ko.   The flowers that bloom in the spring,
                  Tra la,

Have nothing to do with the case.
I've got to take under my wing,
> Tra la,
A most unattractive old thing,
> Tra la,
With a caricature of a face,
> And that's what I mean when I say, or I sing,
> 'Oh, bother the flowers that bloom in the spring.'
>   Tra la la la la la, etc.

ALL. Tra la la la, Tra la la la, etc.

[*Dance and exeunt* NANKI-POO, YUM-YUM, POOH-BAH, PITTI-SING, *and* KO-KO.

Enter KATISHA.

RECITATIVE AND SONG. — KATISHA.

Alone, and yet alive ! Oh, sepulchre !
My soul is still my body's prisoner !
Remote the peace that Death alone can give —
My doom, to wait ! my punishment, to live !

SONG.

Hearts do not break !
They sting and ache
For old love's sake,
> But do not die,
Though with each breath
They long for death
As witnesseth
> The living I !
>   Oh, living I !
>   Come, tell me why,
>   When hope is gone,
>   Dost thou stay on ?
>   Why linger here,
>   Where all is drear ?

> Oh, living I !
> Come, tell me why,
> When hope is gone,
> Dost thou stay on ?
> May not a cheated maiden die ?

Ko. (*entering and approaching her timidly*). Katisha !

KAT. The miscreant who robbed me of my love ! But vengeance pursues — they are heating the cauldron !

Ko. Katisha — behold a suppliant at your feet ! Katisha — mercy !

KAT. Mercy ? Had you mercy on him ? See here, you ! You have slain my love. He did not love *me*, but he would have loved me in time. I am an acquired taste — only the educated palate can appreciate *me*. I was educating *his* palate when he left me. Well, he is dead, and where shall I find another ? It takes years to train a man to love me. Am I to go through the weary round again, and, at the same time, implore mercy for you who robbed me of my prey — I mean my pupil — just as his education was on the point of completion ? Oh, where shall I find another ?

Ko. (*suddenly, and with great vehemence*). Here ! — Here !

KAT. What ! ! !

Ko. (*with intense passion*). Katisha, for years I have loved you with a white-hot passion that is slowly but surely consuming my very vitals ! Ah, shrink not from me ! If there is aught of woman's mercy in your heart, turn not away from a love-sick suppliant whose every fibre thrills at your tiniest touch ! True it is that, under a poor mask of disgust, I have endeavoured to conceal a passion whose inner fires are broiling the soul within me ! But the fire will not be smothered — it defies all attempts at extinction, and, breaking forth, all the more eagerly for its long restraint, it declares itself in words that will not be weighed — that cannot be schooled — that should not be too severely criticised. Katisha, I dare not hope for your love — but I will not live without it ! Darling !

KAT. You, whose hands still reek with the blood of my betrothed, dare to address words of passion to the woman you have so foully wronged !

Ko. I do — accept my love, or I perish on the spot !

KAT. Go to ! Who knows so well as I that no one ever yet died of a broken heart !

KO. You know not what you say. Listen !

SONG — KO-KO.

On a tree by a river a little tom-tit
      Sang 'Willow, titwillow, titwillow !'
And I said to him, 'Dicky-bird, why do you sit
      Singing "Willow, titwillow, titwillow"?'
'Is it weakness of intellect, birdie?' I cried,
'Or a rather tough worm in your little inside?'
With a shake of his poor little head, he replied,
      'Oh, willow, titwillow, titwillow !'

He slapped at his chest, as he sat on that bough,
      Singing 'Willow, titwillow, titwillow !'
And a cold perspiration bespangled his brow,
      Oh, willow, titwillow, titwillow !
He sobbed and he sighed, and a gurgle he gave,
Then he plunged himself into the billowy wave,
And an echo arose from the suicide's grave —
      'Oh, willow, titwillow, titwillow !'

Now I feel just as sure as I'm sure that my name
      Isn't Willow, titwillow, titwillow,
That 'twas blighted affection that made him exclaim,
      'Oh, willow, titwillow, titwillow !'
And if you remain callous and obdurate, I
Shall perish as he did, and you will know why,
Though I probably shall not exclaim as I die,
      'Oh, willow, titwillow, titwillow !'

(*During this song* KATISHA *has been greatly affected, and at the end is almost in tears.*)

KAT. (*whimpering*). Did he really die of love ?

KO. He really did.

KAT. All on account of a cruel little hen ?

KO. Yes.

KAT. Poor little chap !

KO. It's an affecting tale, and quite true. I knew the bird intimately.

KAT. Did you ? He must have been very fond of her.

KO. His devotion was something extraordinary.

KAT. (*still whimpering*). Poor little chap ! And — and if I refuse you, will you go and do the same ?

KO. At once.

KAT. No, no — you mustn't ! Anything but that ! (*Falls on his breast.*) Oh, I'm a silly little goose !

KO. (*making a wry face*). You are !

KAT. And you won't hate me because I'm just a little teeny weeny wee bit bloodthirsty, will you ?

KO. Hate you ? Oh, Katisha ! is there not beauty even in bloodthirstiness ?

KAT. My idea exactly.

DUET — KATISHA *and* KO-KO.

KAT.   There is beauty in the bellow of the blast,
          There is grandeur in the growling of the gale,
             There is eloquent outpouring
             When the lion is a-roaring,
          And the tiger is a-lashing of his tail !

KO.   Yes, I like to see a tiger
             From the Congo or the Niger,
          And especially when lashing of his tail !

KAT.   Volcanoes have a splendour that is grim,
          And earthquakes only terrify the dolts,
             But to him who's scientific
             There's nothing that's terrific
          In the falling of a flight of thunderbolts !

KO.   Yes, in spite of all my meekness,
             If I have a little weakness,
          It's a passion for a flight of thunderbolts !

BOTH.   If that is so,
             Sing derry down derry !
             It's evident, very,
                Our tastes are one.

Away we'll go,
And merrily marry,
Nor tardily tarry
Till day is done !

KO. There is beauty in extreme old age —
Do you fancy you are elderly enough ?
Information I'm requesting
On a subject interesting :
Is a maiden all the better when she's tough ?

KAT. Throughout this wide dominion
It's the general opinion
That she'll last a good deal longer when she's tough.

KO. Are you old enough to marry, do you think ?
Won't you wait till you are eighty in the shade ?
There's a fascination frantic
In a ruin that's romantic ;
Do you think you are sufficiently decayed ?

KAT. To the matter that you mention
I have given some attention,
And I think I am sufficiently decayed.

BOTH. If that is so,
Sing derry down derry !
It's evident, very,
Our tastes are one !
Away we'll go,
And merrily marry,
Nor tardily tarry
Till day is done !

[*Exeunt together.*

Flourish. Enter the MIKADO, *attended by* PISH-TUSH *and Court.*

MIK. Now then, we've had a capital lunch, and we're quite ready. Have all the painful preparations been made ?

PISH. Your Majesty, all is prepared.

MIK. Then produce the unfortunate gentleman and his two well-meaning but misguided accomplices.

Enter Ko-Ko, Katisha, Pooh-Bah, *and* Pitti-Sing. *They throw themselves at the* Mikado's *feet.*

Kat. Mercy ! Mercy for Ko-Ko ! Mercy for Pitti-Sing ! Mercy even for Pooh-Bah !

Mik. I beg your pardon, I don't think I quite caught that remark.

Pooh. Mercy even for Pooh-Bah.

Kat. Mercy ! My husband that was to have been is dead, and I have just married this miserable object.

Mik. Oh ! You've not been long about it !

Ko. We were married before the Registrar.

Pooh. *I* am the Registrar.

Mik. I see. But my difficulty is that, as you have slain the Heir Apparent——

Enter Nanki-Poo *and* Yum-Yum. *They kneel.*

Nanki. The Heir Apparent is *not* slain.

Mik. Bless my heart, my son !

Yum. And your daughter-in-law elected !

Kat. (*seizing* Ko-Ko). Traitor, you have deceived me !

Mik. Yes, you are entitled to a little explanation, but I think he will give it better whole than in pieces.

Ko. Your Majesty, it's like this : It is true that I stated that I had killed Nanki-Poo——

Mik. Yes, with most affecting particulars.

Pooh. Merely corroborative detail intended to give artistic verisimilitude to a bald and——

Ko. *Will* you refrain from putting in your oar ? (*To* Mikado.) It's like this : When your Majesty says, 'Let a thing be done,' it's as good as done — practically, it *is* done — because your Majesty's will is law. Your Majesty says, 'Kill a gentleman,' and a gentleman is told off to be killed. Consequently, that gentleman is as good as dead — practically, he *is* dead — and if he is dead, why not say so ?

Mik. I see. Nothing could possibly be more satisfactory !

FINALE.

Pitti.	For he's gone and married Yum-Yum —
All.	Yum-Yum !

PITTI.	Your anger pray bury, For all will be merry, I think you had better succumb —
ALL.	Cumb — cumb.
PITTI.	And join our expressions of glee !
KO.	On this subject I pray you be dumb —
ALL.	Dumb — dumb !
KO.	Your notions, though many, Are not worth a penny, The word for your guidance is 'Mum' —
ALL.	Mum — Mum !
KO.	You've a very good bargain in me.
ALL.	On this subject we pray you be dumb — Dumb — dumb ! We think you had better succumb — Cumb — cumb ! You'll find there are many Who'll wed for a penny, There are lots of good fish in the sea.
YUM. *and* NANK.	The threatened cloud has passed away, And brightly shines the dawning day; What though the night may come too soon, We've years and years of afternoon !
ALL.	Then let the throng Our joy advance, With laughing song And merry dance, With joyous shout and ringing cheer, Inaugurate our new career ! Then let the throng, etc.

CURTAIN

H.M.S. PINAFORE

OR

THE LASS THAT LOVED A SAILOR

DRAMATIS PERSONÆ

THE RT. HON. SIR JOSEPH PORTER, K.C.B. (*First Lord of the Admiralty*)

CAPTAIN CORCORAN (*Commanding H.M.S. Pinafore*)

TOM TUCKER (*Midshipmite*)

RALPH RACKSTRAW (*Able Seaman*)

DICK DEADEYE (*Able Seaman*)

BILL BOBSTAY (*Boatswain's Mate*)

BOB BECKET (*Carpenter's Mate*)

JOSEPHINE (*the Captain's Daughter*)

HEBE (*Sir Joseph's First Cousin*)

MRS. CRIPPS (LITTLE BUTTERCUP) (*a Portsmouth Bumboat Woman*)

First Lord's Sisters, his Cousins, his Aunts, Sailors, Marines, etc.

SCENE. — Quarter-deck of H.M.S. *Pinafore*, off Portsmouth.

ACT. I. — Noon.   ACT II. — Night.

First produced at the Opéra Comique on May 25, 1878.

H.M.S. PINAFORE

OR

THE LASS THAT LOVED A SAILOR

ACT I

SCENE. — *Quarter-deck of H.M.S. Pinafore. Sailors, led by* BOAT-SWAIN, *discovered cleaning brasswork, splicing rope, etc.*

CHORUS.

We sail the ocean blue,
And our saucy ship's a beauty;
We're sober men and true,
And attentive to our duty.
When the balls whistle free
O'er the bright blue sea,
We stand to our guns all day;
When at anchor we ride
On the Portsmouth tide,
We have plenty of time to play.

Enter LITTLE BUTTERCUP, *with large basket on her arm.*

RECIT.

Hail, men-o'-war's men — safeguards of your nation,
Here is an end, at last, of all privation;
You've got your pay — spare all you can afford
To welcome Little Buttercup on board.

ARIA.

For I'm called Little Buttercup — dear Little Buttercup,
　Though I could never tell why,
But still I'm called Buttercup — poor Little Buttercup,
　Sweet Little Buttercup I !

I've snuff and tobaccy, and excellent jacky,
　I've scissors, and watches, and knives ;
I've ribbons and laces to set off the faces
　Of pretty young sweethearts and wives.

I've treacle and toffee, I've tea and I've coffee,
　Soft tommy and succulent chops ;
I've chickens and conies, and pretty polonies,
　And excellent peppermint drops.

Then buy of your Buttercup — dear Little Buttercup,
　Sailors should never be shy ;
So, buy of your Buttercup — poor Little Buttercup ;
　Come, of your Buttercup buy !

BOAT. Aye, Little Buttercup — and well called — for you're the rosiest, the roundest, and the reddest beauty in all Spithead.

BUT. Red, am I ? and round — and rosy ! May be, for I have dissembled well ! But hark ye, my merry friend — hast ever thought that beneath a gay and frivolous exterior there may lurk a canker-worm which is slowly but surely eating its way into one's very heart ?

BOAT. No, my lass, I can't say I've ever thought that.

Enter DICK DEADEYE. *He pushes through sailors, and comes down.*

DICK. *I* have thought it often. (*All recoil from him.*)

BUT. Yes, you look like it ! What's the matter with the man ? Isn't he well ?

BOAT. Don't take no heed of *him* ; that's only poor Dick Deadeye.

DICK. I say — it's a beast of a name, ain't it — Dick Deadeye ?

But. It's not a nice name.

Dick. I'm ugly too, ain't I?

But. You are certainly plain.

Dick. And I'm three-cornered too, ain't I?

But. You are rather triangular.

Dick. Ha! ha! That's it. I'm ugly, and they hate me for it; for you all hate me, don't you?

All. We do!

Dick. There!

Boat. Well, Dick, we wouldn't go for to hurt any fellow-creature's feelings, but you can't expect a chap with such a name as Dick Deadeye to be a popular character — now can you?

Dick. No.

Boat. It's asking too much, ain't it?

Dick. It is. From such a face and form as mine the noblest sentiments sound like the black utterances of a depraved imagination. It is human nature — I am resigned.

RECIT.

But. (*looking down hatchway*).

> But, tell me — who's the youth whose faltering feet
> With difficulty bear him on his course?

Boat. That is the smartest lad in all the fleet —
> Ralph Rackstraw!

But. Ha! That name! Remorse! remorse!

Enter Ralph *from hatchway.*

MADRIGAL — Ralph.

> The Nightingale
> Sighed for the moon's bright ray
> And told his tale
> In his own melodious way!
> He sang 'Ah, well-a-day!'

All.   He sang 'Ah, well-a-day!'

The lowly vale
For the mountain vainly sighed,
    To his humble wail
The echoing hills replied.
    They sang 'Ah, well-a-day !'

ALL.   They sang 'Ah, well-a-day !'

RECIT.

I know the value of a kindly chorus,
    But choruses yield little consolation
When we have pain and sorrow too before us !
    I love — and love, alas, above my station !

BUT. (*aside*).   He loves — and loves a lass above his station !
ALL (*aside*).   Yes, yes, the lass is much above his station !

[*Exit* LITTLE BUTTERCUP.

BALLAD — RALPH.

A maiden fair to see,
The pearl of minstrelsy,
    A bud of blushing beauty;
For whom proud nobles sigh,
And with each other vie
    To do her menial's duty.

ALL.   To do her menial's duty.

A suitor, lowly born,
With hopeless passion torn,
    And poor beyond denying,
Has dared for her to pine
At whose exalted shrine
    A world of wealth is sighing.

ALL.   A world of wealth is sighing !

Unlearned he in aught
Save that which love has taught
    (For love had been his tutor);
Oh, pity, pity me —
Our captain's daughter she,
    And I that lowly suitor !

ALL.   And he that lowly suitor !

BOAT. Ah, my poor lad, you've climbed too high; our worthy captain's child won't have nothin' to say to a poor chap like you. Will she, lads ?

ALL. No, no !

DICK. No, no, captains' daughters don't marry foremast hands.

ALL (*recoiling from him*). Shame ! shame !

BOAT. Dick Deadeye, them sentiments o' yourn are a disgrace to our common natur'.

RALPH. But it's a strange anomaly, that the daughter of a man who hails from the quarter-deck may not love another who lays out on the fore-yard arm. For a man is but a man, whether he hoists his flag at the main-truck or his slacks on the main-deck.

DICK. Ah, it's a queer world !

RALPH. Dick Deadeye, I have no desire to press hardly on you, but such a revolutionary sentiment is enough to make an honest sailor shudder.

BOAT. My lads, our gallant captain has come on deck; let us greet him as so brave an officer and so gallant a seaman deserves.

Enter CAPTAIN CORCORAN.

RECIT.

CAPT. My gallant crew, good morning.

ALL (*saluting*). Sir, good morning !

CAPT. I hope you're all quite well.

ALL (*as before*). Quite well; and you, sir ?

CAPT. I am in reasonable health, and happy
        To meet you all once more.

ALL (*as before*). You do us proud, sir !

SONG — CAPT.

CAPT.	I am the Captain of the *Pinafore*;
ALL.	And a right good captain, too !
CAPT.	You're very, very good,
	And be it understood,
	I command a right good crew.
ALL.	We're very, very good,
	And be it understood,
	He commands a right good crew.
CAPT.	Though related to a peer,
	I can hand, reef, and steer,
	And ship a selvagee;
	I am never known to quail
	At the fury of a gale,
	And I'm never, never sick at sea !
ALL.	What, never ?
CAPT.	No, never !
ALL.	What, *never* ?
CAPT.	Hardly ever !
ALL.	He's hardly ever sick at sea !
	Then give three cheers, and one cheer more,
	For the hardy Captain of the *Pinafore* !
CAPT.	I do my best to satisfy you all —
ALL.	And with you we're quite content.
CAPT.	You're exceedingly polite,
	And I think it only right
	To return the compliment.
ALL.	We're exceedingly polite,
	And he thinks it's only right
	To return the compliment.
CAPT.	Bad language or abuse,
	I never, never use,
	Whatever the emergency;
	Though 'Bother it' I may
	Occasionally say,
	I never use a big, big D —
ALL.	What, never ?

CAPT.	No, never !
ALL.	What, *never* ?
CAPT.	Hardly ever !
ALL.	Hardly ever swears a big, big D —
	Then give three cheers, and one cheer more,
	For the well-bred Captain of the *Pinafore* !

                     [After song exeunt all but CAPTAIN.

Enter LITTLE BUTTERCUP.

RECITATIVE.

BUT.   Sir, you are sad ! The silent eloquence
          Of yonder tear that trembles on your eyelash
          Proclaims a sorrow far more deep than common;
          Confide in me — fear not — I am a mother !

CAPT.   Yes, Little Buttercup, I'm sad and sorry —
          My daughter, Josephine, the fairest flower
          That ever blossomed on ancestral timber,
          Is sought in marriage by Sir Joseph Porter,
          Our Admiralty's First Lord, but for some reason
          She does not seem to tackle kindly to it.

BUT. (*with emotion*). Ah, poor Sir Joseph ! Ah, I know too well
          The anguish of a heart that loves but vainly !
          But see, here comes your most attractive daughter.
          I go — Farewell !   *[Exit.*
CAPT. (*looking after her*). A plump and pleasing person !   *[Exit.*

Enter JOSEPHINE, *twining some flowers which she carries in a
small basket.*

BALLAD — JOSEPHINE.

Sorry her lot who loves too well,
    Heavy the heart that hopes but vainly,
Sad are the sighs that own the spell,
    Uttered by eyes that speak too plainly;
    Heavy the sorrow that bows the head
    When love is alive and hope is dead !

Sad is the hour when sets the sun —
    Dark is the night to earth's poor daughters,
When to the ark the wearied one
    Flies from the empty waste of waters !
      Heavy the sorrow that bows the head
      When love is alive and hope is dead !

Enter CAPTAIN.

CAPT. My child, I grieve to see that you are a prey to melancholy. You should look your best to-day, for Sir Joseph Porter, K.C.B., will be here this afternoon to claim your promised hand.

Jos. Ah, father, your words cut me to the quick. I can esteem — reverence — venerate Sir Joseph, for he is a great and good man; but oh, I cannot love him ! My heart is already given.

CAPT. (*aside*). It is then as I feared. (*Aloud.*) Given ? And to whom ? Not to some gilded lordling ?

Jos. No, father — the object of my love is no lordling. Oh, pity me, for he is but a humble sailor on board your own ship !

CAPT. Impossible !

Jos. Yes, it is true — too true.

CAPT. A common sailor ? Oh fie !

Jos. I blush for the weakness that allows me to cherish such a passion. I hate myself when I think of the depth to which I have stooped in permitting myself to think tenderly of one so ignobly born, but I love him ! I love him ! I love him ! (*Weeps.*)

CAPT. Come, my child, let us talk this over. In a matter of the heart I would not coerce my daughter — I attach but little value to rank or wealth, but the line must be drawn somewhere. A man in that station may be brave and worthy, but at every step he would commit solecisms that society would never pardon.

Jos. Oh, I have thought of this night and day. But fear not, father, I have a heart, and therefore I love; but I am your daughter, and therefore I am proud. Though I carry my love with me to the tomb, he shall never, never know it.

CAPT. You *are* my daughter after all. But see, Sir Joseph's barge approaches, manned by twelve trusty oarsmen and accompanied by the admiring crowd of sisters, cousins, and aunts that attend him wherever he goes. Retire, my daughter, to your cabin — take this,

his photograph, with you — it may help to bring you to a more reasonable frame of mind.

Jos. My own thoughtful father !

> [*Exit* JOSEPHINE. CAPTAIN *remains and ascends the poop-deck.*

BARCAROLLE (*invisible*).

Over the bright blue sea
Comes Sir Joseph Porter, K.C.B.,
    Wherever he may go
Bang-bang the loud nine-pounders go !
    Shout o'er the bright blue sea
For Sir Joseph Porter, K.C.B.

(*During this the Crew have entered on tiptoe, listening attentively to the song.*)

CHORUS OF SAILORS.

Sir Joseph's barge is seen,
    And its crowd of blushing beauties,
We hope he'll find us clean,
    And attentive to our duties.
We sail, we sail the ocean blue,
    And our saucy ship's a beauty.
We're sober, sober men and true
    And attentive to our duty.
We're smart and sober men,
    And quite devoid of fe-ar,
In all the Royal N.
    None are so smart as we are.

Enter SIR JOSEPH'S FEMALE RELATIVES.

They dance round stage.

REL.
    Gaily tripping,
    Lightly skipping,
    Flock the maidens to the shipping.

SAILORS.
    Flags and guns and pennants dipping !
    All the ladies love the shipping.

REL.   Sailors sprightly
                        Always rightly
                        Welcome ladies so politely.
SAILORS.   Ladies who can smile so brightly,
                        Sailors welcome most politely.
CAPT. (*from poop*). Now give three cheers, I'll lead the way.
ALL.   Hurrah ! hurrah ! hurrah ! hurray !

Enter SIR JOSEPH *with* COUSIN HEBE.

SONG — SIR JOSEPH.

                        I am the monarch of the sea,
                        The ruler of the Queen's Navee,
                        Whose praise Great Britain loudly chants.
COUSIN HEBE.   And we are his sisters, and his cousins, and his
                          aunts !
REL.   And we are his sisters, and his cousins, and his
                          aunts !
SIR JOSEPH.   When at anchor here I ride,
                        My bosom swells with pride,
                        And I snap my fingers at a foeman's taunts;
COUSIN HEBE.   And so do his sisters, and his cousins, and his
                          aunts !
ALL.   And so do his sisters, and his cousins, and his
                          aunts !
SIR JOSEPH.   But when the breezes blow,
                        I generally go below,
                        And seek the seclusion that a cabin grants !
COUSIN HEBE.   And so do his sisters, and his cousins, and his
                          aunts !
ALL.   And so do his sisters, and his cousins, and his
                          aunts !
                        His sisters and his cousins,
                        Whom he reckons up by dozens,
                          And his aunts !

SONG — SIR JOSEPH.

When I was a lad I served a term
As office boy to an Attorney's firm.

I cleaned the windows and I swept the floor,
And I polished up the handle of the big front door.
    I polished up that handle so carefullee
    That now I am the Ruler of the Queen's Navee !
        CHORUS. — He polished, etc.

As office boy I made such a mark
That they gave me the post of a junior clerk.
I served the writs with a smile so bland,
And I copied all the letters in a big round hand —
    I copied all the letters in a hand so free,
    That now I am the Ruler of the Queen's Navee !
        CHORUS. — He copied, etc.

In serving writs I made such a name
That an articled clerk I soon became;
I wore clean collars and a brand-new suit
For the pass examination at the Institute.
        And that pass examination did so well for me,
        That now I am the Ruler of the Queen's Navee !
            CHORUS. — And that pass examination, etc.

Of legal knowledge I acquired such a grip
That they took me into the partnership.
And that junior partnership, I ween,
Was the only ship that I ever had seen.
    But that kind of ship so suited me,
    That now I am the Ruler of the Queen's Navee !
        CHORUS. — But that kind, etc.

I grew so rich that I was sent
By a pocket borough into Parliament.
I always voted at my party's call,
And I never thought of thinking for myself at all.
    I thought so little, they rewarded me
    By making me the Ruler of the Queen's Navee !
        CHORUS. — He thought so little, etc.

Now, landsmen all, whoever you may be,
If you want to rise to the top of the tree,
If your soul isn't fettered to an office stool,
Be careful to be guided by this golden rule —
    Stick close to your desks and never go to sea,
    And you all may be Rulers of the Queen's Navee !
    CHORUS. — Stick close, etc.

SIR JOSEPH. You've a remarkably fine crew, Captain Corcoran.

CAPT. It *is* a fine crew, Sir Joseph.

SIR JOSEPH (*examining a very small midshipman*). A British sailor is a splendid fellow, Captain Corcoran.

CAPT. A splendid fellow indeed, Sir Joseph.

SIR JOSEPH. I hope you treat your crew kindly, Captain Corcoran.

CAPT. Indeed I hope so, Sir Joseph.

SIR JOSEPH. Never forget that they are the bulwarks of England's greatness, Captain Corcoran.

CAPT. So I have always considered them, Sir Joseph.

SIR JOSEPH. No bullying, I trust — no strong language of any kind, eh ?

CAPT. Oh, never, Sir Joseph.

SIR JOSEPH. What, *never* ?

CAPT. Hardly ever, Sir Joseph. They are an excellent crew, and do their work thoroughly without it.

SIR JOSEPH. Don't patronise them, sir — pray, don't patronise them.

CAPT. Certainly not, Sir Joseph.

SIR JOSEPH. That you are their captain is an accident of birth. I cannot permit these noble fellows to be patronised because an accident of birth has placed you above them and them below you.

CAPT. I am the last person to insult a British sailor, Sir Joseph.

SIR JOSEPH. You are the last person who did, Captain Corcoran. Desire that splendid seaman to step forward.

(DICK *comes forward.*)

SIR JOSEPH. No, no, the other splendid seaman.

CAPT. Ralph Rackstraw, three paces to the front — march !

SIR JOSEPH (*sternly*). If what ?

CAPT. I beg your pardon — I don't think I understand you.

SIR JOSEPH. If you *please*.

CAPT. Oh, yes, of course. If you please. (RALPH *steps forward.*)

SIR JOSEPH. You're a remarkably fine fellow.

RALPH. Yes, your honour.

SIR JOSEPH. And a first-rate seaman, I'll be bound.

RALPH. There's not a smarter topman in the Navy, your honour, though I say it who shouldn't.

SIR JOSEPH. Not at all. Proper self-respect, nothing more. Can you dance a hornpipe?

RALPH. No, your honour.

SIR JOSEPH. That's a pity: all sailors should dance hornpipes. I will teach you one this evening, after dinner. Now tell me — don't be afraid — how does your captain treat you, eh?

RALPH. A better captain don't walk the deck, your honour.

ALL. Aye! Aye!

SIR JOSEPH. Good. I like to hear you speak well of your commanding officer; I daresay he don't deserve it, but still it does you credit. Can you sing?

RALPH. I can hum a little, your honour.

SIR JOSEPH. Then hum this at your leisure. (*Giving him MS. music.*) It is a song that I have composed for the use of the Royal Navy. It is designed to encourage independence of thought and action in the lower branches of the service, and to teach the principle that a British sailor is any man's equal, excepting mine. Now, Captain Corcoran, a word with you in your cabin, on a tender and sentimental subject.

CAPT. Aye, aye, Sir Joseph. (*Crossing.*) Boatswain, in commemoration of this joyous occasion, see that extra grog is served out to the ship's company at seven bells.

BOAT. Beg pardon. If what, your honour?

CAPT. If what? I don't think I understand you.

BOAT. If you *please*, your honour.

CAPT. What!

SIR JOSEPH. The gentleman is quite right. If you *please*.

CAPT. (*stamping his foot impatiently*). If you *please*!   [*Exit.*

SIR JOSEPH.   For I hold that on the seas
         The expression, 'if you please',
            A particularly gentlemanly tone implants.

COUSIN HEBE.   And so do his sisters, and his cousins, and his
                      aunts !
ALL.   And so do his sisters, and his cousins, and his
                      aunts !

[*Exeunt* SIR JOSEPH *and* RELATIVES.

BOAT. Ah ! Sir Joseph's a true gentleman; courteous and considerate to the very humblest.

RALPH. True, Boatswain, but we are not the very humblest. Sir Joseph has explained our true position to us. As he says, a British seaman is any man's equal excepting his, and if Sir Joseph says that, is it not our duty to believe him ?

ALL. Well spoke ! well spoke !

DICK. You're on a wrong tack, and so is he. He means well, but he don't know. When people have to obey other people's orders, equality's out of the question.

ALL (*recoiling*). Horrible ! horrible !

BOAT. Dick Deadeye, if you go for to infuriate this here ship's company too far, I won't answer for being able to hold 'em in. I'm shocked ! that's what I am — shocked !

RALPH. Messmates, my mind's made up. I'll speak to the captain's daughter, and tell her, like an honest man, of the honest love I have for her.

ALL. Aye, aye !

RALPH. Is not my love as good as another's ? Is not my heart as true as another's ? Have I not hands and eyes and ears and limbs like another ?

ALL. Aye, aye !

RALPH. True, I lack birth——

BOAT. You've a berth on board this very ship.

RALPH. Well said — I had forgotten that. Messmates — what do you say ? Do you approve my determination ?

ALL. We do.

DICK. *I* don't.

BOAT. What is to be done with this here hopeless chap ? Let us sing him the song that Sir Joseph has kindly composed for us. Perhaps it will bring this here miserable creetur to a proper state of mind.

GLEE — RALPH, BOATSWAIN, BOATSWAIN'S MATE, *and* CHORUS.

> A British tar is a soaring soul,
>> As free as a mountain bird,
> His energetic fist should be ready to resist
>> A dictatorial word.
> His nose should pant and his lip should curl,
> His cheeks should flame and his brow should furl,
> His bosom should heave and his heart should glow,
> And his fist be ever ready for a knock-down blow.
>> CHORUS. — His nose should pant, etc.
>
> His eyes should flash with an inborn fire,
>> His brow with scorn be wrung;
> He never should bow down to a domineering frown,
>> Or the tang of a tyrant tongue.
> His foot should stamp and his throat should growl,
> His hair should twirl and his face should scowl;
> His eyes should flash and his breast protrude,
> And this should be his customary attitude — (*pose*).
>> CHORUS. — His foot should stamp, etc.

(*All dance off excepting* RALPH, *who remains, leaning pensively against bulwark.*)

Enter JOSEPHINE *from cabin.*

JOS. It is useless — Sir Joseph's attentions nauseate me. I know that he is a truly great and good man, for he told me so himself, but to me he seems tedious, fretful, and dictatorial. Yet his must be a mind of no common order, or he would not dare to teach my dear father to dance a hornpipe on the cabin table. (*Sees* RALPH.) Ralph Rackstraw ! (*Overcome by emotion.*)

RALPH. Aye, lady — no other than poor Ralph Rackstraw !

JOS. (*aside*). How my heart beats ! (*Aloud.*) And why poor, Ralph ?

RALPH. I am poor in the essence of happiness, lady — rich only in never-ending unrest. In me there meet a combination of antithetical elements which are at eternal war with one another. Driven hither by objective influences — thither by subjective emotions — wafted one moment into blazing day, by mocking hope — plunged the next into the Cimmerian darkness of tangible despair, I am but a living ganglion of irreconcilable antagonisms. I hope I make myself clear, lady ?

JOS. Perfectly. (*Aside.*) His simple eloquence goes to my heart. Oh, if I dared — but no, the thought is madness ! (*Aloud.*) Dismiss these foolish fancies, they torture you but needlessly. Come, make one effort.

RALPH (*aside*). I will — one. (*Aloud.*) Josephine !

JOS. (*indignantly*). Sir !

RALPH. Aye, even though Jove's armoury were launched at the head of the audacious mortal whose lips, unhallowed by relationship, dared to breathe that precious word, yet would I breathe it once, and then perchance be silent evermore. Josephine, in one brief breath I will concentrate the hopes, the doubts, the anxious fears of six weary months. Josephine, I am a British sailor, and I love you !

JOS. Sir, this audacity ! (*Aside.*) Oh, my heart, my beating heart ! (*Aloud.*) This unwarrantable presumption on the part of a common sailor ! (*Aside.*) Common ! oh, the irony of the word ! (*Crossing, aloud.*) Oh, sir, you forget the disparity in our ranks.

RALPH. I forget nothing, haughty lady. I love you desperately, my life is in your hand — I lay it at your feet ! Give me hope, and what I lack in education and polite accomplishments, that I will endeavour to acquire. Drive me to despair, and in death alone I shall look for consolation. I am proud and cannot stoop to implore. I have spoken and I wait your word.

JOS. You shall not wait long. Your proffered love I haughtily reject. Go, sir, and learn to cast your eyes on some village maiden in your own poor rank — they should be lowered before your captain's daughter !

DUET — JOSEPHINE *and* RALPH.

JOS.   Refrain, audacious tar,
                          Your suit from pressing,
                    Remember what you are,
                          And whom addressing !

(*Aside.*)   I'd laugh my rank to scorn
                       In union holy,
                   Were he more highly born
                       Or I more lowly !

RALPH.   Proud lady, have your way,
                       Unfeeling beauty !
                   You speak and I obey,
                       It is my duty !
                   I am the lowliest tar
                       That sails the water,
                   And you, proud maiden, are
                       My captain's daughter !

(*Aside.*)   My heart with anguish torn
                       Bows down before her,
                   She laughs my love to scorn,
                       Yet I adore her !

[*Repeat refrain, ensemble, then exit* JOSEPHINE *into cabin.*

RALPH (*Recit.*)   Can I survive this overbearing
                   Or live a life of mad despairing,
                   My proffered love despised, rejected ?
                   No, no, it's not to be expected !
                               (*Calling off.*)
                   Messmates, ahoy !
                       Come here ! Come here !

Enter SAILORS, HEBE, *and* RELATIVES.

ALL.   Aye, aye, my boy,
                   What cheer, what cheer ?
                       Now tell us, pray,
                       Without delay,
                       What does she say —
                   What cheer, what cheer ?

RALPH (*to* COUSIN HEBE).
            The maiden treats my suit with scorn,
                Rejects my humble gift, my lady;
            She says I am ignobly born,
                And cuts my hopes adrift, my lady.

ALL.   Oh, cruel one.
DICK.   She spurns your suit ? Oho ! Oho !
               I told you so, I told you so.
SAILORS *and* RELATIVES.

               Shall $\left\{ \begin{array}{c} \text{we} \\ \text{they} \end{array} \right\}$ submit ? Are $\left\{ \begin{array}{c} \text{we} \\ \text{they} \end{array} \right\}$ but slaves ?
                    Love comes alike to high and low —
                    Britannia's sailors rule the waves,
                         And shall they stoop to insult ? No !
DICK.   You must submit, you are but slaves;
                    A lady she ! Oho ! Oho !
               You lowly toilers of the waves,
                    She spurns you all — I told you so !
RALPH.   My friends, my leave of life I'm taking,
               For oh, my heart, my heart is breaking.
               When I am gone, oh, prithee tell
               The maid that, as I died, I loved her well !
ALL (*turning away, weeping*).
                    Of life, alas ! his leave he's taking,
                    For ah ! his faithful heart is breaking;
                    When he is gone we'll surely tell
                    The maid that, as he died, he loved her well.

     (*During Chorus* BOATSWAIN *has loaded pistol, which he
                         hands to* RALPH.)

RALPH.   Be warned, my messmates all
                    Who love in rank above you —
               For Josephine I fall !

     (*Puts pistol to his head. All the sailors stop their ears.*)

                    Enter JOSEPHINE *on deck.*

JOS.   Ah ! stay your hand ! I love you !
ALL.   Ah ! stay your hand — she loves you !
RALPH (*incredulously*). Loves me ?
JOS.   Loves you !
ALL.   Yes, yes — ah, yes, — she loves you !

ENSEMBLE.

SAILORS *and* RELATIVES *and* JOSEPHINE.

Oh joy, oh rapture unforeseen,
For now the sky is all serene;
The god of day — the orb of love —
Has hung his ensign high above,
    The sky is all ablaze.

With wooing words and loving song,
We'll chase the lagging hours along,
And if $\left\{ \begin{array}{l} \text{I find} \\ \text{we find} \end{array} \right\}$ the maiden coy,
$\left. \begin{array}{l} \text{I'll} \\ \text{We'll} \end{array} \right\}$ murmur forth decorous joy
    In dreamy roundelays !

DICK DEADEYE.

He thinks he's won his Josephine,
But though the sky is now serene,
A frowning thunderbolt above
May end their ill-assorted love
    Which now is all ablaze.

Our captain, ere the day is gone,
Will be extremely down upon
The wicked men who art employ
To make his Josephine less coy
    In many various ways.   [*Exit* DICK.

JOS.	This very night,
HEBE.	With bated breath
RALPH.	And muffled oar —
JOS.	Without a light,
HEBE.	As still as death,
RALPH.	We'll steal ashore
JOS.	A clergyman
RALPH.	Shall make us one

BOAT.	At half-past ten,
JOS.	And then we can
RALPH.	Return, for none
BOAT.	Can part them then !
ALL.	This very night, etc.

(DICK *appears at hatchway.*)

DICK.   Forbear, nor carry out the scheme you've planned;
           She is a lady — you a foremast hand !
           Remember, she's your gallant captain's daughter,
           And you the meanest slave that crawls the water !

ALL.   Back, vermin, back,
                           Nor mock us !
                       Back, vermin, back,
                           You shock us !

                                        [*Exit* DICK.

           Let's give three cheers for the sailor's bride
           Who casts all thought of rank aside —
           Who gives up home and fortune too
           For the honest love of a sailor true !
               For a British tar is a soaring soul
                   As free as a mountain bird !
               His energetic fist should be ready to resist
                   A dictatorial word !
     His foot should stamp and his throat should growl,
     His hair should twirl and his face should scowl,
     His eyes should flash and his breast protrude,
     And this should be his customary attitude — (*pose*).

                   GENERAL DANCE.

                   END OF ACT I

ACT II

Same Scene. Night. Awning removed. Moonlight.

CAPTAIN *discovered singing on poop-deck, and accompanying himself on a mandolin.* LITTLE BUTTERCUP *seated on quarter-deck, gazing sentimentally at him.*

SONG — CAPTAIN.

Fair moon, to thee I sing,
   Bright regent of the heavens,
Say, why is everything
   Either at sixes or at sevens?
I have lived hitherto
   Free from breath of slander,
Beloved by all my crew —
   A really popular commander.
But now my kindly crew rebel,
   My daughter to a tar is partial,
Sir Joseph storms, and, sad to tell,
   He threatens a court martial!
   Fair moon, to thee I sing,
      Bright regent of the heavens,
   Say, why is everything
      Either at sixes or at sevens?

BUT. How sweetly he carols forth his melody to the unconscious moon! Of whom is he thinking? Of some high-born beauty? It may be! Who is poor Little Buttercup that she should expect his glance to fall on one so lowly! And yet if he knew — if he only knew!

CAPT. (*coming down*). Ah! Little Buttercup, still on board? That is not quite right, little one. It would have been more respectable to have gone on shore at dusk.

79

But. True, dear Captain — but the recollection of your sad pale face seemed to chain me to the ship. I would fain see you smile before I go.

Capt. Ah ! Little Buttercup, I fear it will be long before I recover my accustomed cheerfulness, for misfortunes crowd upon me, and all my old friends seem to have turned against me !

But. Oh no — do not say 'all', dear Captain. That were unjust to one, at least.

Capt. True, for you are staunch to me. (*Aside.*) If ever I gave my heart again, methinks it would be to such a one as this ! (*Aloud.*) I am touched to the heart by your innocent regard for me, and were we differently situated, I think I could have returned it. But as it is, I fear I can never be more to you than a friend.

But. I understand ! You hold aloof from me because you are rich and lofty — and I poor and lowly. But take care ! The poor bumboat woman has gipsy blood in her veins, and she can read destinies.

Capt. Destinies ?

But. There is a change in store for you !

Capt. A change ?

But. Aye — be prepared !

DUET — Little Buttercup *and* Captain.

But.   Things are seldom what they seem,
                  Skim milk masquerades as cream;
                  Highlows pass as patent leathers;
                  Jackdaws strut in peacock's feathers.

Capt. (*puzzled*).   Very true,
                          So they do.

But.   Black sheep dwell in every fold;
                  All that glitters is not gold;
                  Storks turn out to be but logs;
                  Bulls are but inflated frogs.

Capt. (*puzzled*). So they be,
                    Frequentlee.

But.   Drops the wind and stops the mill;
                  Turbot is ambitious brill;

Gild the farthing if you will,
Yet it is a farthing still.

CAPT. (*puzzled*).   Yes, I know,
    That is so.
Though to catch your drift I'm striving,
    It is shady — it is shady;
I don't see at what you're driving,
    Mystic lady — mystic lady.

(*Aside.*)   Stern conviction's o'er me stealing,
That the mystic lady's dealing
In oracular revealing.

BUT. (*aside*).   Stern conviction's o'er him stealing,
That the mystic lady's dealing
In oracular revealing.

BOTH.   Yes, I know —
    That is so !

CAPT.   Though I'm anything but clever,
I could talk like that for ever:
Once a cat was killed by care;
Only brave deserve the fair.

BUT.   Very true,
    So they do.

CAPT.   Wink is often good as nod;
Spoils the child who spares the rod;
Thirsty lambs run foxy dangers;
Dogs are found in many mangers.

BUT.   Frequentlee,
    I agree.

CAPT.   Paw of cat the chestnut snatches;
Worn-out garments show new patches;
Only count the chick that hatches;
Men are grown-up catchy-catchies.

BUT.   Yes, I know,
    That is so.

(*Aside.*)   Though to catch my drift he's striving,
    I'll dissemble — I'll dissemble;
When he sees at what I'm driving,
    Let him tremble — let him tremble !

ENSEMBLE.

Though a mystic tone $\left\{ \begin{matrix} I \\ you \end{matrix} \right\}$ borrow,

You will
I shall $\left. \right\}$ learn the truth with sorrow,

Here to-day and gone to-morrow;

    Yes, I know —

    That is so !

[*At the end exit* LITTLE BUTTERCUP *melodramatically.*

CAPT. Incomprehensible as her utterances are, I nevertheless feel that they are dictated by a sincere regard for me. But to what new misery is she referring ? Time alone can tell !

Enter SIR JOSEPH.

SIR JOSEPH. Captain Corcoran, I am much disappointed with your daughter. In fact, I don't think she will do.

CAPT. She won't do, Sir Joseph !

SIR JOSEPH. I'm afraid not. The fact is, that although I have urged my suit with as much eloquence as is consistent with an official utterance, I have done so hitherto without success. How do you account for this ?

CAPT. Really, Sir Joseph, I hardly know. Josephine is of course sensible of your condescension.

SIR JOSEPH. She naturally would be.

CAPT. But perhaps your exalted rank dazzles her.

SIR JOSEPH. You think it does ?

CAPT. I can hardly say; but she is a modest girl, and her social position is far below your own. It may be that she feels she is not worthy of you.

SIR JOSEPH. That is really a very sensible suggestion, and displays more knowledge of human nature than I had given you credit for.

CAPT. See, she comes. If your lordship would kindly reason with her and assure her officially that it is a standing rule at the Admiralty that love levels all ranks, her respect for an official utterance might induce her to look upon your offer in its proper light.

SIR JOSEPH. It is not unlikely. I will adopt your suggestion. But soft, she is here. Let us withdraw, and watch our opportunity.

Enter JOSEPHINE *from cabin.* FIRST LORD *and* CAPTAIN *retire.*

SCENA — JOSEPHINE.

The hours creep on apace,
  My guilty heart is quaking !
Oh, that I might retrace
  The step that I am taking !
Its folly it were easy to be showing,
What I am giving up and whither going.
On the one hand, papa's luxurious home,
  Hung with ancestral armour and old brasses,
Carved oak and tapestry from distant Rome,
  Rare 'blue and white' Venetian finger-glasses,
Rich oriental rugs, luxurious sofa pillows,
And everything that isn't old, from Gillow's.
And on the other, a dark and dingy room,
  In some back street with stuffy children crying,
Where organs yell, and clacking housewives fume,
  And clothes are hanging out all day a-drying.
With one cracked looking-glass to see your face in,
And dinner served up in a pudding basin !

A simple sailor, lowly born,
  Unlettered and unknown,
Who toils for bread from early morn
  Till half the night has flown !
No golden rank can he impart —
  No wealth of house or land —
No fortune save his trusty heart
  And honest brown right hand !
And yet he is so wondrous fair
That love for one so passing rare,
So peerless in his manly beauty,
Were little else than solemn duty !
Oh, god of love, and god of reason, say,
Which of you twain shall my poor heart obey !

SIR JOSEPH *and* CAPTAIN *enter.*

SIR JOSEPH. Madam, it has been represented to me that you are
appalled by my exalted rank. I desire to convey to you officially
my assurance, that if your hesitation is attributable to that circumstance, it is uncalled for.

Jos. Oh ! then your lordship is of opinion that married happiness
is *not* inconsistent with discrepancy in rank ?

SIR JOSEPH. I am officially of that opinion.

Jos. That the high and the lowly may be truly happy together,
provided that they truly love one another ?

SIR JOSEPH. Madam, I desire to convey to you officially my
opinion that love is a platform upon which all ranks meet.

Jos. I thank you, Sir Joseph. I *did* hesitate, but I will hesitate no
longer. (*Aside.*) He little thinks how eloquently he has pleaded his
rival's cause !

TRIO.

FIRST LORD, CAPTAIN, *and* JOSEPHINE.

CAPT.	Never mind the why and wherefore,
	Love can level ranks, and therefore,
	Though his lordship's station's mighty,
	Though stupendous be his brain,
	Though your tastes are mean and flighty
	And your fortune poor and plain,
CAPT. *and*	Ring the merry bells on board-ship,
SIR JOSEPH.	Rend the air with warbling wild,
	For the union of $\left\{\begin{array}{c} \text{his} \\ \text{my} \end{array}\right\}$ lordship
	With a humble captain's child !
CAPT.	For a humble captain's daughter —
Jos.	For a gallant captain's daughter —
SIR JOSEPH.	And a lord who rules the water —
Jos. (*aside*).	And a *tar* who ploughs the water !
ALL.	Let the air with joy be laden,
	Rend with songs the air above,
	For the union of a maiden
	With the man who owns her love !

SIR JOSEPH.
    Never mind the why and wherefore,
    Love can level ranks, and therefore,
    Though your nautical relation (*alluding to* CAPT.)
    In my set could scarcely pass —
    Though you occupy a station
    In the lower middle class —

CAPT. *and*
SIR JOSEPH.
    Ring the merry bells on board-ship,
    Rend the air with warbling wild,

$$\text{For the union of} \left\{ \begin{matrix} \text{my} \\ \text{his} \end{matrix} \right\} \text{lordship}$$

    With a humble captain's child !

CAPT.
    For a humble captain's daughter —
JOS.
    For a gallant captain's daughter —
SIR JOSEPH.
    And a lord who rules the water —
JOS. (*aside*).
    And a *tar* who ploughs the water !
ALL.
    Let the air with joy be laden,
    Rend with songs the air above,
    For the union of a maiden
    With the man who owns her love !

JOS.
    Never mind the why and wherefore,
    Love can level ranks, and therefore
    I admit the jurisdiction;
    Ably have you played your part;
    You have carried firm conviction
    To my hesitating heart.

CAPT. *and*
SIR JOSEPH.
    Ring the merry bells on board-ship,
    Rend the air with warbling wild,

$$\text{For the union of} \left\{ \begin{matrix} \text{my} \\ \text{his} \end{matrix} \right\} \text{lordship}$$

    With a humble captain's child !

CAPT.
    For a humble captain's daughter —
JOS.
    For a gallant captain's daughter —
SIR JOSEPH.
    And a lord who rules the water —
JOS. (*aside*).
    And a *tar* who ploughs the water !
(*Aloud.*)
    Let the air with joy be laden.
CAPT. *and* SIR JOSEPH.
    Ring the merry bells on board-ship —
JOS.
    For the union of a maiden —
CAPT. *and* SIR JOSEPH.
    For her union with his lordship.

ALL.   Rend with songs the air above
                    For the man who owns her love !

                                                    [*Exit* Jos.

CAPT. Sir Joseph, I cannot express to you my delight at the happy
result of your eloquence. Your argument was unanswerable.

SIR JOSEPH. Captain Corcoran, it is one of the happiest characteristics of this glorious country that official utterances are invariably
regarded as unanswerable.   [*Exit* SIR JOSEPH.

CAPT. At last my fond hopes are to be crowned. My only
daughter is to be the bride of a Cabinet Minister. The prospect is
Elysian. (*During this speech* DICK DEADEYE *has entered.*)

DICK. Captain.

CAPT. Deadeye ! You here ? Don't ! (*Recoiling from him.*)

DICK. Ah, don't shrink from me, Captain. I'm unpleasant to
look at, and my name's agin me, but I ain't as bad as I seem.

CAPT. What would you with me ?

DICK (*mysteriously*). I'm come to give you warning.

CAPT. Indeed ! do you propose to leave the Navy then ?

DICK. No, no, you misunderstand me ; listen !

DUET.

CAPTAIN *and* DICK DEADEYE.

DICK.   Kind Captain, I've important information,
                Sing hey, the kind commander that you are,
            About a certain intimate relation,
                Sing hey, the merry maiden and the tar.
BOTH.   The merry maiden and the tar.

CAPT.   Good fellow, in conundrums you are speaking,
                Sing hey, the mystic sailor that you are ;
            The answer to them vainly I am seeking ;
                Sing hey, the merry maiden and the tar.
BOTH.   The merry maiden and the tar.

DICK.   Kind Captain, your young lady is a-sighing,
                Sing hey, the simple captain that you are,
            This very night with Rackstraw to be flying ;

Sing hey, the merry maiden and the tar.

BOTH. The merry maiden and the tar.

CAPT. Good fellow, you have given timely warning,
Sing hey, the thoughtful sailor that you are,
I'll talk to Master Rackstraw in the morning:
Sing hey, the cat-o'-nine-tails and the tar.

(Producing a 'cat'.)

BOTH. The merry cat-o'-nine-tails and the tar !

CAPT. Dick Deadeye — I thank you for your warning — I will at once take means to arrest their flight. This boat cloak will afford me ample disguise — So ! *(Envelops himself in a mysterious cloak, holding it before his face.)*

DICK. Ha, ha ! They are foiled — foiled — foiled !

Enter Crew on tiptoe, with RALPH *and* BOATSWAIN *meeting* JOSEPHINE, *who enters from cabin on tiptoe, with bundle of necessaries, and accompanied by* LITTLE BUTTERCUP.

ENSEMBLE.

Carefully on tiptoe stealing,
Breathing gently as we may,
Every step with caution feeling,
We will softly steal away.
*(*CAPTAIN *stamps.)* — *Chord.*

ALL *(much alarmed)*. Goodness me —
Why, what was that ?

DICK. Silent be,
It was the cat !

ALL *(reassured)*. It was — it was the cat !

CAPT. *(producing cat-o'-nine-tails)*. They're right, it was the cat !

ALL. Pull ashore, in fashion steady,
Hymen will defray the fare,
For a clergyman is ready
To unite the happy pair !
(Stamp as before, and Chord.)

ALL.   Goodness me,
                        Why, what was that ?
DICK.   Silent be,
                        Again the cat !
ALL.   It was again that cat !
CAPT. (*aside*).   They're right, it was the cat !
CAPT. (*throwing off cloak*). Hold ! (*All start.*)
             Pretty daughter of mine,
                I insist upon knowing
                Where you may be going
             With these sons of the brine,
                For my excellent crew,
             Though foes they could thump any,
             Are scarcely fit company,
                My daughter, for you.
CREW.   Now, hark at that, do !
             Though foes we could thump any,
             We are scarcely fit company
               For a lady like you !
RALPH. Proud officer, that haughty lip uncurl !
        Vain man, suppress that supercilious sneer,
    For I have dared to love your matchless girl,
     A fact well known to all my messmates here !
CAPT.   Oh, horror !
RALPH *and* JOS. { I,
                   He, } humble, poor, and lowly born,

             The meanest in the port division —
               The butt of epauletted scorn —
            The mark of quarter-deck derision —
            Have }
            Has } dared to raise { my
                         his } wormy eyes

       Above the dust to which you'd mould { me
                                him

        In manhood's glorious pride to rise,
            I am }
            He is } an Englishman — behold { me !
                                him !
ALL.   He is an Englishman !
BOAT.   He is an Englishman !

| | For he himself has said it,
| | And it's greatly to his credit,
| | That he is an Englishman !
ALL. | That he is an Englishman !
BOAT. | For he might have been a Roosian,
| | A French, or Turk, or Proosian,
| | Or perhaps Itali-an !
ALL. | Or perhaps Itali-an !
BOAT. | But in spite of all temptations
| | To belong to other nations,
| | He remains an Englishman !
ALL. | For in spite of all temptations, etc.
CAPT. (*trying to repress his anger*).
| | In uttering a reprobation
| | To any British tar,
| | I try to speak with moderation,
| | But you have gone too far.
| | I'm very sorry to disparage
| | A humble foremast lad,
| | But to seek your captain's child in marriage,
| | Why, damme, it's too bad !

During this, COUSIN HEBE *and* FEMALE RELATIVES
have entered.

ALL (*shocked*). Oh !
CAPT.   Yes, damme, it's too bad !
ALL.   Oh !
CAPT. *and* DICK DEADEYE.   Yes, damme, it's too bad.

During this, SIR JOSEPH *has appeared on poop-deck. He is
horrified at the bad language.*

HEBE.   Did you hear him — did you hear him ?
| | Oh, the monster overbearing !
| | Don't go near him — don't go near him —
| | He is swearing — he is swearing !
SIR JOSEPH. My pain and my distress,
| | I find it is not easy to express ;
| | My amazement — my surprise —
| | You may learn from the expression of my eyes !

CAPT.   My lord — one word — the facts are not before you;
                 The word was injudicious, I allow —
                 But hear my explanation, I implore you,
                 And you will be indignant too, I vow!

SIR JOSEPH.   I will hear of no defence,
                       Attempt none if you're sensible.
                    That word of evil sense
                       Is wholly indefensible.
                    Go, ribald, get you hence
                       To your cabin with celerity.
                    This is the consequence
                       Of ill-advised asperity!
                 [*Exit* CAPTAIN, *disgraced, followed by* JOSEPHINE.

ALL.   This is the consequence
                       Of ill-advised asperity!

SIR JOSEPH.   For I'll teach you all, ere long,
                       To refrain from language strong,
                    For I haven't any sympathy for ill-bred taunts!

HEBE.   No more have his sisters, nor his cousins, nor his aunts.

ALL.   For he is an Englishman, etc.

SIR JOSEPH. Now, tell me, my fine fellow — for you *are* a fine fellow——

RALPH. Yes, your honour.

SIR JOSEPH. How came your captain so far to forget himself? I am quite sure you had given him no cause for annoyance.

RALPH. Please your honour, it was thus-wise. You see I'm only a topman — a mere foremast hand ——

SIR JOSEPH. Don't be ashamed of that. Your position as a top-man is a very exalted one.

RALPH. Well, your honour, love burns as brightly in the fo'c'sle as it does on the quarter-deck, and Josephine is the fairest bud that ever blossomed upon the tree of a poor fellow's wildest hopes.

Enter JOSEPHINE; *she rushes to* RALPH'S *arms.*

JOS. Darling! (SIR JOSEPH *horrified.*)

RALPH. She is the figurehead of my ship of life — the bright beacon that guides me into my port of happiness — the rarest, the purest gem that ever sparkled on a poor but worthy fellow's trusting brow !

ALL. Very pretty, very pretty !

SIR JOSEPH. Insolent sailor, you shall repent this outrage. Seize him ! (*Two Marines seize him and handcuff him.*)

JOS. Oh, Sir Joseph, spare him, for I love him tenderly.

SIR JOSEPH. Pray, don't. I will teach this presumptuous mariner to discipline his affections. Have you such a thing as a dungeon on board ?

ALL. We have !

DICK. They have !

SIR JOSEPH. Then load him with chains and take him there at once !

OCTETTE.

RALPH.
    Farewell, my own,
        Light of my life, farewell !
    For crime unknown
        I go to a dungeon cell.

JOS.
    I will atone.
        In the meantime farewell !
    And all alone
        Rejoice in your dungeon cell !

SIR JOSEPH.
    A bone, a bone
        I'll pick with this sailor fell ;
    Let him be shown
        At once to his dungeon cell.

BOATSWAIN, DICK DEADEYE, *and* COUSIN HEBE.
        He'll hear no tone
            Of the maiden he loves so well !
        No telephone
            Communicates with his cell !

BUT. (*mysteriously*).   But when is known
            The secret I have to tell,
        Wide will be thrown
            The door of his dungeon cell.

D

ALL.   For crime unknown
                  He goes to a dungeon cell !

                              [RALPH *is led off in custody.*

SIR JOSEPH.   My pain and my distress
                  Again it is not easy to express.
                  My amazement, my surprise,
                  Again you may discover from my eyes.

ALL.   How terrible the aspect of his eyes !

BUT.   Hold ! Ere upon your loss
                  You lay much stress,
                A long-concealèd crime
                I would confess.

SONG — BUTTERCUP.

        A many years ago,
     When I was young and charming,
        As some of you may know,
     I practised baby-farming.

ALL.   Now this is most alarming !
                When she was young and charming,
                She practised baby-farming,
                A many years ago.

BUT.   Two tender babes I nussed :
                One was of low condition,
                The other, upper crust,
                A regular patrician.

ALL (*explaining to each other*).
                Now, this is the position :
                One was of low condition,
                The other a patrician,
                A many years ago.

BUT.   Oh, bitter is my cup !
                However could I do it ?
                I mixed those children up,
                And not a creature knew it !

ALL.   However could you do it ?
                Some day, no doubt, you'll rue it,

Although no creature knew it,
     So many years ago.

BUT.   In time each little waif
          Forsook his foster-mother,
     The well-born babe was Ralph —
          Your captain was the other ! ! !

ALL.   They left their foster-mother,
     The one was Ralph, our brother,
     Our captain was the other,
          A many years ago.

SIR JOSEPH. Then I am to understand that Captain Corcoran and Ralph were exchanged in childhood's happy hour — that Ralph is really the Captain, and the Captain is Ralph ?

BUT. That is the idea I intended to convey, officially !

SIR JOSEPH. And very well you have conveyed it.

BUT. Aye ! aye ! yer 'onour.

SIR JOSEPH. Dear me ! Let them appear before me, at once !

RALPH *enters as* CAPTAIN ; CAPTAIN *as a common sailor.* JOSEPHINE *rushes to his arms.*

JOS. My father — a common sailor !

CAPT. It is hard, is it not, my dear ?

SIR JOSEPH. This is a very singular occurrence ; I congratulate you both. (*To* RALPH.) Desire that remarkably fine seaman to step forward.

RALPH. Corcoran. Three paces to the front — march !

CAPT. If what ?

RALPH. If what ? I don't think I understand you.

CAPT. If you please.

SIR JOSEPH. The gentleman is quite right. If you *please.*

RALPH. Oh ! If you *please.* (CAPTAIN *steps forward.*)

SIR JOSEPH (*to* CAPTAIN). You are an extremely fine fellow.

CAPT. Yes, your honour.

SIR JOSEPH. So it seems that you were Ralph, and Ralph was you.

CAPT. So it seems, your honour.

SIR JOSEPH. Well, I need not tell you that after this change in your condition, a marriage with your daughter will be out of the question.

CAPT. Don't say that, your honour — love levels all ranks.

SIR JOSEPH. It does to a considerable extent, but it does not level them as much as that. (*Handing* JOSEPHINE *to* RALPH.) Here — take her, sir, and mind you treat her kindly.

RALPH *and* JOS. Oh bliss, oh rapture !

CAPT. *and* BUT. Oh rapture, oh bliss !

SIR JOSEPH.   Sad my lot and sorry,
          What shall I do ?   I cannot live alone !

HEBE.   Fear nothing — while I live I'll not desert you.
          I'll soothe and comfort your declining days.

SIR JOSEPH. No, don't do that.

HEBE.   Yes, but indeed I'd rather —

SIR JOSEPH (*resigned*). To-morrow morn our vows shall all be plighted,
          Three loving pairs on the same day united !

QUARTETTE.

JOSEPHINE, HEBE, RALPH, *and* DEADEYE.

Oh joy, oh rapture unforeseen,
The clouded sky is now serene,
The god of day — the orb of love,
Has hung his ensign high above,
     The sky is all ablaze.

With wooing words and loving song,
We'll chase the lagging hours along,
And if $\left\{ \begin{array}{l} \text{he finds} \\ \text{I find} \end{array} \right\}$ the maiden coy,
We'll murmur forth decorous joy,
     In dreamy roundelay.

CAPT.   For he's the Captain of the *Pinafore*.

ALL.   And a right good captain too !

CAPT.   And though before my fall
               I was captain of you all,
          I'm a member of the crew.

ALL.   Although before his fall, etc.

CAPT.	I shall marry with a wife,
	In my humble rank of life ! (*turning to* BUT.)
	And you, my own, are she —
	I must wander to and fro,
	But wherever I may go,
	I shall never be untrue to thee !
ALL.	What, never ?
CAPT.	No, never !
ALL.	What, *never* ?
CAPT.	Hardly ever !
ALL.	Hardly ever be untrue to thee.
	Then give three cheers, and one cheer more
	For the former Captain of the *Pinafore*.

BUT.	For he loves Little Buttercup, dear Little Buttercup,
	Though I could never tell why;
	But still he loves Buttercup, poor Little Buttercup,
	Sweet Little Buttercup, aye !
ALL.	For he loves, etc.

SIR JOSEPH.	I'm the monarch of the sea,
	And when I've married thee (*to* HEBE),
	I'll be true to the devotion that my love implants,
HEBE.	Then good-bye to his sisters, and his cousins, and his aunts,
	Especially his cousins,
	Whom he reckons up by dozens,
	His sisters, and his cousins, and his aunts !

ALL.	For he is an Englishman,
	And he himself hath said it,
	And it's greatly to his credit
	That he is an Englishman !

CURTAIN

THE GONDOLIERS

OR

THE KING OF BARATARIA

DRAMATIS PERSONÆ

THE DUKE OF PLAZA-TORO (*a Grandee of Spain*)
LUIZ (*his Attendant*)
DON ALHAMBRA DEL BOLERO (*the Grand Inquisitor*)
MARCO PALMIERI
GIUSEPPE PALMIERI
ANTONIO
FRANCESCO } (*Venetian Gondoliers*)
GIORGIO
ANNIBALE
THE DUCHESS OF PLAZA-TORO
CASILDA (*her Daughter*)
GIANETTA
TESSA
FIAMETTA } (*Contadine*)
VITTORIA
GIULIA
INEZ (*the King's Foster-mother*)
*Chorus of Gondoliers and Contadine, Men-at-Arms, Heralds,
and Pages.*

———

ACT I. — The Piazzetta, Venice.

ACT II. — Pavilion in the Palace of Barataria.

(*An interval of three months is supposed to elapse between
Acts I. and II.*)

Date 1750.

First produced at the Savoy Theatre on December 7, 1889.

THE GONDOLIERS

OR

THE KING OF BARATARIA

ACT I

SCENE. — THE PIAZZETTA, VENICE. *The Ducal Palace on the right.*

FIAMETTA, GIULIA, VITTORIA, *and other Contadine discovered, each tying a bouquet of roses.*

CHORUS OF CONTADINE.

List and learn, ye dainty roses,
    Roses white and roses red,
Why we bind you into posies
    Ere your morning bloom has fled.
By a law of maiden's making,
Accents of a heart that's aching,
Even though that heart be breaking,
    Should by maiden be unsaid:
Though they love with love exceeding,
They must seem to be unheeding —
Go ye then and do their pleading,
    Roses white and roses red !

FIAMETTA.

Two there are for whom, in duty,
    Every maid in Venice sighs —
Two so peerless in their beauty
    That they shame the summer skies.

> We have hearts for them, in plenty,
> > They have hearts, but all too few,
> We, alas, are four-and-twenty !
> > They, alas, are only two !
> We, alas !

CHORUS.	Alas !
FIA.	Are four-and-twenty,
	They, alas !
CHORUS.	Alas !
FIA.	Are only two.
CHORUS.	They, alas, are only two, alas !

> Now ye know, ye dainty roses,
> Why we bind you into posies,
> > Ere your morning bloom has fled,
> > Roses white and roses red !

During this chorus ANTONIO, FRANCESCO, GIORGIO, *and other Gondoliers have entered unobserved by the Girls — at first two, then
two more, then four, then half a dozen, then the remainder of the
Chorus.*

SOLI.

FRANC.	Good morrow, pretty maids ; for whom prepare ye
	These floral tributes extraordinary ?
FIA.	For Marco and Giuseppe Palmieri,
	The pink and flower of all the Gondolieri.
GIU.	They're coming here, as we have heard but lately,
	To choose two brides from us who sit sedately.
ANT.	Do all you maidens love them ?
ALL.	Passionately !
ANT.	These gondoliers are to be envied greatly !
GIOR.	But what of us, who one and all adore you ?
	Have pity on our passion, we implore you !
FIA.	These gentlemen must make their choice before you ;
VIT.	In the meantime we tacitly ignore you.
GIU.	When they have chosen two that leaves you plenty —
	Two dozen we, and ye are four-and-twenty.
FIA. *and* VIT.	Till then, enjoy your *dolce far niente*.
ANT.	With pleasure, nobody *contradicente* !

SONG — Antonio *and* Chorus.

For the merriest fellows are we, tra la,
That ply on the emerald sea, tra la;
    With loving and laughing,
    And quipping and quaffing,
We're happy as happy can be, tra la —
    As happy as happy can be !

With sorrow we've nothing to do, tra la,
And care is a thing to pooh-pooh, tra la;
    And Jealousy yellow,
    Unfortunate fellow,
We drown in the shimmering blue, tra la —
    We drown in the shimmering blue !

FIA. (*looking off*). See, see, at last they come to make their
      choice —
    Let us acclaim them with united voice.

(MARCO *and* GIUSEPPE *appear in gondola at back.*)

CHORUS (*Girls*). Hail, hail ! gallant gondolieri, ben venuti !
    Accept our love, our homage, and our duty.

(MARCO *and* GIUSEPPE *jump ashore — the Girls salute them.*)

DUET — MARCO *and* GIUSEPPE, *with*
CHORUS OF GIRLS.

MAR. *and* GIU.	Buon' giorno, signorine !
GIRLS.	Gondolieri carissimi !
	Siamo contadine !
MAR. *and* GIU. (*bowing*).	Servitori umilissimi !
	Per chi questi fiori —
	Questi fiori bellissimi ?
GIRLS.	Per voi, bei signori,
	O eccellentissimi !

(*The Girls present their bouquets to* MARCO *and* GIUSEPPE, *who are overwhelmed with them, and carry them with difficulty.*)

MAR. *and* GIU. (*their arms full of flowers*).	O ciel' !
GIRLS.	Buon' giorno, cavalieri !
MAR. *and* GIU. (*deprecatingly*).	Siamo gondolieri.
(*To* FIA. *and* VIT.)	Signorina, io t' amo !
GIRLS (*deprecatingly*).	Contadine siamo.
MAR. *and* GIU.	Signorine !
GIRLS (*deprecatingly*).	Contadine !
(*Curtseying to* MAR. *and* GIU.)	Cavalieri.
MAR. *and* GIU. (*deprecatingly*).	Gondolieri !
	Poveri gondolieri !
CHORUS.	Buon' giorno, signorine, etc.

DUET — MARCO *and* GIUSEPPE.

We're called *gondolieri*,
But that's a vagary,
It's quite honorary
        The trade that we ply.
For gallantry noted
Since we were short-coated,
To beauty devoted,
        Giuseppe } and I;
        Are Marco }
When morning is breaking,
Our couches forsaking,
To greet their awaking
        With carols we come.
At summer day's nooning,
When weary lagooning,
Our mandolins tuning,
        We lazily thrum.
When vespers are ringing,
To hope ever clinging,
With songs of our singing
        A vigil we keep,

When daylight is fading,
Enwrapt in night's shading,
With soft serenading
    We sing them to sleep.
We're called *gondolieri*, etc.

RECIT. — MARCO *and* GIUSEPPE.

MAR.	And now to choose our brides !
GIU.	As all are young and fair,
	And amiable besides,
BOTH.	We really do not care
	A preference to declare.
MAR.	A bias to disclose
	Would be indelicate —
GIU.	And therefore we propose
	To let impartial Fate
	Select for us a mate !
ALL.	Viva !
GIRLS.	A bias to disclose
	Would be indelicate —
MEN.	But how do they propose
	To let impartial Fate
	Select for them a mate ?
GIU.	These handkerchiefs upon our eyes be good enough to bind,
MAR.	And take good care that both of us are absolutely blind ;
BOTH.	Then turn us round — and we, with all convenient despatch,
	Will undertake to marry any two of you we catch !
ALL.	Viva !

They undertake to marry any two of $\begin{cases} \text{us they catch !} \\ \text{them they catch !} \end{cases}$

(*The Girls prepare to bind their eyes as directed.*)

FIA. (*to* MARCO).	Are you peeping ?
	Can you see me ?
MAR.	Dark I'm keeping,
	Dark and dreamy !
	(MARCO *slyly lifts bandage.*)

VIT. (*to* GIUSEPPE). If you're blinded
      Truly, say so.
GIU.   All right-minded
      Players play so ! (*slyly lifts bandage*).
FIA. (*detecting* MARCO). Conduct shady !
      They are cheating !
      Surely they de-
      Serve a beating ! (*replaces bandage*).
VIT. (*detecting* GIUSEPPE). This too much is ;
      Maidens mocking —
      Conduct such is
      Truly shocking ! (*replaces bandage*).
ALL.   You can spy, sir !
      Shut your eye, sir !
    You may use it by and by, sir !
      You can see, sir !
      Don't tell me, sir !
    That will do — now let it be, sir !
CHORUS OF My papa he keeps three horses,
 GIRLS.   Black, and white, and dapple grey, sir ;
    Turn three times, then take your courses,
    Catch whichever girl you may, sir !
CHORUS OF MEN. My papa, etc.

(MARCO *and* GIUSEPPE *turn round, as directed, and try to catch the
girls. Business of blind-man's buff. Eventually* MARCO *catches*
GIANETTA, *and* GIUSEPPE *catches* TESSA. *The two girls try to
escape, but in vain. The two men pass their hands over the girls'
faces to discover their identity.*)

GIU.   I've at length achieved a capture !
 (*Guessing.*) This is Tessa ! (*removes bandage*). Rapture,
     rapture !
MAR. (*guessing*). To me Gianetta fate has granted ! (*removes
     bandage*).
     Just the very girl I wanted !
GIU. (*politely to* MAR.). If you'd rather change——
TESS.   My goodness !
     This indeed is simple rudeness.

MAR. (*politely to* GIU.).　I've no preference whatever —
GIA.　　　　　　　　　　Listen to him ! Well, I never !

(*Each man kisses each girl.*)

GIA.　　　　　Thank you, gallant *gondolieri* !
　　　　　　　　　In a set and formal measure
　　　　　　　It is scarcely necessary
　　　　　　　　　To express our pleasure.
　　　　　　　　　Each of us to prove a treasure,
　　　　　　　Conjugal and monetary,
　　　　　　　Gladly will devote our leisure,
　　　　　　　Gay and gallant *gondolieri.*
　　　　　　　　　Tra, la, la, la, la, la, etc.

TESS.　　　　Gay and gallant *gondolieri,*
　　　　　　　　　Take us both and hold us tightly,
　　　　　　　You have luck extraordinary ;
　　　　　　　　　We might both have been unsightly !
　　　　　　　　　If we judge your conduct rightly,
　　　　　　　'Twas a choice involuntary ;
　　　　　　　　　Still we thank you most politely,
　　　　　　　Gay and gallant *gondolieri* !
　　　　　　　　　Tra, la, la, la, la, la, etc.

CHORUS OF　 Thank you, gallant *gondolieri* ;
　GIRLS.　　　　　In a set and formal measure,
　　　　　　　It is scarcely necessary
　　　　　　　　　To express our pleasure.
　　　　　　　　　Each of us to prove a treasure
　　　　　　　Gladly will devote our leisure,
　　　　　　　Gay and gallant *gondolieri* !
　　　　　　　　　Tra, la, la, la, la, la, etc.

ALL.　　　　　Fate in this has put his finger —
　　　　　　　　　Let us bow to Fate's decree,
　　　　　　　Then no longer let us linger,
　　　　　　　　　To the altar hurry we !
　　　　　　[*They all dance off two and two* — GIANETTA *with* MARCO,
　　　　　　TESSA *with* GIUSEPPE.

*Flourish. A gondola arrives at the Piazzetta steps, from which enter
the* DUKE OF PLAZA-TORO, *the* DUCHESS, *their daughter* CASILDA,

and their attendant LUIZ, *who carries a drum. All are dressed in pompous but old and faded clothes.*

Entrance of DUKE, DUCHESS, CASILDA, *and* LUIZ.

DUKE.   From the sunny Spanish shore,
        The Duke of Plaza-Tor' —
DUCH.   And His Grace's Duchess true —
CAS.   And His Grace's daughter, too —
LUIZ.   And His Grace's private drum
        To Venetia's shores have come:
ALL.   If ever, ever, ever
            They get back to Spain,
        They will never, never, never
            Cross the sea again —
DUKE.   Neither that Grandee from the Spanish shore,
        The noble Duke of Plaza Tor' —
DUCH.   Nor His Grace's Duchess, staunch and true —
CAS.   You may add, His Grace's daughter, too —
LUIZ.   Nor His Grace's own particular drum
        To Venetia's shores will come:
ALL.   If ever, ever, ever
            They get back to Spain,
        They will never, never, never
            Cross the sea again !

DUKE. At last we have arrived at our destination. This is the Ducal Palace, and it is here that the Grand Inquisitor resides. As a Castilian hidalgo of ninety-five quarterings, I regret that I am unable to pay my state visit on a horse. As a Castilian hidalgo of that description, I should have preferred to ride through the streets of Venice; but owing, I presume, to an unusually wet season, the streets are in such a condition that equestrian exercise is impracticable. No matter. Where is our suite ?

LUIZ (*coming forward*). Your Grace, I am here.

DUCH. Why do you not do yourself the honour to kneel when you address His Grace ?

DUKE. My love, it is so small a matter ! (*To* LUIZ.) Still, you may as well do it. (LUIZ *kneels.*)

CAS. The young man seems to entertain but an imperfect appreciation of the respect due from a menial to a Castilian hidalgo.

DUKE. My child, you are hard upon our suite.

CAS. Papa, I've no patience with the presumption of persons in his plebeian position. If he does not appreciate that position, let him be whipped until he does.

DUKE. Let us hope the omission was not intended as a slight. I should be much hurt if I thought it was. So would he. (*To* LUIZ.) Where are the halberdiers who were to have had the honour of meeting us here, that our visit to the Grand Inquisitor might be made in becoming state?

LUIZ. Your Grace, the halberdiers are mercenary people who stipulated for a trifle on account.

DUKE. How tiresome! Well, let us hope the Grand Inquisitor is a blind gentleman. And the band who were to have had the honour of escorting us? I see no band!

LUIZ. Your Grace, the band are sordid persons who required to be paid in advance.

DUCH. That's so like a band!

DUKE (*annoyed*). Insuperable difficulties meet me at every turn!

DUCH. But surely they know His Grace?

LUIZ. Exactly — they know His Grace.

DUKE. Well, let us hope that the Grand Inquisitor is a deaf gentleman. A cornet-à-piston would be something. You do not happen to possess the accomplishment of tootling like a cornet-à-piston?

LUIZ. Alas, no, Your Grace! But I can imitate a farmyard.

DUKE (*doubtfully*). I don't see how that would help us. I don't see how we could bring it in.

CAS. It would not help us in the least. We are not a parcel of graziers come to market, dolt!

DUKE. My love, our suite's feelings! (*To* LUIZ.) Be so good as to ring the bell and inform the Grand Inquisitor that his Grace the Duke of Plaza-Toro, Count Matadoro, Baron Picadoro——

DUCH. And suite—

DUKE. And suite — have arrived at Venice, and seek——

CAS. Desire—

DUCH. Demand!

DUKE. And demand an audience.

LUIZ. Your Grace has but to command. (*Rising.*)

DUKE (*much moved*). I felt sure of it — I felt sure of it ! (*Exit* LUIZ *into Ducal Palace.*) And now, my love — (*aside to* DUCHESS) Shall we tell her ? I think so — (*aloud to* CASILDA) And now, my love, prepare for a magnificent surprise. It is my agreeable duty to reveal to you a secret which should make you the happiest young lady in Venice !

CAS. A secret ?

DUCH. A secret which, for State reasons, it has been necessary to preserve for twenty years.

DUKE. When you were a prattling babe of six months old you were married by proxy to no less a personage than the infant son and heir of His Majesty the immeasurably wealthy King of Barataria !

CAS. Married to the infant son of the King of Barataria ? Was I consulted ? (DUKE *shakes his head.*) Then it was a most unpardonable liberty !

DUKE. Consider his extreme youth and forgive him. Shortly after the ceremony that misguided monarch abandoned the creed of his forefathers, and became a Wesleyan Methodist of the most bigoted and persecuting type. The Grand Inquisitor, determined that the innovation should not be perpetuated in Barataria, caused your smiling and unconscious husband to be stolen and conveyed to Venice. A fortnight since the Methodist Monarch and all his Wesleyan Court were killed in an insurrection, and we are here to ascertain the whereabouts of your husband, and to hail you, our daughter, as Her Majesty, the reigning Queen of Barataria ! (*Kneels.*)

During this speech LUIZ *re-enters.*

DUCH. Your Majesty ! (*Kneels.*)

DUKE. It is at such moments as these that one feels how necessary it is to travel with a full band.

CAS. I, the Queen of Barataria ! But I've nothing to wear ! We are practically penniless !

DUKE. That point has not escaped me. Although I am unhappily in straitened circumstances at present, my social influence is something enormous ; and a Company, to be called the Duke of Plaza-Toro, Limited, is in course of formation to work me. An influential directorate has been secured, and I shall myself join the Board after allotment.

Cas. Am I to understand that the Queen of Barataria may be called upon at any time to witness her honoured sire in process of liquidation ?

Duch. The speculation is not exempt from that drawback. If your father should stop, it will, of course, be necessary to wind him up.

Cas. But it's so undignified—it's so degrading! A Grandee of Spain turned into a public company ! Such a thing was never heard of !

Duke. My child, the Duke of Plaza-Toro does not follow fashions — he leads them. He always leads everybody. When he was in the army he led his regiment. He occasionally led them into action. He invariably led them out of it.

SONG — Duke of Plaza-Toro.

In enterprise of martial kind,
　　When there was any fighting,
He led his regiment from behind —
　　He found it less exciting.
But when away his regiment ran,
　　His place was at the fore, O —
　　　　That celebrated,
　　　　Cultivated,
　　　　Underrated,
　　　　　　Nobleman,
　　The Duke of Plaza-Toro !

All.　　　In the first and foremost flight, ha, ha !
You always found that knight, ha, ha !
　　　　That celebrated,
　　　　Cultivated,
　　　　Underrated
　　　　　　Nobleman,
　　The Duke of Plaza-Toro !

When, to evade Destruction's hand,
　　To hide they all proceeded,
No soldier in that gallant band
　　Hid half as well as he did.

   He lay concealed throughout the war,
    And so preserved his gore, O !
     That unaffected,
     Undetected,
     Well-connected
      Warrior,
    The Duke of Plaza-Toro !

ALL.   In every doughty deed, ha, ha !
   He always took the lead, ha, ha !
     That unaffected,
     Undetected,
     Well-connected
      Warrior,
    The Duke of Plaza-Toro !

   When told that they would all be shot
    Unless they left the service,
   That hero hesitated not,
    So marvellous his nerve is.
   He sent his resignation in,
    The first of all his corps, O !
     That very knowing,
     Overflowing,
     Easy-going
      Paladin,
    The Duke of Plaza-Toro !

ALL.   To men of grosser clay, ha, ha !
   He always showed the way, ha, ha !
     That very knowing,
     Overflowing,
     Easy-going
      Paladin,
    The Duke of Plaza-Toro !

[*Exeunt* DUKE *and* DUCHESS *into Ducal Palace.
As soon as they have disappeared,* LUIZ *and*
CASILDA *rush to each other's arms.*

RECIT. AND DUET — CASILDA *and* LUIZ.

> O rapture, when alone together
>> Two loving hearts and those that bear them
> May join in temporary tether,
>> Though Fate apart should rudely tear them.

CAS. Necessity, Invention's mother,
>> Compelled me to a course of feigning —
> But, left alone with one another,
>> I will atone for my disdaining !

>> Ah, well-beloved,
>> Mine angry frown
>> Is but a gown
>> That serves to dress
>> My gentleness !

LUIZ.
>> Ah, well-beloved,
>> Thy cold disdain,
>> It gives no pain —
>> 'Tis mercy, played
>> In masquerade !

BOTH.
>> Ah, well-beloved, etc.

CAS. O Luiz, Luiz — what have you said ? What have I done ? What have I allowed you to do ?

LUIZ. Nothing, I trust, that you will ever have reason to repent. (*Offering to embrace her.*)

CAS. (*withdrawing from him*). Nay, Luiz, it may not be. I have embraced you for the last time.

LUIZ (*amazed*). Casilda !

CAS. I have just learnt, to my surprise and indignation, that I was wed in babyhood to the infant son of the King of Barataria !

LUIZ. The son of the King of Barataria ? The child who was stolen in infancy by the Inquisition ?

CAS. The same. But, of course, you know his story.

LUIZ. Know his story? Why, I have often told you that my mother was the nurse to whose charge he was entrusted!

CAS. True. I had forgotten. Well, he has been discovered, and my father has brought me here to claim his hand.

LUIZ. But you will not recognize this marriage? It took place when you were too young to understand its import.

CAS. Nay, Luiz, respect my principles and cease to torture me with vain entreaties. Henceforth my life is another's.

LUIZ. But stay — the present and the future — *they* are another's; but the past — that at least is ours, and none can take it from us. As we may revel in naught else, let us revel in that!

CAS. I don't think I grasp your meaning.

LUIZ. Yet it is logical enough. You say you cease to love me?

CAS. (*demurely*). I say I *may* not love you.

LUIZ. Ah, but you do not say you *did* not love me?

CAS. I loved you with a frenzy that words are powerless to express — and that but ten brief minutes since!

LUIZ. Exactly. My own — that is, until ten minutes since, my own — my lately loved, my recently adored — tell me that until, say a quarter of an hour ago, I was all in all to thee! (*Embracing her.*)

CAS. I see your idea. It's ingenious, but don't do that. (*Releasing herself.*)

LUIZ. There can be no harm in revelling in the past.

CAS. None whatever, but an embrace cannot be taken to act retrospectively.

LUIZ. Perhaps not!

CAS. We may recollect an embrace — I recollect many — but we must not repeat them.

LUIZ. Then let us recollect a few! (*A moment's pause, as they recollect, then both heave a deep sigh.*)

LUIZ. Ah, Casilda, you were to me as the sun is to the earth!

CAS. A quarter of an hour ago?

LUIZ. About that.

CAS. And to think that, but for this miserable discovery, you would have been my own for life!

LUIZ. Through life to death — a quarter of an hour ago!

CAS. How greedily my thirsty ears would have drunk the golden melody of those sweet words a quarter — well, it's now about twenty minutes since. (*Looking at her watch.*)

LUIZ. About that. In such a matter one cannot be too precise.

CAS. And now our love, so full of life, is but a silent, solemn memory !

LUIZ. Must it be so, Casilda ?

CAS. Luiz, it must be so !

DUET — CASILDA *and* LUIZ.

LUIZ.

There was a time —
    A time for ever gone — ah, woe is me !
It was no crime
    To love but thee alone — ah, woe is me !
One heart, one life, one soul,
    One aim, one goal —
Each in the other's thrall,
    Each all in all, ah, woe is me !

BOTH.

Oh, bury, bury — let the grave close o'er
The days that were — that never will be more !
Oh, bury, bury love that all condemn,
And let the whirlwind mourn its requiem !

CAS.

Dead as the last year's leaves —
    As gathered flowers — ah, woe is me !
Dead as the garnered sheaves,
    That love of ours — ah, woe is me !
Born but to fade and die
    When hope was high,
Dead and as far away
    As yesterday ! — ah, woe is me !

BOTH.

Oh, bury, bury — let the grave close o'er, etc.

[*Re-enter from the Ducal Palace the* DUKE *and* DUCHESS, *followed by* DON ALHAMBRA DEL BOLERO, *the Grand Inquisitor*.

DUKE. My child, allow me to present to you His Distinction Don Alhambra del Bolero, the Grand Inquisitor of Spain. It was His

Distinction who so thoughtfully abstracted your infant husband and brought him to Venice.

DON AL. So this is the little lady who is so unexpectedly called upon to assume the functions of Royalty ! And a very nice little lady, too !

DUKE. Jimp, isn't she ?

DON AL. Distinctly jimp. Allow me ! (*Offers his hand. She turns away scornfully.*) Naughty temper !

DUKE. You must make some allowance. Her Majesty's head is a little turned by her access of dignity.

DON AL. I could have wished that Her Majesty's access of dignity had turned it in this direction.

DUCH. Unfortunately, if I am not mistaken, there appears to be some little doubt as to His Majesty's whereabouts.

CAS. (*aside*). A doubt as to his whereabouts ? Then we may yet be saved !

DON AL. A doubt ? Oh dear, no — no doubt at all ! He is here, in Venice, plying the modest but picturesque calling of a gondolier. I can give you his address — I see him every day ! In the entire annals of our history there is absolutely no circumstance so entirely free from all manner of doubt of any kind whatever ! Listen, and I'll tell you all about it.

SONG — DON ALHAMBRA (*with* DUKE, DUCHESS,
CASILDA, *and* LUIZ).

I stole the Prince, and I brought him here,
  And left him gaily prattling
With a highly respectable gondolier,
Who promised the Royal babe to rear,
And teach him the trade of a timoneer
  With his own beloved bratling.

   Both of the babes were strong and stout,
    And, considering all things, clever.
   Of that there is no manner of doubt —
   No probable, possible shadow of doubt —
    No possible doubt whatever.

But owing, I'm much disposed to fear,
    To his terrible taste for tippling,
That highly respectable gondolier
Could never declare with a mind sincere
Which of the two was his offspring dear,
    And which the Royal stripling !

            Which was which he could never make out
                Despite his best endeavour.
            Of *that* there is no manner of doubt —
            No probable, possible shadow of doubt —
                No possible doubt whatever.

Time sped, and when at the end of a year
    I sought that infant cherished,
That highly respectable gondolier
Was lying a corpse on his humble bier —
I dropped a Grand Inquisitor's tear —
    That gondolier had perished.

            A taste for drink, combined with gout,
                Had doubled him up for ever.
            Of *that* there is no manner of doubt —
            No probable, possible shadow of doubt —
                No possible doubt whatever.

The children followed his old career —
    (This statement can't be parried)
Of a highly respectable gondolier :
Well, one of the two (who will soon be here) —
But *which* of the two is not quite clear —
    Is the Royal Prince you married !

            Search in and out and round about,
                And you'll discover never
            A tale so free from every doubt —
            All probable, possible shadow of doubt —
                All possible doubt whatever !

CAS. Then do you mean to say that I am married to one of two gondoliers, but it is impossible to say which?

DON AL. Without any doubt of any kind whatever. But be re-assured: the nurse to whom your husband was entrusted is the mother of the musical young man who is such a past-master of that delicately modulated instrument (*indicating the drum*). She can, no doubt, establish the King's identity beyond all question.

LUIZ. Heavens, how did he know that?

DON AL. My young friend, a Grand Inquisitor is always up to date. (*To* CAS.) His mother is at present the wife of a highly res-pectable and old-established brigand, who carries on an extensive practice in the mountains around Cordova. Accompanied by two of my emissaries, he will set off at once for his mother's address. She will return with them, and if she finds any difficulty in making up her mind, the persuasive influence of the torture chamber will jog her memory.

RECIT. — CASILDA *and* DON ALHAMBRA.

CAS. But, bless my heart, consider my position!
    I am the wife of one, that's very clear;
    But who can tell, except by intuition,
      Which is the Prince, and which the Gondolier?

DON AL. Submit to Fate without unseemly wrangle:
      Such complications frequently occur —
    Life is one closely complicated tangle:
      Death is the only true unraveller!

QUINTET — DUKE, DUCHESS, CASILDA, LUIZ, *and* GRAND INQUISITOR.

ALL.   Try we life-long, we can never
      Straighten out life's tangled skein,
      Why should we, in vain endeavour,
        Guess and guess and guess again?
LUIZ.   Life's a pudding full of plums,
DUCH.   Care's a canker that benumbs.

ALL.
> Life's a pudding full of plums,
>> Care's a canker that benumbs.
> Wherefore waste our elocution
> On impossible solution ?
> Life's a pleasant institution,
>> Let us take it as it comes !

> Set aside the dull enigma,
>> We shall guess it all too soon;
> Failure brings no kind of stigma —
>> Dance we to another tune !

LUIZ.   String the lyre and fill the cup,
DUCH.   Lest on sorrow we should sup.
ALL.   String the lyre and fill the cup,
> Lest on sorrow we should sup.
> Hop and skip to Fancy's fiddle,
> Hands across and down the middle —
> Life's perhaps the only riddle
>> That we shrink from giving up !

> [*Exeunt all into Ducal Palace except* LUIZ, *who goes off in gondola.*

Enter Gondoliers and Contadine, followed by MARCO,
GIANETTA, GIUSEPPE, *and* TESSA.

CHORUS.
> Bridegroom and bride !
>> Knot that's insoluble,
>> Voices all voluble
> Hail it with pride.
> Bridegroom and bride !
>> We in sincerity
>> Wish you prosperity,
> Bridegroom and bride !

SONG — TESSA.

TESS.
> When a merry maiden marries,
> Sorrow goes and pleasure tarries;

Every sound becomes a song,
　　All is right, and nothing's wrong !
From to-day and ever after
Let our tears be tears of laughter.
　　Every sigh that finds a vent
　　Be a sigh of sweet content !
When you marry, merry maiden,
Then the air with love is laden;
　　Every flower is a rose,
　　　　Every goose becomes a swan,
　　Every kind of trouble goes
　　　　Where the last year's snows have gone !

CHORUS.　　Sunlight takes the place of shade
　　　　　　When you marry, merry maid !

TESS.　　　When a merry maiden marries,
　　　　　　Sorrow goes and pleasure tarries;
　　　　　　　　Every sound becomes a song,
　　　　　　　　All is right, and nothing's wrong.
　　　　　　Gnawing Care and aching Sorrow,
　　　　　　Get ye gone until to-morrow;
　　　　　　　　Jealousies in grim array,
　　　　　　　　Ye are things of yesterday !
　　　　　　When you marry, merry maiden,
　　　　　　Then the air with joy is laden;
　　　　　　　　All the corners of the earth
　　　　　　　　　　Ring with music sweetly played,
　　　　　　　　Worry is melodious mirth,
　　　　　　　　　　Grief is joy in masquerade;

CHORUS.　　Sullen night is laughing day —
　　　　　　All the year is merry May !

At the end of the song, DON ALHAMBRA *enters at back. The Gondoliers and Contadine shrink from him, and gradually go off,
much alarmed.*

GIU. And now our lives are going to begin in real earnest! What's a bachelor? A mere nothing — he's a chrysalis. He can't be said to live — he exists.

MAR. What a delightful institution marriage is! Why have we wasted all this time? Why didn't we marry ten years ago?

TESS. Because you couldn't find anybody nice enough.

GIA. Because you were waiting for *us*.

MAR. I suppose that *was* the reason. We were waiting for you without knowing it. (DON ALHAMBRA *comes forward*.) Hallo!

DON AL. Good morning.

GIU. If this gentleman is an undertaker, it's a bad omen.

DON AL. Ceremony of some sort going on?

GIU. (*aside*). He *is* an undertaker! (*Aloud*.) No — a little unimportant family gathering. Nothing in *your* line.

DON AL. Somebody's birthday, I suppose?

GIA. Yes, mine!

TESS. And mine!

MAR. And mine!

GIU. And mine!

DON AL. Curious coincidence! And how old may you all be?

TESS. It's a rude question — but about ten minutes.

DON AL. Remarkably fine children! But surely you are jesting?

TESS. In other words, we were married about ten minutes since.

DON AL. Married! You don't mean to say you are married?

MAR. Oh yes, we are married.

DON AL. What, both of you?

ALL. All four of us.

DON AL. (*aside*). Bless my heart, how extremely awkward!

GIA. You don't mind, I suppose?

TESS. You were not thinking of either of us for yourself, I presume? Oh, Giuseppe, look at him — he was. He's heart-broken!

DON AL. No, no, I wasn't! I wasn't!

GIU. Now, my man (*slapping him on the back*), we don't want anything in your line to-day, and if your curiosity's satisfied — you can go!

DON AL. You mustn't call me your man. It's a liberty. I don't think you know who I am.

GIU. Not we, indeed! We are jolly gondoliers, the sons of Baptisto Palmieri, who led the last revolution. Republicans, heart and soul, we hold all men to be equal. As we abhor oppression, we abhor kings: as we detest vain-glory, we detest rank: as we despise effeminacy, we despise wealth. We are Venetian gondoliers — your equals in everything except our calling, and in that at once your masters and your servants.

DON AL. Bless my heart, how unfortunate! One of you may be Baptisto's son, for anything I know to the contrary; but the other is no less a personage than the only son of the late King of Barataria.

ALL. What!

DON AL. And I trust — I *trust* it was that one who slapped me on the shoulder and called me his man!

GIU. One of us a king!
MAR. Not brothers!
TESS. The King of Barataria! } *Together.*
GIA. Well, who'd have thought it!

MAR. But which is it?

DON AL. What does it matter? As you are both Republicans, and hold kings in detestation, of course you'll abdicate at once. Good morning! (*Going.*)

GIA. *and* TESS. Oh, don't do that! (MARCO *and* GIUSEPPE *stop him.*)

GIU. Well, as to that, of course there are kings and kings. When I say that I detest kings, I mean I detest *bad* kings.

DON AL. I see. It's a delicate distinction.

GIU. Quite so. Now I can conceive a kind of king — an ideal king — the creature of my fancy, you know — who would be absolutely unobjectionable. A king, for instance, who would abolish taxes and make everything cheap, except gondolas——

MAR. And give a great many free entertainments to the gondoliers——

GIU. And let off fireworks on the Grand Canal, and engage all the gondolas for the occasion——

MAR. And scramble money on the Rialto among the gondoliers.

GIU. Such a king would be a blessing to his people, and if I were a king, that is the sort of king I would be.

MAR. And so would I!

DON AL. Come, I'm glad to find your objections are not insuperable.

MAR. *and* GIU. Oh, they're not insuperable.

GIA. *and* TESS. No, they're not insuperable.

GIU. Besides, we are open to conviction.

GIA. Yes; they are open to conviction.

TESS. Oh! they've often been convicted.

GIU. Our views may have been hastily formed on insufficient grounds. They may be crude, ill-digested, erroneous. I've a very poor opinion of the politician who is not open to conviction.

TESS. (*to* GIA.). Oh, he's a fine fellow!

GIA. Yes, that's the sort of politician for *my* money!

DON AL. Then we'll consider it settled. Now, as the country is in a state of insurrection, it is absolutely necessary that you should assume the reins of Government at once; and, until it is ascertained which of you is to be king, I have arranged that you will reign jointly, so that no question can arise hereafter as to the validity of any of your acts.

MAR. As one individual?

DON AL. As one individual.

GIU. (*linking himself with* MARCO). Like this?

DON AL. Something like that.

MAR. And we may take our friends with us, and give them places about the Court?

DON AL. Undoubtedly. That's always done!

MAR. I'm convinced!

GIU. So am I!

TESS. Then the sooner we're off the better.

GIA. We'll just run home and pack up a few things (*going*)——

DON AL. Stop, stop — that won't do at all — ladies are not admitted.

ALL. What!

DON AL. Not admitted. Not at present. Afterwards, perhaps. We'll see.

GIU. Why, you don't mean to say you are going to separate us from our wives!

DON AL. (*aside*). This is very awkward! (*Aloud.*) Only for a time — a few months. After all, what is a few months?

TESS. But we've only been married half an hour! (*Weeps.*)

FINALE, ACT I.

SONG — GIANETTA.

Kind sir, you cannot have the heart
　　　Our lives to part
From those to whom an hour ago
　　　We were united !
Before our flowing hopes you stem,
　　　Ah, look at them,
And pause before you deal this blow,
　　　All uninvited !
You men can never understand
　　　That heart and hand
Cannot be separated when
　　　We go a-yearning ;
You see, you've only women's eyes
　　　To idolize
And only women's hearts, poor men,
　　　To set *you* burning !
Ah me, you men will never understand
That woman's heart is one with woman's hand !

Some kind of charm you seem to find
　　　In womankind —
Some source of unexplained delight
　　　(Unless you're jesting),
But what attracts you, I confess,
　　　I cannot guess,
To me a woman's face is quite
　　　Uninteresting !
If from my sister I were torn,
　　　It could be borne —
I should, no doubt, be horrified,
　　　But I could bear it ; —
But Marco's quite another thing —
　　　He is my King,

He has my heart and none beside
                    Shall ever share it !
Ah me, you men will never understand
That woman's heart is one with woman's hand !

RECIT. — DON ALHAMBRA.

Do not give way to this uncalled-for grief,
Your separation will be very brief.
                    To ascertain which is the King
                        And which the other,
                    To Barataria's Court I'll bring
                        His foster-mother;
                    Her former nurseling to declare
                        She'll be delighted.
                    That settled, let each happy pair
                        Be reunited.

MAR., GIU., GIA., TESS.		
	Viva !	His argument is strong !
	Viva !	We'll not be parted long !
	Viva !	It will be settled soon !
	Viva !	Then comes our honeymoon !

[*Exit* DON ALHAMBRA.

QUARTET — MARCO, GIUSEPPE, GIANETTA, TESSA.

GIA.   Then one of us will be a Queen,
                    And sit on a golden throne,
                        With a crown instead
                        Of a hat on her head,
                    And diamonds all her own !
            With a beautiful robe of gold and green,
                    I've always understood;
                        I wonder whether
                        She'd wear a feather ?
                    I rather think she should !

ALL.   Oh, 'tis a glorious thing, I ween,
            To be a regular Royal Queen !
            No half-and-half affair, I mean,
            But a right-down regular Royal Queen !

E

MAR.   She'll drive about in a carriage and pair,
            With the King on her left-hand side,
                And a milk-white horse,
                As a matter of course,
            Whenever she wants to ride !
        With beautiful silver shoes to wear
            Upon her dainty feet;
                With endless stocks
                Of beautiful frocks
            And as much as she wants to eat !

ALL.   Oh, 'tis a glorious thing, I ween, etc.

TESS.   Whenever she condescends to walk,
            Be sure she'll shine at that,
                With her haughty stare
                And her nose in the air,
            Like a well-born aristocrat !
        At elegant high society talk
            She'll bear away the bell,
                With her 'How de do ?'
                And her 'How are you ?'
            And 'I trust I see you well !'

ALL.   Oh, 'tis a glorious thing, I ween, etc.

GIU.   And noble lords will scrape and bow,
            And double themselves in two,
                And open their eyes
                In blank surprise
            At whatever she likes to do.
        And everybody will roundly vow
            She's fair as flowers in May,
                And say, 'How clever !'
                At whatsoever
            She condescends to say !

ALL.   Oh, 'tis a glorious thing, I ween,
        To be a regular Royal Queen !
        No half-and-half affair, I mean,
        But a right-down regular Royal Queen !

        Enter Chorus of Gondoliers and Contadine.

CHORUS.

Now, pray, what is the cause of this remarkable hilarity ?
  This sudden ebullition of unmitigated jollity ?
Has anybody blessed you with a sample of his charity ?
  Or have you been adopted by a gentleman of quality ?

MAR. *and* GIU.   Replying, we sing
                         As one individual,
                    As I find I'm a king,
                         To my kingdom I bid you all.
                    I'm aware you object
                         To pavilions and palaces,
                    But you'll find I respect
                         Your Republican fallacies.

CHORUS.   As they know we object
                         To pavilions and palaces,
                    How can they respect
                         Our Republican fallacies ?

MARCO *and* GIUSEPPE.

MAR.   For every one who feels inclined,
            Some post we undertake to find
            Congenial with his frame of mind —
                 And all shall equal be.

GIU.   The Chancellor in his peruke —
            The Earl, the Marquis, and the Dook,
            The Groom, the Butler, and the Cook —
                 They all shall equal be.

MAR.   The Aristocrat who banks with Coutts —
            The Aristocrat who hunts and shoots —
            The Aristocrat who cleans our boots —
                 They all shall equal be !

GIU.   The Noble Lord who rules the State —
            The Noble Lord who cleans the plate —

MAR.   The Noble Lord who scrubs the grate —
                 They all shall equal be !

GIU.   The Lord High Bishop orthodox —
           The Lord High Coachman on the box —

MAR.   The Lord High Vagabond in the stocks —
              They all shall equal be !

BOTH.   For every one, etc.

                Sing high, sing low,
                Wherever they go,
                    They all shall equal be !

CHORUS.   Sing high, sing low,
                Wherever they go,
                    They all shall equal be !

           The Earl, the Marquis, and the Dook,
           The Groom, the Butler, and the Cook,
           The Aristocrat who banks with Coutts,
           The Aristocrat who cleans the boots,
           The Noble Lord who rules the State,
           The Noble Lord who scrubs the grate,
           The Lord High Bishop orthodox,
           The Lord High Vagabond in the stocks —

           For every one, etc.

                Sing high, sing low,
                Wherever they go,
                    They all shall equal be !
                Then hail ! O King,
                    Whichever you may be,
                To you we sing,
                    But do not bend the knee.
                Then hail ! O King.

               MARCO *and* GIUSEPPE (*together*).

Come, let's away — our island crown awaits me —
    Conflicting feelings rend my soul apart !
The thought of Royal dignity elates me,
    But leaving thee behind me breaks my heart !
                        (*Addressing* GIANETTA *and* TESSA.)

GIANETTA *and* TESSA (*together*).

Farewell, my love; on board you must be getting;
  But while upon the sea you gaily roam,
Remember that a heart for thee is fretting —
  The tender little heart you've left at home !

GIA.
    Now, Marco dear,
    My wishes hear:
      While you're away
    It's understood
    You will be good,
      And not too gay.
    To every trace
    Of maiden grace
      You will be blind,
    And will not glance
    By any chance
      On womankind !

    If you are wise,
    You'll shut your eyes
      Till we arrive,
    And not address
    A lady less
      Than forty-five.
    You'll please to frown
    On every gown
      That you may see;
    And, O my pet,
    You won't forget
      You've married me !

And O my darling, O my pet,
Whatever else you may forget,
In yonder isle beyond the sea,
Do not forget you've married me.

TESS.   You'll lay your head
                        Upon your bed
                          At set of sun.
                        You will not sing
                        Of anything
                          To any one.
                        You'll sit and mope
                        All day, I hope,
                          And shed a tear
                        Upon the life
                        Your little wife
                          Is passing here.

                        And if so be
                        You think of me,
                          Please tell the moon !
                        I'll read it all
                        In rays that fall
                          On the lagoon :
                        You'll be so kind
                        As tell the wind
                          How you may be,
                        And send me words
                        By little birds
                          To comfort me !

                    And O my darling, O my pet,
                    Whatever else you may forget,
                    In yonder isle beyond the sea,
                    Do not forget you've married me.

QUARTET.   O my darling, O my pet, etc.

          CHORUS (*during which a 'Xebeque' is hauled
                    alongside the quay*).

          Then away we go to an island fair
              That lies in a Southern sea :
          We know not where, and we don't much care,
              Wherever that isle may be.

THE MEN (*hauling on boat*).   One, two, three,
                                      Haul !
                                      One, two, three,
                                      Haul !
                                      One, two, three,
                                      Haul !
                                      With a will !

ALL.   When the breezes are a-blowing
              The ship will be going,
                   When they don't we shall all stand still !
              Then away we go to an island fair,
              We know not where, and we don't much care,
                   Wherever that isle may be.

                   SOLO — MARCO.

              Away we go
              To a balmy isle,
              Where the roses blow
              All the winter while.

ALL (*hoisting sail*).   Then away we go to an island fair
                                That lies in a Southern sea :
                                Then away we go to an island fair,
                                Then away, then away, then away !

(*The men embark on the 'Xebeque'. MARCO and GIUSEPPE embracing GIANETTA and TESSA. The girls wave a farewell to the men as the curtain falls.*)

                   END OF ACT I

ACT II

SCENE. — *Pavilion in the Court of Barataria.* MARCO *and* GIUSEPPE, *magnificently dressed, are seated on two thrones, occupied in cleaning the crown and the sceptre. The Gondoliers are discovered, dressed, some as courtiers, officers of rank, etc., and others as private soldiers and servants of various degrees. All are enjoying themselves without reference to social distinctions — some playing cards, others throwing dice, some reading, others playing cup and ball, 'morra', etc.*

CHORUS OF MEN *with* MARCO *and* GIUSEPPE.

> Of happiness the very pith
> > In Barataria you may see:
> A monarchy that's tempered with
> > Republican Equality.
> This form of government we find
> The beau-ideal of its kind —
> A despotism strict, combined
> > With absolute equality !

MARCO *and* GIUSEPPE.

> Two kings, of undue pride bereft,
> > Who act in perfect unity,
> Whom you can order right and left
> > With absolute impunity.
> Who put their subjects at their ease
> By doing all they can to please !
> And thus, to earn their bread-and-cheese,
> > Seize every opportunity.

CHORUS.   Of happiness the very pith, etc.

MAR. Gentlemen, we are much obliged to you for your expressions

130

of satisfaction and good feeling — I say, we are much obliged to you for your expressions of satisfaction and good feeling.

ALL. We heard you.

MAR. We are delighted, at any time, to fall in with sentiments so charmingly expressed.

ALL. That's all right.

GIU. At the same time there is just one little grievance that we should like to ventilate.

ALL (*angrily*). What?

GIU. Don't be alarmed — it's not serious. It is arranged that, until it is decided which of us two is the actual King, we are to act as one person.

GIORGIO. Exactly.

GIU. Now, although we act as *one* person, we are, in point of fact, *two* persons.

ANNIBALE. Ah, I don't think we can go into that. It is a legal fiction, and legal fictions are solemn things. Situated as we are, we can't recognize two independent responsibilities.

GIU. No; but you can recognize two independent appetites. It's all very well to say we act as one person, but when you supply us with only one ration between us, I should describe it as a legal fiction carried a little too far.

ANNI. It's rather a nice point. I don't like to express an opinion off-hand. Suppose we reserve it for argument before the full Court?

MAR. Yes, but what are we to do in the meantime?

MAR. *and* GIU. We want our tea.

ANNI. I think we may make an interim order for double rations on their Majesties entering into the usual undertaking to indemnify in the event of an adverse decision?

GIOR. That, I think, will meet the case. But you must work hard — stick to it — nothing like work.

GIU. Oh, certainly. We quite understand that a man who holds the magnificent position of King should do something to justify it. We are called 'Your Majesty', we are allowed to buy ourselves magnificent clothes, our subjects frequently nod to us in the streets, the sentries always return our salutes, and we enjoy the inestimable privilege of heading the subscription lists to all the principal charities. In return for these advantages the least we can do is to make ourselves useful about the Palace.

SONG — GIUSEPPE *with* CHORUS.

Rising early in the morning,
    We proceed to light the fire,
Then our Majesty adorning
    In its workaday attire,
        We embark without delay
        On the duties of the day.

First, we polish off some batches
Of political despatches,
    And foreign politicians circumvent;
Then, if business isn't heavy,
We may hold a Royal *levée*,
    Or ratify some Acts of Parliament.
Then we probably review the household troops —
With the usual 'Shalloo humps !' and 'Shalloo hoops !'
Or receive with ceremonial and state
An interesting Eastern potentate.
        After that we generally
        Go and dress our private *valet* —
(It's a rather nervous duty — he's a touchy little man) —
        Write some letters literary
        For our private secretary —
He is shaky in his spelling, so we help him if we can.
        Then, in view of cravings inner,
        We go down and order dinner;
Then we polish the Regalia and the Coronation Plate —
        Spend an hour in titivating
        All our Gentlemen-in-Waiting;
Or we run on little errands for the Ministers of State.

        Oh, philosophers may sing
        Of the troubles of a King;
Yet the duties are delightful, and the privileges great;
        But the privilege and pleasure
        That we treasure beyond measure
Is to run on little errands for the Ministers of State.

CHORUS.   Oh, philosophers may sing, etc.

After luncheon (making merry
On a bun and glass of sherry),
   If we've nothing in particular to do,
We may make a Proclamation,
Or receive a deputation —
   Then we possibly create a Peer or two.
Then we help a fellow-creature on his path
With the Garter or the Thistle or the Bath,
Or we dress and toddle off in semi-state
To a festival, a function, or a *fête*.
   Then we go and stand as sentry
   At the Palace (private entry),
Marching hither, marching thither, up and down and to and fro,
   While the warrior on duty
   Goes in search of beer and beauty
(And it generally happens that he hasn't far to go).
   He relieves us, if he's able,
   Just in time to lay the table,
Then we dine and serve the coffee, and at half-past twelve or one,
   With a pleasure that's emphatic,
   We retire to our attic
With the gratifying feeling that our duty has been done !

   Oh, philosophers may sing
   Of the troubles of a King,
But of pleasures there are many and of worries there are none ;
   And the culminating pleasure
   That we treasure beyond measure
Is the gratifying feeling that our duty has been done !

CHORUS.   Oh, philosophers may sing, etc.
                       [Exeunt all but MARCO *and* GIUSEPPE.

GIU. Yes, it really is a very pleasant existence. They're all so singularly kind and considerate. You don't find them wanting to do this, or wanting to do that, or saying 'It's my turn now'. No, they let us have all the fun to ourselves, and never seem to grudge it.

MAR. It makes one feel quite selfish. It almost seems like taking advantage of their good nature.

GIU. How nice they were about the double rations.

MAR. Most considerate. Ah! there's only one thing wanting to make us thoroughly comfortable.

GIU. And that is?

MAR. The dear little wives we left behind us three months ago.

GIU. Yes, it *is* dull without female society. We can do without everything else, but we can't do without that.

MAR. And if we have that in perfection, we have everything. There is only one recipe for perfect happiness.

SONG — MARCO

Take a pair of sparkling eyes,
 Hidden, ever and anon,
  In a merciful eclipse —
Do not heed their mild surprise —
  Having passed the Rubicon,
  Take a pair of rosy lips;
Take a figure trimly planned —
 Such as admiration whets —
  (Be particular in this);
Take a tender little hand,
 Fringed with dainty fingerettes,
  Press it — in parenthesis; —
Ah! Take all these, you lucky man —
Take and keep them, if you can!

Take a pretty little cot —
 Quite a miniature affair —
  Hung about with trellised vine,
Furnish it upon the spot
 With the treasures rich and rare
  I've endeavoured to define.
Live to love and love to live —
 You will ripen at your ease,
  Growing on the sunny side —
Fate has nothing more to give.

You're a dainty man to please
If you are not satisfied.
Ah ! Take my counsel, happy man ;
Act upon it, if you can !

Enter Chorus of Contadine, running in, led by FIAMETTA *and* VIT-
TORIA. *They are met by all the Ex-Gondoliers, who welcome
them heartily.*

SCENA — CHORUS OF GIRLS, QUARTET, DUET *and* CHORUS.

Here we are, at the risk of our lives,
From ever so far, and we've brought your wives —
And to that end we've crossed the main,
And don't intend to return again !

FIA.
Though obedience is strong,
Curiosity's stronger —
We waited for long,
Till we couldn't wait longer.

VIT.
It's imprudent, we know,
But without your society
Existence was slow,
And we wanted variety —

ALL.
So here we are, at the risk of our lives,
From ever so far, and we've brought your wives —
And to that end we've crossed the main,
And don't intend to return again !

Enter GIANETTA *and* TESSA. *They rush to the
arms of* MARCO *and* GIUSEPPE.

GIU. Tessa !
TESS.   Giuseppe !   *Embrace.*
GIA. Marco !
MAR.   Gianetta !

TESSA *and* GIANETTA.

TESS.	After sailing to this island —
GIA.	Tossing in a manner frightful,
TESS.	We are all once more on dry land —
GIA.	And we find the change delightful,
TESS.	As at home we've been remaining —
	We've not seen you both for ages,
GIA.	Tell me, are you fond of reigning ? —
	How's the food, and what's the wages ?
TESS.	Does your new employment please ye ? —
GIA.	How does Royalizing strike you ?
TESS.	Is it difficult or easy ? —
GIA.	Do you think your subjects like you ?
TESS.	I am anxious to elicit,
	Is it plain and easy steering ?
GIA.	Take it altogether, is it
	Better fun than gondoliering ?
BOTH.	We shall both go on requesting
	Till you tell us, never doubt it ;
	Everything is interesting,
	Tell us, tell us all about it !
CHORUS.	They will both go on requesting, etc.
TESS.	Is the populace exacting ?
GIA.	Do they keep you at a distance ?
TESS.	All unaided are you acting,
GIA.	Or do they provide assistance ?
TESS.	When you're busy, have you got to
	Get up early in the morning ?
GIA.	If you do what you ought not to,
	Do they give the usual warning ?
TESS.	With a horse do they equip you ?
GIA.	Lots of trumpeting and drumming ?
TESS.	Do the Royal tradesmen tip you ?
GIA.	Ain't the livery becoming !
TESS.	Does your human being inner
	Feed on everything that nice is ?

GIA.	Do they give you wine for dinner;
	Peaches, sugar-plums, and ices ?
BOTH.	We shall both go on requesting
	Till you tell us, never doubt it;
	Everything is interesting,
	Tell us, tell us all about it !

CHORUS.   They will both go on requesting, etc.

MAR. This is indeed a most delightful surprise !

TESS. Yes, we thought you'd like it. You see, it was like this. After you left we felt very dull and mopey, and the days crawled by, and you never wrote; so at last I said to Gianetta, 'I can't stand this any longer; those two poor Monarchs haven't got any one to mend their stockings or sew on their buttons or patch their clothes — at least, I hope they haven't — let us all pack up a change and go and see how they're getting on.' And she said, 'Done', and they all said, 'Done'; and we asked old Giacopo to lend us his boat, and *he* said, 'Done'; and we've crossed the sea, and, thank goodness, *that's* done; and here we are, and — and — *I've* done !

GIA. And now — which of you is King ?

TESS. And which of us is Queen ?

GIU. That we shan't know until Nurse turns up. But never mind that — the question is, how shall we celebrate the commencement of our honeymoon ? Gentlemen, will you allow us to offer you a magnificent banquet ?

ALL. We will !

GIU. Thanks very much; and, ladies, what do you say to a dance ?

TESS. A banquet *and* a dance ! Oh, it's too much happiness !

CHORUS *and* DANCE.

Dance a cachucha, fandango, bolero,
Xeres we'll drink — Manzanilla, Montero —
Wine, when it runs in abundance, enhances
The reckless delight of that wildest of dances !
    To the pretty pitter-pitter-patter,
    And the clitter-clitter-clitter-clatter —
        Clitter — clitter — clatter,

Pitter — pitter — patter,
Patter, patter, patter, patter, we'll dance.
Old Xeres we'll drink — Manzanilla, Montero;
For wine, when it runs in abundance, enhances
The reckless delight of that wildest of dances !

CACHUCHA.

The dance is interrupted by the unexpected appearance of Don
Alhambra, *who looks on with astonishment.* Marco *and*
Giuseppe *appear embarrassed. The others run off, except Drum-
mer Boy, who is driven off by* Don Alhambra.

Don Al. Good evening. Fancy ball ?

Giu. No, not exactly. A little friendly dance. That's all. Sorry
you're late.

Don Al. But I saw a groom dancing, and a footman !

Mar. Yes. That's the Lord High Footman.

Don Al. And, dear me, a common little drummer boy !

Giu. Oh no ! That's the Lord High Drummer Boy.

Don Al. But surely, surely the servants'-hall is the place for these
gentry ?

Giu. Oh dear no ! *We* have appropriated the servants'-hall. It's
the Royal Apartment, and accessible only by tickets obtainable at
the Lord Chamberlain's office.

Mar. We really must have some place that we can call our
own.

Don Al. (*puzzled*). I'm afraid I'm not quite equal to the intellectual pressure of the conversation.

Giu. You see, the Monarchy has been re-modelled on Republican
principles.

Don Al. What !

Giu. All departments rank equally, and everybody is at the head
of his department.

Don Al. I see.

Mar. I'm afraid you're annoyed.

Don Al. No. I won't say that. It's not quite what I expected.

Giu. I'm awfully sorry.

Mar. So am I.

Giu. By the by, can I offer you anything after your voyage ? A plate of macaroni and a rusk ?

Don Al. (*preoccupied*). No, no — nothing — nothing.

Giu. Obliged to be careful ?

Don Al. Yes — gout. You see, in every Court there are distinctions that must be observed.

Giu. (*puzzled*). There are, are there ?

Don Al. Why, of course. For instance, you wouldn't have a Lord High Chancellor play leapfrog with his own cook.

Mar. Why not ?

Don Al. Why not ! Because a Lord High Chancellor is a personage of great dignity, who should never, under any circumstances, place himself in the position of being told to tuck in his tuppenny, except by noblemen of his own rank. A Lord High Archbishop, for instance, might tell a Lord High Chancellor to tuck in his tuppenny, but certainly not a cook, gentlemen, certainly not a cook.

Giu. Not even a Lord High Cook ?

Don Al. My good friend, that is a rank that is not recognized at the Lord Chamberlain's office. No, no, it won't do. I'll give you an instance in which the experiment was tried.

SONG — Don Alhambra, *with* Marco *and* Giuseppe.

Don Al.   There lived a King, as I've been told,
            In the wonder-working days of old,
            When hearts were twice as good as gold,
                And twenty times as mellow.
            Good-temper triumphed in his face,
            And in his heart he found a place
            For all the erring human race
                And every wretched fellow.
            When he had Rhenish wine to drink
            It made him very sad to think
            That some, at junket or at jink,
                Must be content with toddy.

Mar. *and* Giu.   With toddy, must be content with toddy.

DON AL.			He wished all men as rich as he
				(And he was rich as rich could be),
				So to the top of every tree
					Promoted everybody.

MAR. *and* GIU.		Now, that's the kind of King for me —
				He wished all men as rich as he,
				So to the top of every tree
					Promoted everybody !

DON AL.			Lord Chancellors were cheap as sprats,
				And Bishops in their shovel hats
				Were plentiful as tabby cats —
					In point of fact, too many.
				Ambassadors cropped up like hay,
				Prime Ministers and such as they
				Grew like asparagus in May,
					And Dukes were three a penny.
				On every side Field-Marshals gleamed,
				Small beer were Lords-Lieutenant deemed,
				With Admirals the ocean teemed
					All round his wide dominions.

MAR. *and* GIU.		With Admirals all round his wide dominions.

DON AL.			And Party Leaders you might meet
				In twos and threes in every street
				Maintaining, with no little heat,
					Their various opinions.

MAR. *and* GIU.		Now that's a sight you couldn't beat —
				Two Party Leaders in each street
				Maintaining, with no little heat,
					Their various opinions.

DON AL.			That King, although no one denies
				His heart was of abnormal size,
				Yet he'd have acted otherwise
					If he had been acuter.

> The end is easily foretold,
> When every blessed thing you hold
> Is made of silver, or of gold,
>   You long for simple pewter.
> When you have nothing else to wear
> But cloth of gold and satins rare,
> For cloth of gold you cease to care —
>   Up goes the price of shoddy.

MAR. *and* GIU.   Of shoddy, up goes the price of shoddy.

DON AL.   In short, whoever you may be,
> To this conclusion you'll agree,
> When every one is somebodee,
>   Then no one's anybody !

MAR. *and* GIU.   Now that's as plain as plain can be,
> To this conclusion we agree —

ALL.   When every one is somebodee,
>   Then no one's anybody !

GIANETTA *and* TESSA *enter unobserved. The two girls, impelled by curiosity, remain listening at the back of the stage.*

DON AL. And now I have some important news to communicate. His Grace the Duke of Plaza-Toro, Her Grace the Duchess, and their beautiful daughter Casilda — I say their beautiful daughter Casilda——

GIU. We heard you.

DON AL. Have arrived at Barataria, and may be here at any moment.

MAR. The Duke and Duchess are nothing to us.

DON AL. But the daughter — the beautiful daughter ! Aha ! Oh, you're a lucky dog, one of you !

GIU. I think you're a very incomprehensible old gentleman.

DON AL. Not a bit — I'll explain. Many years ago when you (whichever you are) were a baby, you (whichever you are) were married to a little girl who has grown up to be the most beautiful

young lady in Spain. That beautiful young lady will be here to claim
you (whichever you are) in half an hour, and I congratulate that one
(whichever it is) with all my heart.

MAR. Married when a baby !

GIU. But we were married three months ago !

DON AL. One of you — only one. The other (whichever it is) is
an unintentional bigamist.

GIA. *and* TESS. (*coming forward*). Well, upon my word !

DON AL. Eh ? Who are these young people ?

TESS. Who are we ? Why, their wives, of course. We've just
arrived.

DON AL. Their wives ! Oh dear, this is very unfortunate ! Oh
dear, this complicates matters ! Dear, dear, what will Her Majesty
say ?

GIA. And do you mean to say that one of these Monarchs was
already married ?

TESS. And that neither of us will be a Queen ?

DON AL. That is the idea I intended to convey. (TESSA *and*
GIANETTA *begin to cry.*)

GIU. (*to* TESSA). Tessa, my dear, dear child——

TESS. Get away ! perhaps it's you !

MAR. (*to* GIA). My poor, poor little woman !

GIA. Don't ! Who knows whose husband you are ?

TESS. And pray, why didn't you tell us all about it before they
left Venice ?

DON AL. Because, if I had, no earthly temptation would have
induced these gentlemen to leave two such extremely fascinating and
utterly irresistible little ladies !

TESS. There's something in that.

DON AL. I may mention that you will not be kept long in suspense, as the old lady who nursed the Royal child is at present in
the torture chamber, waiting for me to interview her.

GIU. Poor old girl. Hadn't you better go and put her out of her
suspense ?

DON AL. Oh no — there's no hurry — she's all right. She has all
the illustrated papers. However, I'll go and interrogate her, and, in
the meantime, may I suggest the absolute propriety of your regarding
yourselves as single young ladies. Good evening !

[*Exit* DON ALHAMBRA.

GIA. Well, here's a pleasant state of things !

MAR. Delightful. One of us is married to two young ladies, and nobody knows which; and the other is married to one young lady whom nobody can identify !

GIA. And one of us is married to one of you, and the other is married to nobody.

TESS. But which of you is married to which of us, and what's to become of the other ? (*About to cry.*)

GIU. It's quite simple. Observe. Two husbands have managed to acquire three wives. Three wives — two husbands. (*Reckoning up.*) That's two-thirds of a husband to each wife.

TESS. O Mount Vesuvius, here we are in arithmetic ! My good sir, one can't marry a vulgar fraction !

GIU. You've no right to call me a vulgar fraction.

MAR. We are getting rather mixed. The situation is entangled. Let's try and comb it out.

QUARTET — MARCO, GIUSEPPE, GIANETTA, TESSA.

> In a contemplative fashion,
>   And a tranquil frame of mind,
> Free from every kind of passion,
>   Some solution let us find.
> Let us grasp the situation,
>   Solve the complicated plot —
> Quiet, calm deliberation
>   Disentangles every knot.

TESS. I, no doubt, Giuseppe wedded —
    That's, of course, a slice of luck.
He is rather dunder-headed,
    Still distinctly, he's a duck.

THE OTHERS. In a contemplative fashion, etc.

GIA. I, a victim, too, of Cupid,
    Marco married — that is clear.
He's particularly stupid,
    Still distinctly, he's a dear.

THE OTHERS. Let us grasp the situation, etc.

MAR. To Gianetta I was mated;
    I can prove it in a trice:
Though her charms are overrated,
    Still I own she's rather nice.

THE OTHERS. In a contemplative fashion, etc.

GIU. I to Tessa, willy-nilly,
    All at once a victim fell.
She is what is called a silly,
    Still she answers pretty well.

THE OTHERS. Let us grasp the situation, etc.

MAR.	Now when we were pretty babies Some one married us, that's clear —
GIA.	And if I can catch her I'll pinch her and scratch her And send her away with a flea in her ear.
GIU.	He whom that young lady married, To receive her can't refuse.
TESS.	If I overtake her I'll warrant I'll make her To shake in her aristocratical shoes !
GIA. (*to* TESS.).	If she married your Giuseppe You and he will have to part —
TESS. (*to* GIA.).	If I have to do it I'll warrant she'll rue it — I'll teach her to marry the man of my heart !
TESS. (*to* GIA.).	If she married Messer Marco You're a spinster, that is plain —
GIA. (*to* TESS.).	No matter — no matter. If I can get at her I doubt if her mother will know her again !
ALL.	Quiet, calm deliberation Disentangles every knot !

[*Exeunt, pondering.*

MARCH. *Enter procession of Retainers, heralding approach of* DUKE, DUCHESS, *and* CASILDA. *All three are now dressed with the utmost magnificence.*

CHORUS OF MEN, *with* DUKE *and* DUCHESS.

With ducal pomp and ducal pride
        (Announce these comers,
            O ye kettle-drummers !)
Comes Barataria's high-born bride.
        (Ye sounding cymbals clang !)

> She comes to claim the Royal hand —
>> (Proclaim their Graces,
>> O ye double basses !)
> Of the King who rules this goodly land.
>> (Ye brazen brasses bang !)

DUKE *and*   This polite attention touches
DUCH.   Heart of Duke and heart of Duchess
>> Who resign their pet
>> With profound regret.
> She of beauty was a model
> When a tiny tiddle-toddle,
>> And at twenty-one
>> She's excelled by none !

CHORUS.   With ducal pomp and ducal pride, etc.

DUKE (*to his attendants*). Be good enough to inform His Majesty that His Grace the Duke of Plaza-Toro, Limited, has arrived, and begs——

CAS. Desires——

DUCH. Demands——

DUKE. And demands an audience. (*Exeunt attendants.*) And now, my child, prepare to receive the husband to whom you were united under such interesting and romantic circumstances.

CAS. But which is it ? There are two of them !

DUKE. It is true that at present His Majesty is a double gentleman; but as soon as the circumstances of his marriage are ascertained, he will, *ipso facto*, boil down to a single gentleman — thus presenting a unique example of an individual who becomes a single man and a married man by the same operation.

DUCH. (*severely*). I have known instances in which the characteristics of both conditions existed concurrently in the same individual.

DUKE. Ah, he couldn't have been a Plaza-Toro.

DUCH. Oh ! couldn't he, though !

CAS. Well, whatever happens, I shall, of course, be a dutiful wife, but I can never love my husband.

DUKE. I don't know. It's extraordinary what unprepossessing people one can love if one gives one's mind to it.

DUCH. I loved your father.

DUKE. My love — that remark is a little hard, I think? Rather cruel, perhaps? Somewhat uncalled-for, I venture to believe?

DUCH. It was very difficult, my dear; but I said to myself, 'That man is a Duke, and I *will* love him.' Several of my relations bet me I couldn't, but I did — desperately!

SONG — DUCHESS.

On the day when I was wedded
    To your admirable sire,
I acknowledge that I dreaded
    An explosion of his ire.
I was overcome with panic —
For his temper was volcanic,
    And I didn't dare revolt,
    For I feared a thunderbolt!
I was always very wary,
    For his fury was ecstatic —
His refined vocabulary
    Most unpleasantly emphatic.
        To the thunder
            Of this Tartar
        I knocked under
            Like a martyr;
        When intently
            He was fuming,
        I was gently
            Unassuming —
        When reviling
            Me completely,
        I was smiling
            Very sweetly:
Giving him the very best, and getting back the very worst —
That is how I tried to tame your great progenitor — at first!

But I found that a reliance
    On my threatening appearance,

And a resolute defiance
    Of marital interference,
And a gentle intimation
    Of my firm determination
        To see what I could do
        To be wife and husband too
Was the only thing required
    For to make his temper supple,
And you couldn't have desired
    A more reciprocating couple.
            Ever willing
                To be wooing,
            We were billing —
                We were cooing;
            When I merely
                From him parted,
            We were nearly
                Broken-hearted —
            When in sequel
                Reunited,
            We were equal-
                Ly delighted.
So with double-shotted guns and colours nailed unto the mast,
I tamed your insignificant progenitor — at last !

CAS. My only hope is that when my husband sees what a shady family he has married into he will repudiate the contract altogether.

DUKE. Shady ? A nobleman shady, who is blazing in the lustre of unaccustomed pocket-money ? A nobleman shady, who can look back upon ninety-five quarterings ? It is not every nobleman who is ninety-five quarters in arrear — I mean, who can look back upon ninety-five of them ! And this, just as I have been floated at a premium ! Oh fie !

DUCH. Your Majesty is surely unaware that directly Your Majesty's father came before the public he was applied for over and over again.

DUKE. My dear, Her Majesty's father was in the habit of being applied for over and over again — and very urgently applied for, too — long before he was registered under the Limited Liability Act.

RECIT. — Duke.

To help unhappy commoners, and add to their enjoyment,
Affords a man of noble rank congenial employment;
Of our attempts we offer you examples illustrative:
The work is light, and, I may add, it's most remunerative.

DUET — Duke *and* Duchess.

DUKE.	Small titles and orders For Mayors and Recorders I get — and they're highly delighted —
DUCH.	They're highly delighted !
DUKE.	M.P.'s baronetted, Sham Colonels gazetted, And second-rate Aldermen knighted —
DUCH.	Yes, Aldermen knighted.
DUKE.	Foundation-stone laying I find very paying: It adds a large sum to my makings —
DUCH.	Large sums to his makings.
DUKE.	At charity dinners The best of speech-spinners, I get ten per cent on the takings —
DUCH.	One-tenth of the takings.
DUCH.	I present any lady Whose conduct is shady Or smacking of doubtful propriety —
DUKE.	Doubtful propriety.

DUCH.	When Virtue would quash her, I take and whitewash her, And launch her in first-rate society —
DUKE.	First-rate society !
DUCH.	I recommend acres Of clumsy dressmakers — Their fit and their finishing touches —
DUKE.	Their finishing touches.
DUCH.	A sum in addition They pay for permission To say that they make for the Duchess —
DUKE.	They make for the Duchess !
DUKE.	Those pressing prevailers, The ready-made tailors, Quote me as their great double-barrel —
DUCH.	Their great double-barrel.
DUKE.	I allow them to do so, Though Robinson Crusoe Would jib at their wearing apparel —
DUCH.	Such wearing apparel !
DUKE.	I sit, by selection, Upon the direction Of several Companies bubble —
DUCH.	All Companies bubble !
DUKE.	As soon as they're floated I'm freely bank-noted — I'm pretty well paid for my trouble —

Duch.   He's paid for his trouble !

Duch.   At middle-class party
          I play at *écarté* —
               And I'm by no means a beginner —

Duke (*significantly*). She's not a beginner.

Duch.   To one of my station
          The remuneration —
               Five guineas a night and my dinner —

Duke.   And wine with her dinner.

Duch.   I write letters blatant
          On medicines patent —
               And use any other you mustn't —

Duke.   Believe me, you mustn't —

Duch.   And vow my complexion
          Derives its perfection
               From somebody's soap — which it doesn't —

Duke (*significantly*). It certainly doesn't !

Duke.   We're ready as witness
          To any one's fitness
               To fill any place or preferment —

Duch.   A place or preferment.

Duch.   We're often in waiting
          At junket or *fêting*,
               And sometimes attend an interment —

Duke.   We enjoy an interment.

BOTH.	In short, if you'd kindle
	The spark of a swindle,
	Lure simpletons into your clutches —
	Yes; into your clutches.
	Or hoodwink a debtor,
	You cannot do better

DUCH.   Than trot out a Duke or a Duchess —

DUKE.   A Duke or a Duchess !

Enter MARCO *and* GIUSEPPE.

DUKE. Ah ! Their Majesties. Your Majesty ! (*Bows with great ceremony.*)

MAR. The Duke of Plaza-Toro, I believe ?

DUKE. The same. (MARCO *and* GIUSEPPE *offer to shake hands with him. The* DUKE *bows ceremoniously. They endeavour to imitate him.*) Allow me to present——

GIU. The young lady one of us married ?

(MARCO *and* GIUSEPPE *offer to shake hands with her.* CASILDA *curtsies formally. They endeavour to imitate her.*)

CAS. Gentlemen, I am the most obedient servant of one of you. (*Aside.*) Oh, Luiz !

DUKE. I am now about to address myself to the gentleman whom my daughter married; the other may allow his attention to wander if he likes, for what I am about to say does not concern him. Sir, you will find in this young lady a combination of excellences which you would search for in vain in any young lady who had not the good fortune to be my daughter. There is some little doubt as to which of you is the gentleman I am addressing, and which is the gentleman who is allowing his attention to wander; but when that doubt is solved, I shall say (still addressing the attentive gentleman), 'Take her, and may she make you happier than her mother has made me.'

DUCH. Sir !

DUKE. If possible. And now there is a little matter to which I think I am entitled to take exception. I come here in state with Her Grace the Duchess and Her Majesty my daughter, and what do I find ? Do I find, for instance, a guard of honour to receive me ? No !

MAR. *and* GIU. No.

DUKE. The town illuminated ? No !

MAR. *and* GIU. No.

DUKE. Refreshment provided ? No !

MAR. *and* GIU. No.

DUKE. A Royal salute fired ? No !

MAR. *and* GIU. No.

DUKE. Triumphal arches erected ? No !

MAR. *and* GIU. No.

DUKE. The bells set ringing ?

MAR. *and* GIU. No.

DUKE. Yes — one — the Visitors', and I rang it myself. It is not enough ! It is not enough !

GIU. Upon my honour, I'm very sorry; but you see, I was brought up in a gondola, and my ideas of politeness are confined to taking off my cap to my passengers when they tip me.

DUCH. That's all very well in its way, but it is not enough.

GIU. I'll take off anything else in reason.

DUKE. But a Royal Salute to my daughter — it costs so little.

CAS. Papa, I don't want a salute.

GIU. My dear sir, as soon as we know which of us is entitled to take that liberty she shall have as many salutes as she likes.

MAR. As for guards of honour and triumphal arches, you don't know our people — they wouldn't stand it.

GIU. They are very off-hand with us — very off-hand indeed.

DUKE. Oh, but you mustn't allow that — you must keep them in proper discipline, you must impress your Court with your importance. You want deportment — carriage——

GIU. We've got a carriage.

DUKE. Manner — dignity. There must be a good deal of this sort of thing — (*business*) — and a little of this sort of thing — (*business*) — and possibly just a *soupçon* of this sort of thing ! — (*business*) — and so on. Oh, it's very useful, and most effective. Just attend to me. You are a King — I am a subject. Very good——

GAVOTTE.

DUKE, DUCHESS, CASILDA, MARCO, GIUSEPPE.

DUKE.
I am a courtier grave and serious
Who is about to kiss your hand:
Try to combine a pose imperious
With a demeanour nobly bland.

MAR. *and*
GIU.
Let us combine a pose imperious
With a demeanour nobly bland.

(MARCO *and* GIUSEPPE *endeavour to carry out his instructions.*)

DUKE.
That's, if anything, *too* unbending —
Too aggressively stiff and grand;

(*They suddenly modify their attitudes.*)

Now to the other extreme you're tending —
Don't be so deucedly condescending !

DUCH. *and*
CAS.
Now to the other extreme you're tending —
Don't be so dreadfully condescending !

MAR. *and*
GIU.
Oh, hard to please some noblemen seem !
At first, if anything, *too* unbending;
Off we go to the other extreme —
Too confoundedly condescending !

DUKE.
Now a gavotte perform sedately —
Offer your hand with conscious pride;
Take an attitude not too stately,
Still sufficiently dignified.

MAR. *and*
GIU.
Now for an attitude not too stately,
Still sufficiently dignified.

(*They endeavour to carry out his instructions.*)

DUKE (*beating time*).
                Oncely, twicely — oncely, twicely —
                Bow impressively ere you glide.

                                            (*They do so.*)
                Capital both — you've caught it nicely !
                That is the style of thing precisely !

DUCH. *and*   Capital both — they've caught it nicely !
  CAS.   That is the style of thing precisely !

MAR. *and*   Oh, sweet to earn a nobleman's praise !
  GIU.   Capital both — we've caught it nicely !
                Supposing he's right in what he says,
                This is the style of thing precisely !

      [GAVOTTE. *At the end exeunt* DUKE *and* DUCHESS,
          leaving CASILDA *with* MARCO *and* GIUSEPPE.

GIU. (*to* MARCO). The old birds have gone away and left the young chickens together. That's called tact.

MAR. It's very awkward. We really ought to tell her how we are situated. It's not fair to the girl.

GIU. Then why don't you do it ?

MAR. I'd rather not — you.

GIU. I don't know how to begin. (*To* CASILDA.) A — Madam — I — we, that is, several of us——

CAS. Gentlemen, I am bound to listen to you; but it is right to tell you that, not knowing I was married in infancy I am over head and ears in love with somebody else.

GIU. Our case exactly ! *We* are over head and ears in love with somebody else ! (*Enter* GIANETTA *and* TESSA.) In point of fact, with our wives !

CAS. Your wives ! Then you are married ?

TESS. It's not our fault.

GIA. We knew nothing about it.

BOTH. We are sisters in misfortune.

CAS. My good girls, I don't blame you. Only before we go any further we must really arrive at some satisfactory arrangement, or we shall get hopelessly complicated.

QUINTET AND FINALE.

MARCO, GIUSEPPE, CASILDA, GIANETTA, TESSA.

ALL.

Here is a case unprecedented !
Here are a King and Queen ill-starred !
Ever since marriage was first invented
Never was known a case so hard !

MAR. *and*
GIU.

I may be said to have been bisected,
By a profound catastrophe !

CAS., GIA.,
TESS.

Through a calamity unexpected
I am divisible into three !

ALL.

O moralists all,
How can you call
Marriage a state of unitee,
When excellent husbands are bisected,
And wives divisible into three ?
O moralists all,
How can you call
Marriage a state of union true ?

CAS., GIA.,
TESS.

One-third of myself is married to half of ye or
you.

MAR. *and*
GIU.

When half of myself has married one-third of ye or
you ?

Enter DON ALHAMBRA, *followed by* DUKE, DUCHESS,
and all the CHORUS.

FINALE.

RECIT. — DON ALHAMBRA.

Now let the loyal lieges gather round —
The Prince's foster-mother has been found !
She will declare, to silver clarion's sound,
The rightful King — let him forthwith be crowned !

F

CHORUS.   She will declare, etc.

(DON ALHAMBRA *brings forward* INEZ, *the Prince's
foster-mother.*)

TESS.   Speak, woman, speak —
DUKE.   We're all attention !
GIA.   The news we seek —
DUCH.   This moment mention.
CAS.   To us they bring —
DON AL.   His foster-mother.
MAR.   Is he the King ?
GIU.   Or this my brother ?

ALL.   Speak, woman, speak, etc.

RECIT. — INEZ.

The Royal Prince was by the King entrusted
To my fond care, ere I grew old and crusted;
When traitors came to steal his son reputed,
My own small boy I deftly substituted !
The villains fell into the trap completely —
I hid the Prince away — still sleeping sweetly:
I called him 'son' with pardonable slyness —
His name, Luiz ! Behold his Royal Highness !

(*Sensation.* LUIZ *ascends the throne, crowned
and robed as King.*)

CAS. (*rushing to his arms*). Luiz.
LUIZ. Casilda ! (*Embrace.*)

ALL.   Is this indeed the King ?
                    Oh, wondrous revelation !
                    Oh, unexpected thing !
                    Unlooked-for situation !

MAR., GIA., GIU., TESS.	This statement we receive

MAR., GIA., GIU., TESS.

This statement we receive
   With sentiments conflicting;
Our hearts rejoice and grieve,
   Each other contradicting;
To those whom we adore
   We can be reunited —
On one point rather sore,
   But, on the whole, delighted !

LUIZ.

When others claimed thy dainty hand,
   I waited — waited — waited,

DUKE.

As prudence (so I understand)
   Dictated — tated — tated.

CAS.

By virtue of our early vow
   Recorded — corded — corded,

DUCH.

Your pure and patient love is now
   Rewarded — warded — warded.

ALL.

Then hail, O King of a Golden Land,
And the high-born bride who claims his hand !
The past is dead, and you gain your own,
A royal crown and a golden throne !

(*All kneel:* LUIZ *crowns* CASILDA.)

ALL.

   Once more *gondolieri*,
   Both skilful and wary,
   Free from this quandary
      Contented are we.
   From Royalty flying,
   Our gondolas plying,
   And merrily crying
      Our '*premé*,' '*stalì*!'

So good-bye, cachucha, fandango, bolero —
We'll dance a farewell to that measure —
Old Xeres, adieu — Manzanilla — Montero —
We leave you with feelings of pleasure !

CURTAIN

PATIENCE

OR

BUNTHORNE'S BRIDE

DRAMATIS PERSONÆ

COLONEL CALVERLEY ⎫ (*Officers of*
MAJOR MURGATROYD ⎬ *Dragoon*
LIEUT. THE DUKE OF DUNSTABLE ⎭ *Guards*)
REGINALD BUNTHORNE (*a Fleshly Poet*)
ARCHIBALD GROSVENOR (*an Idyllic Poet*)
MR. BUNTHORNE'S SOLICITOR
THE LADY ANGELA ⎫
THE LADY SAPHIR ⎬ (*Rapturous Maidens*)
THE LADY ELLA ⎪
THE LADY JANE ⎭
PATIENCE (*a Dairy Maid*)

Chorus of Rapturous Maidens and Officers of Dragoon Guards.

———

ACT I. — Exterior of Castle Bunthorne.

ACT II. — A Glade.

First produced at the Opéra Comique on April 23, 1881.

PATIENCE

OR

BUNTHORNE'S BRIDE

ACT I

SCENE. — *Exterior of Castle Bunthorne. Entrance to Castle by draw-bridge over moat. Young ladies dressed in æsthetic draperies are grouped about the stage. They play on lutes, mandolins, etc., as they sing, and all are in the last stage of despair.* ANGELA, ELLA, *and* SAPHIR *lead them.*

CHORUS.

Twenty love-sick maidens we,
    Love-sick all against our will.
Twenty years hence we shall be
    Twenty love-sick maidens still.
Twenty love-sick maidens we,
And we die for love of thee.

SOLO — ANGELA.

Love feeds on hope, they say, or love will die —
ALL.   Ah, miserie !
Yet my love lives, although no hope have I !
ALL.   Ah, miserie !
Alas, poor heart, go hide thyself away —
To weeping concords tune thy roundelay !
                    Ah, miserie !

CHORUS.

All our love is all for one,
　　Yet that love he heedeth not,
He is coy and cares for none,
　　Sad and sorry is our lot !
　　　　　　　　　　Ah, miserie !

SOLO — ELLA.

Go, breaking heart,
　　Go, dream of love requited;
Go, foolish heart,
　　Go, dream of lovers plighted;
Go, madcap heart,
　　Go, dream of never waking;
And in thy dream
　　Forget that thou art breaking !

CHORUS.	Ah, miserie !
ELLA.	Forget that thou art breaking !
CHORUS.	Twenty love-sick maidens, etc.

ANG. There is a strange magic in this love of ours ! Rivals as
we all are in the affections of our Reginald, the very hopelessness of
our love is a bond that binds us to one another !

SAPH. Jealousy is merged in misery. While he, the very cynosure
of our eyes and hearts, remains icy insensible — what have we to
strive for ?

ELLA. The love of maidens is, to him, as interesting as the taxes !

SAPH. Would that it were ! He pays his taxes.

ANG. And cherishes the receipts !

Enter LADY JANE.

SAPH. Happy receipts !

JANE (*suddenly*). Fools !

ANG. I beg your pardon ?

JANE. Fools and blind ! The man loves — wildly loves !

ANG. But whom ? None of us !

JANE. No, none of us. His weird fancy has lighted, for the nonce, on Patience, the village milkmaid !

SAPH. On Patience ? Oh, it cannot be !

JANE. Bah ! But yesterday I caught him in her dairy, eating fresh butter with a tablespoon. To-day he is not well !

SAPH. But Patience boasts that she has never loved — that love is, to her, a sealed book ! Oh, he cannot be serious !

JANE. 'Tis but a fleeting fancy — 'twill quickly pass away. (*Aside.*) Oh, Reginald, if you but knew what a wealth of golden love is waiting for you, stored up in this rugged old bosom of mine, the milkmaid's triumph would be short indeed !

(PATIENCE *appears on an eminence. She looks down with pity on the despondent Ladies.*)

RECIT. — PATIENCE.

Still brooding on their mad infatuation !
 I thank thee, Love, thou comest not to me !
Far happier I, free from thy ministration,
 Than dukes or duchesses who love can be !

SAPH. (*looking up*). 'Tis Patience — happy girl ! Loved by a Poet !
PA.   Your pardon, ladies. I intrude upon you. (*Going.*)
ANG.   Nay, pretty child, come hither. Is it true
      That you have never loved ?

PA.   Most true indeed.
SOPRANOS. Most marvellous !
CONTRALTOS.   And most deplorable !

SONG — PATIENCE.

I cannot tell what this love may be
That cometh to all, but not to me.
It cannot be kind as they'd imply,
 Or why do these ladies sigh ?
It cannot be joy and rapture deep,
 Or why do these gentle ladies weep ?
It cannot be blissful as 'tis said,
 Or why are their eyes so wondrous red ?

Though everywhere true love I see
A-coming to all, but not to me,
I cannot tell what this love may be !
  For I am blithe and I am gay,
  While they sit sighing night and day.
  Think of the gulf 'twixt them and me,
  'Fal la la la !' — and 'Miserie !'

CHORUS.   Yes, she is blithe, etc.

PA.   If love is a thorn, they show no wit
           Who foolishly hug and foster it.
           If love is a weed, how simple they
           Who gather it, day by day !
           If love is a nettle that makes you smart,
           Then why do you wear it next your heart ?
           And if it be none of these, say I,
           Ah, why do you sit and sob and sigh ?
               Though everywhere, etc.

CHORUS.   For she is blithe, etc.

ANG. Ah, Patience, if you have never loved, you have never known true happiness ! (*All sigh.*)

PA. But the truly happy always seem to have so much on their minds. The truly happy never seem quite well.

JANE. There is a transcendentality of delirium — an acute accentuation of supremest ecstasy — which the earthy might easily mistake for indigestion. But it is *not* indigestion — it is æsthetic transfiguration ! (*To the others.*) Enough of babble. Come !

PA. But stay, I have some news for you. The 35th Dragoon Guards have halted in the village, and are even now on their way to this very spot.

ANG. The 35th Dragoon Guards !

SAPH. They are fleshly men, of full habit !

ELLA. We care nothing for Dragoon Guards !

PA. But, bless me, you were all engaged to them a year ago !

SAPH. A year ago !

ANG. My poor child, you don't understand these things. A year ago they were very well in our eyes, but since then our tastes have been etherealized, our perceptions exalted. (*To others.*) Come, it is time to lift up our voices in morning carol to our Reginald. Let us to his door.

> [*The Ladies go off, two and two, into the Castle, singing refrain of 'Twenty love-sick maidens we', and accompanying themselves on harps and mandolins.* PATIENCE *watches them in surprise, as she climbs the rock by which she entered.*

March. Enter Officers of Dragoon Guards, led by MAJOR.

CHORUS OF DRAGOONS.

The soldiers of our Queen
    Are linked in friendly tether;
Upon the battle scene
    They fight the foe together.
There every mother's son
    Prepared to fight and fall is;
The enemy of one
    The enemy of all is !

Enter COLONEL.

SONG — COLONEL.

If you want a receipt for that popular mystery,
    Known to the world as a Heavy Dragoon,
Take all the remarkable people in history,
    Rattle them off to a popular tune.
The pluck of Lord Nelson on board of the *Victory* —
Genius of Bismarck devising a plan —
The humour of Fielding (which sounds contradictory) —
    Coolness of Paget about to trepan —
The science of Jullien, the eminent musico —
    Wit of Macaulay, who wrote of Queen Anne —
The pathos of Paddy, as rendered by Boucicault —
    Style of the Bishop of Sodor and Man —

The dash of a D'Orsay, divested of quackery —
Narrative powers of Dickens and Thackeray —
Victor Emmanuel — peak-haunting Peveril —
Thomas Aquinas, and Doctor Sacheverell —
  Tupper and Tennyson — Daniel Defoe —
  Anthony Trollope and Mr. Guizot !
      Take of these elements all that is fusible,
      Melt them all down in a pipkin or crucible,
      Set them to simmer and take off the scum,
      And a Heavy Dragoon is the residuum !

CHORUS.   Yes ! yes ! yes ! yes !
               A Heavy Dragoon is the residuum !

COL.   If you want a receipt for this soldier-like paragon,
         Get at the wealth of the Czar (if you can) —
       The family pride of a Spaniard from Arragon —
         Force of Mephisto pronouncing a ban —
       A smack of Lord Waterford, reckless and rollicky —
         Swagger of Roderick, heading his clan —
       The keen penetration of Paddington Pollaky —
         Grace of an Odalisque on a divan —
       The genius strategic of Cæsar or Hannibal —
       Skill of Sir Garnet in thrashing a cannibal —
       Flavour of Hamlet — the Stranger, a touch of him —
       Little of Manfred (but not very much of him) —
         Beadle of Burlington — Richardson's show —
         Mr. Micawber and Madame Tussaud !
            Take of these elements all that is fusible,
            Melt them all down in a pipkin or crucible,
            Set them to simmer and take off the scum,
            And a Heavy Dragoon is the residuum !

ALL.   Yes ! yes ! yes ! yes !
               A Heavy Dragoon is the residuum !

    COL. Well, here we are once more on the scene of our former
triumphs. But where's the Duke ?

                Enter DUKE, *listlessly, and in low spirits.*

DUKE. Here I am ! (*Sighs.*)

COL. Come, cheer up, don't give way !

DUKE. Oh, for that, I'm as cheerful as a poor devil can be expected to be who has the misfortune to be a duke, with a thousand a day !

MAJ. Humph ! Most men would envy you !

DUKE. Envy *me* ? Tell me, Major, are you fond of toffee ?

MAJ. Very !

COL. We are all fond of toffee.

ALL. We are !

DUKE. Yes, and toffee in moderation is a capital thing. But to *live* on toffee — toffee for breakfast, toffee for dinner, toffee for tea — to have it supposed that you care for nothing *but* toffee, and that you would consider yourself insulted if anything but toffee were offered to you — how would you like *that* ?

COL. I can quite believe that, under those circumstances, even toffee would become monotonous.

DUKE. For 'toffee' read flattery, adulation, and abject deference, carried to such a pitch that I began, at last, to think that man was born bent at an angle of forty-five degrees ! Great Heavens, what is there to adulate in me ! Am I particularly intelligent, or remarkably studious, or excruciatingly witty, or unusually accomplished, or exceptionally virtuous ?

COL. You're about as commonplace a young man as ever I saw.

ALL. You are !

DUKE. Exactly ! That's it exactly ! That describes me to a T ! Thank you all very much ! Well, I couldn't stand it any longer, so I joined this second-class cavalry regiment. In the Army, thought I, I shall be occasionally snubbed, perhaps even bullied, who knows ? The thought was rapture, and here I am.

COL. (*looking off*). Yes, and here are the ladies !

DUKE. But who is the gentleman with the long hair ?

COL. I don't know.

DUKE. He seems popular !

COL. He *does* seem popular !

BUNTHORNE *enters, followed by Ladies, two and two, singing and playing on harps as before. He is composing a poem, and quite absorbed. He sees no one, but walks across the stage, followed by Ladies. They take no notice of Dragoons — to the surprise and indignation of those Officers.*

CHORUS OF LADIES.

In a doleful train
        Two and two we walk all day —
For we love in vain !
        None so sorrowful as they
                Who can only sigh and say,
                Woe is me, alackaday !

CHORUS OF DRAGOONS.

Now is not this ridiculous — and is not this preposterous ?
    A thorough-paced absurdity — explain it if you can.
Instead of rushing eagerly to cherish us and foster us,
    They all prefer this melancholy literary man.
            Instead of slyly peering at us,
            Casting looks endearing at us,
    Blushing at us, flushing at us — flirting with a fan ;
    They're actually sneering at us, fleering at us, jeering at us !
            Pretty sort of treatment for a military man !
            Pretty sort of treatment for a military man !

ANG.   Mystic poet, hear our prayer,
                    Twenty love-sick maidens we —
                Young and wealthy, dark and fair —
                    All of country family.
                        And we die for love of thee —
                        Twenty love-sick maidens we !

CHORUS OF LADIES.   Yes, we die for love of thee —
                        Twenty love-sick maidens we !

BUN. (*aside — slyly*).   Though my book I seem to scan
                        In a rapt ecstatic way,
                    Like a literary man
                        Who despises female clay,
                    I hear plainly all they say,
                    Twenty love-sick maidens they !

OFFICERS (*to each other*).   He hears plainly, etc.

SAPH.   Though so excellently wise,
                  For a moment mortal be,
              Deign to raise thy purple eyes
                  From thy heart-drawn poesy.
              Twenty love-sick maidens see —
              Each is kneeling on her knee !   (*All kneel.*)

CHORUS OF LADIES.   Twenty love-sick, etc.

BUN. (*aside*).   Though, as I remarked before,
                  Any one convinced would be
              That some transcendental lore
                  Is monopolizing me,
              Round the corner I can see
              Each is kneeling on her knee !

OFFICERS (*to each other*).   Round the corner, etc.

ENSEMBLE.

OFFICERS	LADIES.
Now is not this ridiculous, etc.	Mystic poet, hear our prayer, etc.

COL. Angela ! what is the meaning of this ?

ANG. Oh, sir, leave us; our minds are but ill-tuned to light love-talk.

MAJ. But what in the world has come over you all ?

JANE. Bunthorne ! *He* has come over us. He has come among us, and he has idealized us.

DUKE. Has he succeeded in idealizing *you* ?

JANE. He has !

DUKE. Good old Bunthorne !

JANE. My eyes are open; I droop despairingly; I am soulfully intense; I am limp and I cling !

(*During this* BUNTHORNE *is seen in all the agonies of composition. The Ladies are watching him intently as he writhes. At last he hits on the word he wants and writes it down. A general sense of relief.*)

BUN. Finished ! At last ! Finished !

(*He staggers, overcome with the mental strain, into arms of* COLONEL.)

COL. Are you better now ?

BUN. Yes — oh, it's you — I am better now. The poem is finished, and my soul had gone out into it. That was all. It was nothing worth mentioning, it occurs three times a day. (*Sees* PATIENCE, *who has entered during this scene.*) Ah, Patience ! Dear Patience ! (*Holds her hand; she seems frightened.*)

ANG. Will it please you read it to us, sir ?

SAPH. This we supplicate. (*All kneel.*)

BUN. Shall I ?

ALL THE DRAGOONS. No !

BUN. (*annoyed — to* PATIENCE). I will read it if *you* bid me !

PA. (*much frightened*). You can if you like !

BUN. It is a wild, weird, fleshly thing; yet very tender, very yearning, very precious. It is called, 'Oh, Hollow ! Hollow ! Hollow !'

PA. Is it a hunting song ?

BUN. A hunting song ? No, it is *not* a hunting song. It is the wail of the poet's heart on discovering that everything is commonplace. To understand it, cling passionately to one another and think of faint lilies. (*They do so as he recites*) —

'OH, HOLLOW ! HOLLOW ! HOLLOW !'

What time the poet hath hymned
The writhing maid, lithe-limbed,
    Quivering on amaranthine asphodel,
How can he paint her woes,
Knowing, as well he knows,
    That all can be set right with calomel ?

When from the poet's plinth
The amorous colocynth
    Yearns for the aloe, faint with rapturous thrills,

How can he hymn their throes
Knowing, as well he knows,
   That they are only uncompounded pills ?

Is it, and can it be,
Nature hath this decree,
   Nothing poetic in the world shall dwell ?
Or that in all her works
Something poetic lurks,
   Even in colocynth and calomel ?
             I cannot tell.

                       [*Exit* BUNTHORNE.

ANG. How purely fragrant !

SAPH. How earnestly precious !

PA. Well, it seems to me to be nonsense.

SAPH. Nonsense, yes, perhaps — but oh, what precious nonsense !

COL. This is all very well, but you seem to forget that you are engaged to us.

SAPH. It can never be. You are not Empyrean. You are not Della Cruscan. You are not even Early English. Oh, be Early English ere it is too late ! (*Officers look at each other in astonishment.*)

JANE (*looking at uniform*). Red and Yellow ! Primary colours ! Oh, South Kensington !

DUKE. We didn't design our uniforms, but we don't see how they could be improved.

JANE. No, you wouldn't. Still, there *is* a cobwebby grey velvet, with a tender bloom like cold gravy, which, made Florentine fourteenth-century, trimmed with Venetian leather and Spanish altar lace, and surmounted with something Japanese — it matters not what — would at least be Early English ! Come, maidens.

    [*Exeunt Maidens, two and two, singing refrain of 'Twenty
        love-sick maidens we'. The Officers watch them off in
        astonishment.*

DUKE. Gentlemen, this is an insult to the British uniform——

COL. A uniform that has been as successful in the courts of Venus as on the field of Mars !

SONG — Colonel.

When I first put this uniform on,
　I said, as I looked in the glass,
　　'It's one to a million
　　That any civilian
My figure and form will surpass.
　　Gold lace has a charm for the fair,
　　And I've plenty of that, and to spare,
　　　While a lover's professions,
　　　When uttered in Hessians,
　　Are eloquent everywhere !'
　　　　A fact that I counted upon,
　　　　When I first put this uniform on !

Chorus of Dragoons.

By a simple coincidence, few
　　Could ever have counted upon,
The same thing occurred to me, too,
　　When I first put this uniform on !

Col.　　I said, when I first put it on,
　　'It is plain to the veriest dunce
　　　That every beauty
　　　Will feel it her duty
To yield to its glamour at once.
They will see that I'm freely gold-laced
In a uniform handsome and chaste' —
　　　But the peripatetics
　　　Of long-haired æsthetics
Are very much more to their taste —
　　　Which I never counted upon,
　　　When I first put this uniform on !

Chorus.　　By a simple coincidence, few
　　Could ever have reckoned upon,
I didn't anticipate that,
　　When I first put this uniform on !

　　　　　　　　　　　[*The Dragoons go off angrily.*

Enter BUNTHORNE, *who changes his manner and becomes intensely melodramatic.*

RECIT. AND SONG — BUNTHORNE.

Am I alone,
 And unobserved ? I am !
Then let me own
 I'm an æsthetic sham !
This air severe
 Is but a mere
   Veneer !
This cynic smile
 Is but a wile
   Of guile !
This costume chaste
 Is but good taste
   Misplaced !
 Let me confess !
A languid love for lilies does *not* blight me !
Lank limbs and haggard cheeks do *not* delight me !
 I do *not* care for dirty greens
  By any means.

 I do *not* long for all one sees
  That's Japanese.
 I am *not* fond of uttering platitudes
  In stained-glass attitudes.
 In short, my mediævalism's affectation,
 Born of a morbid love of admiration !

SONG.

If you're anxious for to shine in the high æsthetic line as a man of
 culture rare,
You must get up all the germs of the transcendental terms, and
 plant them everywhere.
You must lie upon the daisies and discourse in novel phrases of
 your complicated state of mind,
The meaning doesn't matter if it's only idle chatter of a transcendental kind.

> And every one will say,
> As you walk your mystic way,
'If this young man expresses himself in terms too deep for *me*,
Why, what a very singularly deep young man this deep young
    man must be !'

Be eloquent in praise of the very dull old days which have long since
    passed away,
And convince 'em, if you can, that the reign of good Queen Anne
    was Culture's palmiest day.
Of course you will pooh-pooh whatever's fresh and new, and declare
    it's crude and mean,
For Art stopped short in the cultivated court of the Empress Jose-
    phine.

> And every one will say,
> As you walk your mystic way,
'If that's not good enough for him which is good enough for
    me,
Why, what a very cultivated kind of youth this kind of youth must
    be !'

Then a sentimental passion of a vegetable fashion must excite your
    languid spleen,
An attachment *à la* Plato for a bashful young potato, or a not-too-
    French French bean !
Though the Philistines may jostle, you will rank as an apostle in
    the high æsthetic band,
If you walk down Piccadilly with a poppy or a lily in your mediæval
    hand.

> And every one will say,
> As you walk your flowery way,
'If he's content with a vegetable love which would certainly not
    suit *me*,
Why, what a most particularly pure young man this pure young man
    must be !'

At the end of his song PATIENCE *enters. He sees her.*

BUN. Ah ! Patience, come hither. I am pleased with thee. The bitter-hearted one, who finds all else hollow, is pleased with thee. For you are not hollow. *Are* you?

PA. No, thanks, I have dined; but — I beg your pardon — I interrupt you.

BUN. Life is made up of interruptions. The tortured soul, yearning for solitude, writhes under them. Oh, but my heart is a-weary! Oh, I am a cursed thing! Don't go.

PA. Really, I'm very sorry——

BUN. Tell me, girl, do you ever yearn?

PA. (*misunderstanding him*). I earn my living.

BUN. (*impatiently*). No, no! Do you know what it is to be heart-hungry? Do you know what it is to yearn for the Indefinable, and yet to be brought face to face, daily, with the Multiplication Table? Do you know what it is to seek oceans and to find puddles? — to long for whirlwinds and yet to have to do the best you can with the bellows? That's my case. Oh, I am a cursed thing! Don't go.

PA. If you please, I don't understand you — you frighten me!

BUN. Don't be frightened — it's only poetry.

PA. Well, if that's poetry, I don't like poetry.

BUN. (*eagerly*). Don't you? (*Aside.*) Can I trust her? (*Aloud.*) Patience, you don't like poetry — well, between you and me, *I* don't like poetry. It's hollow, unsubstantial — unsatisfactory. What's the use of yearning for Elysian Fields when you know you can't get 'em, and would only let 'em out on building leases if you had 'em?

PA. Sir, I——

BUN. Patience, I have long loved you. Let me tell you a secret. I am not as bilious as I look. If you like, I will cut my hair. There is more innocent fun within me than a casual spectator would imagine. You have never seen me frolicsome. Be a good girl — a very good girl — and one day you shall. If you are fond of touch-and-go jocularity — this is the shop for it.

PA. Sir, I will speak plainly. In the matter of love I am untaught. I have never loved but my great-aunt. But I am quite certain that, under any circumstances, I couldn't possibly love *you*.

BUN. Oh, you think not?

PA. I'm quite sure of it. Quite sure. Quite.

BUN. Very good. Life is henceforth a blank. I don't care what becomes of me. I have only to ask that you will not abuse my confidence; though *you* despise me, I am extremely popular with the other young ladies.

PA. I only ask that you will leave me and never renew the subject.

BUN. Certainly. Broken-hearted and desolate, I go. (*Recites.*)

> 'Oh, to be wafted away
>   From this black Aceldama of sorrow,
> Where the dust of an earthy to-day
>   Is the earth of a dusty to-morrow!'

It is a little thing of my own. I call it 'Heart Foam'. I shall not publish it. Farewell! Patience, Patience, farewell!

[*Exit* BUNTHORNE.

PA. What on earth does it all mean? Why does he love me? Why does he expect me to love him? He's not a relation! It frightens me!

Enter ANGELA.

ANG. Why, Patience, what is the matter?

PA. Lady Angela, tell me two things. Firstly, what on earth is this love that upsets everybody; and, secondly, how is it to be distinguished from insanity?

ANG. Poor blind child! Oh, forgive her, Eros! Why, love is of all passions the most essential! It is the embodiment of purity, the abstraction of refinement! It is the one unselfish emotion in this whirlpool of grasping greed!

PA. Oh, dear, oh! (*Beginning to cry.*)

ANG. Why are you crying?

PA. To think that I have lived all these years without having experienced this ennobling and unselfish passion! Why, what a wicked girl I must be! For it *is* unselfish, isn't it?

ANG. Absolutely! Love that is tainted with selfishness is no love. Oh, try, try, try to love! It really isn't difficult if you give your whole mind to it.

PA. I'll set about it at once. I won't go to bed until I'm head over ears in love with somebody.

ANG. Noble girl! But is it possible that you have never loved anybody?

PA. Yes, one.

ANG. Ah ! Whom ?

PA. My great-aunt——

ANG. Great-aunts don't count.

PA. Then there's nobody. At least — no, nobody. Not since I was a baby. But *that* doesn't count, I suppose.

ANG. I don't know. Tell me all about it.

DUET — PATIENCE *and* ANGELA.

> Long years ago — fourteen, maybe —
> When but a tiny babe of four,
> Another baby played with me,
> My elder by a year or more;
> A little child of beauty rare,
> With marvellous eyes and wondrous hair,
> Who, in my child-eyes, seemed to me
> All that a little child should be !
> Ah, how we loved, that child and I !
> How pure our baby joy !
> How true our love — and, by the by,
> *He* was a little boy !

ANG.

> Ah, old, old tale of Cupid's touch !
> I thought as much — I thought as much !
> He *was* a little boy !

PA. (*shocked*).

> Pray don't misconstrue what I say —
> Remember, pray — remember, pray,
> He was a *little* boy !

ANG.

> No doubt ! Yet, spite of all your pains,
> The interesting fact remains —
> He was a little *boy* !

ENSEMBLE. $\left\{ \begin{matrix} \text{Ah, yes, in} \\ \text{No doubt ! Yet,} \end{matrix} \right\}$ spite of all $\left\{ \begin{matrix} \text{my} \\ \text{your} \end{matrix} \right\}$ pains, etc.

[*Exit* ANGELA.

PA. It's perfectly dreadful to think of the appalling state I must be in ! I had no idea that love was a duty. No wonder they all look so unhappy ! Upon my word, I hardly like to associate with myself. I don't think I'm respectable. I'll go at once and fall in love with—— (*Enter* GROSVENOR.) A stranger !

DUET — PATIENCE *and* GROSVENOR.

GROS. Prithee, pretty maiden — prithee, tell me true,
    (Hey, but I'm doleful, willow willow waly !)
Have you e'er a lover a-dangling after you ?
    Hey willow waly O !
        I would fain discover
        If you have a lover ?
    Hey willow waly O !

PA. Gentle sir, my heart is frolicsome and free —
    (Hey, but he's doleful, willow willow waly !)
Nobody I care for comes a-courting me —
    Hey willow waly O !
        Nobody I care for
        Comes a-courting — therefore,
    Hey willow waly O !

GROS. Prithee, pretty maiden, will you marry me ?
    (Hey, but I'm hopeful, willow willow waly !)
I may say, at once, I'm a man of propertee —
    Hey willow waly O !
        Money, I despise it ;
        Many people prize it,
    Hey willow waly O !

PA. Gentle sir, although to marry I design —
    (Hey, but he's hopeful, willow willow waly !)
As yet I do not know you, and so I must decline.
    Hey willow waly O !
        To other maidens go you —
        As yet I do not know you,
    Hey willow waly O !

GROS. Patience ! Can it be that you don't recognise me ?
PA. Recognise you ? No, indeed I don't !

GROS. Have fifteen years so greatly changed me ?

PA. Fifteen years ? What do you mean ?

GROS. Have you forgotten the friend of your youth, your Archibald ? — your little playfellow ? Oh, Chronos, Chronos, this is too bad of you !

PA. Archibald ! Is it possible ? Why, let me look ! It is ! It is ! It must be ! Oh, how happy I am ! I thought we should never meet again ! And how you've grown !

GROS. Yes, Patience, I am much taller and much stouter than I was.

PA. And how you've improved !

GROS. Yes, Patience, I am very beautiful ! (*Sighs.*)

PA. But surely *that* doesn't make you unhappy ?

GROS. Yes, Patience. Gifted as I am with a beauty which probably has not its rival on earth, I am, nevertheless, utterly and completely miserable.

PA. Oh — but why ?

GROS. My child-love for you has never faded. Conceive, then, the horror of my situation when I tell you that it is my hideous destiny to be madly loved at first sight by every woman I come across !

PA. But why do you make yourself so picturesque ? Why not disguise yourself, disfigure yourself, anything to escape this persecution ?

GROS. No, Patience, that may not be. These gifts — irksome as they are — were given to me for the enjoyment and delectation of my fellow-creatures. I am a trustee for Beauty, and it is my duty to see that the conditions of my trust are faithfully discharged.

PA. And you, too, are a Poet ?

GROS. Yes, I am the Apostle of Simplicity. I am called 'Archibald the All-Right' — for I am infallible !

PA. And is it possible that you condescend to love such a girl as I ?

GROS. Yes, Patience, is it not strange ? I have loved you with a Florentine fourteenth-century frenzy for full fifteen years !

PA. Oh, marvellous ! I have hitherto been deaf to the voice of love. I seem now to know what love is ! It has been revealed to me — it is Archibald Grosvenor !

Gros. Yes, Patience, it is !

Pa. (*as in a trance*). We will never, never part !

Gros. We will live and die together !

Pa. I swear it !

Gros. We both swear it !

Pa. (*recoiling from him*). But — oh, horror !

Gros. What's the matter ?

Pa. Why, you are perfection ! A source of endless ecstasy to all who know you !

Gros. I know I am. Well ?

Pa. Then, bless my heart, there can be nothing unselfish in loving *you* !

Gros. Merciful powers ! I never thought of that !

Pa. To monopolize those features on which all women love to linger ! It would be unpardonable !

Gros. Why, so it would ! Oh, fatal perfection, again you interpose between me and my happiness !

Pa. Oh, if you were but a thought less beautiful than you are !

Gros. Would that I were ; but candour compels me to admit that I'm not !

Pa. Our duty is clear ; we must part, and for ever !

Gros. Oh, misery ! And yet I cannot question the propriety of your decision. Farewell, Patience !

Pa. Farewell, Archibald ! But stay !

Gros. Yes, Patience ?

Pa. Although I may not love *you* — for you are perfection — there is nothing to prevent your loving *me*. I am plain, homely, unattractive !

Gros. Why, that's true !

Pa. The love of such a man as you for such a girl as I must be unselfish !

Gros. Unselfishness itself !

DUET — Patience *and* Grosvenor.

Pa.	Though to marry you would very selfish be —
Gros.	Hey, but I'm doleful — willow willow waly !
Pa.	You may, all the same, continue loving me —
Gros.	Hey willow waly O !

BOTH.   All the world ignoring,
                      You'll ⎫
                          I'll ⎬ go on adoring —
              Hey willow waly O !

[At the end, exeunt despairingly, in opposite directions.

FINALE — ACT I.

Enter BUNTHORNE, *crowned with roses and hung about with garlands, and looking very miserable. He is led by* ANGELA *and* SAPHIR *(each of whom holds an end of the rose-garland by which he is bound), and accompanied by procession of Maidens. They are dancing classically, and playing on cymbals, double pipes, and other archaic instruments.*

CHORUS.

Let the merry cymbals sound,
    Gaily pipe Pandæan pleasure,
With a Daphnephoric bound
    Tread a gay but classic measure.
Every heart with hope is beating,
For at this exciting meeting
    Fickle Fortune will decide
    Who shall be our Bunthorne's bride !

Enter Dragoons, led by COLONEL, MAJOR, *and* DUKE.
They are surprised at proceedings.

CHORUS OF DRAGOONS.
Now tell us, we pray you,
Why thus they array you —
Oh, poet, how say you —
    What is it you've done ?

DUKE.   Of rite sacrificial,
By sentence judicial,
This seems the initial,
    Then why don't you run ?

COL.   They cannot have led you
                     To hang or behead you,
                     Nor may they *all* wed you,
                          Unfortunate one !

                     CHORUS OF DRAGOONS.
                     Then tell us, we pray you,
                     Why thus they array you —
                     Oh, poet, how say you —
                          What is it you've done ?

                     RECIT. — BUNTHORNE.

Heart-broken at my Patience's barbarity,
     By the advice of my solicitor (*introducing his Solicitor*),
In aid — in aid of a deserving charity,
     I've put myself up to be raffled for !

MAIDENS.   By the advice of his solicitor
                     He's put himself up to be raffled for !

DRAGOONS.   Oh, horror ! urged by his solicitor,
                     He's put himself up to be raffled for !

MAIDENS.   Oh, heaven's blessing on his solicitor !

DRAGOONS.   A hideous curse on his solicitor !

     [*The* SOLICITOR, *horrified at the Dragoons' curse, rushes off.*

COL.   Stay, we implore you,
                     Before our hopes are blighted ;
                 You see before you
                     The men to whom you're plighted !

                     CHORUS OF DRAGOONS.

                     Stay, we implore you,
                     For we adore you ;
                     To us you're plighted
                     To be united —
                          Stay, we implore you !

SOLO — DUKE.

Your maiden hearts, ah, do not steel
To pity's eloquent appeal,
Such conduct British soldiers feel.
(Aside to Dragoons.)   Sigh, sigh, all sigh !

(They all sigh.)

To foeman's steel we rarely see
A British soldier bend the knee,
Yet, one and all, they kneel to ye —
(Aside to Dragoons.)   Kneel, kneel, all kneel !

(They all kneel.)

Our soldiers very seldom cry,
And yet — I need not tell you why —
A tear-drop dews each martial eye !
(Aside to Dragoons.)   Weep, weep, all weep !

(They all weep.)

ENSEMBLE.

Our soldiers very seldom cry,
And yet — I need not tell you why —
A tear-drop dews each manly eye !
Weep, weep, all weep !

BUNTHORNE *(who has been impatient during this appeal).*

Come, walk up, and purchase with avidity,
Overcome your diffidence and natural timidity,
Tickets for the raffle should be purchased with avidity,
  Put in half a guinea and a husband you may gain —
Such a judge of blue-and-white and other kinds of pottery —
From early Oriental down to modern terra-cotta-ry —
Put in half a guinea — you may draw him in a lottery —
  Such an opportunity may not occur again.

CHORUS.   Such a judge of blue-and-white, etc.

*(Maidens crowd up to purchase tickets; during this Dragoons dance
in single file round stage, to express their indifference.)*

DRAGOONS.	We've been thrown over, we're aware,
	But we don't care — but we don't care !
	There's fish in the sea, no doubt of it,
	As good as ever came out of it,
	And some day we shall get our share,
	So we don't care — so we don't care !

During this the Maidens have been buying tickets. At last JANE
presents herself. BUNTHORNE *looks at her with aversion.*

RECIT.

BUN.	And are *you* going a ticket for to buy ?
JANE (*surprised*).	Most certainly I am; why shouldn't I ?
BUN. (*aside*).	Oh, Fortune, this is hard ! (*Aloud.*) Blindfold your eyes;
	Two minutes will decide who wins the prize !
	(*Maidens blindfold themselves.*)

CHORUS OF MAIDENS.

Oh, Fortune, to my aching heart be kind !
Like us, thou art blindfolded, but not blind ! (*Each uncovers one eye.*)
Just raise your bandage, thus, that you may see,
And give the prize, and give the prize to me ! (*They cover their eyes again.*)

BUN.	Come, Lady Jane, I pray you draw the first !
JANE (*joyfully*).	He loves me best !
BUN. (*aside*).	I want to know the worst !

JANE *puts hand in bag to draw ticket.* PATIENCE
enters and prevents her doing so.

PA.	Hold ! Stay your hand !
ALL (*uncovering their eyes*).	What means this interference ?
	Of this bold girl I pray you make a clearance !
JANE.	Away with you, and to your milk-pails go !
BUN. (*suddenly*).	She wants a ticket ! Take a dozen !
PA.	No !

SOLO — PATIENCE (*kneeling to* BUNTHORNE).

> If there be pardon in your breast
>   For this poor penitent,
> Who, with remorseful thought opprest,
>   Sincerely doth repent;
> If you, with one so lowly, still
>   Desire to be allied,
> Then you may take me, if you will,
>   For I will be your bride !

ALL.

> Oh, shameless one !
>   Oh, bold-faced thing !
> Away you run,
>   Go, take you wing,
> You shameless one !
>   You bold-faced thing !

BUN.
How strong is love ! For many and many a week
She's loved me fondly and has feared to speak,
But Nature, for restraint too mighty far,
Has burst the bonds of Art — and here we are !

PA.
No, Mr. Bunthorne, no — you're wrong again;
Permit me — I'll endeavour to explain !

SONG — PATIENCE.

PA. True love must single-hearted be —
BUN. Exactly so !
PA. From every selfish fancy free —
BUN. Exactly so !
PA. No idle thought of gain or joy
A maiden's fancy should employ —
True love must be without alloy.
ALL. Exactly so !

PA. Imposture to contempt must lead —
COL. Exactly so !

PA.   Blind vanity's dissension's seed —
MAJ.   Exactly so !
PA.   It follows, then, a maiden who
           Devotes herself to loving *you* (*indicating*
               BUNTHORNE)
           Is prompted by no selfish view —
ALL.   Exactly so !

   SAPH.   Are you resolved to wed this shameless one ?
   ANG.   Is there no chance for any other ?
   BUN. (*decisively*).   None ! (*Embraces* PATIENCE.)
                    [*Exeunt* PATIENCE *and* BUNTHORNE.

(ANGELA, SAPHIR, *and* ELLA *take* COLONEL, DUKE, *and* MAJOR *down*,
    while Girls gaze fondly at other Officers.)

SESTETTE.

           I hear the soft note of the echoing voice
               Of an old, old love, long dead —
           It whispers my sorrowing heart 'rejoice' —
               For the last sad tear is shed —
           The pain that is all but a pleasure will change
               For the pleasure that's all but pain,
           And never, oh never, this heart will range
               From that old, old love again !
                            (*Girls embrace Officers.*)

CHORUS.   Yes, the pain that is all, etc.   (*Embrace.*)

               Enter PATIENCE *and* BUNTHORNE.

As the Dragoons and Girls are embracing, enter GROSVENOR, *reading.
    He takes no notice of them, but comes slowly down, still reading.
    The Girls are all strangely fascinated by him, and gradually with-
    draw from Dragoons.*

ANG.   But who is this, whose god-like grace
               Proclaims he comes of noble race ?
               And who is this, whose manly face
               Bears sorrow's interesting trace ?

ENSEMBLE — Tutti.

Yes, who is this, etc.

GROS. I am a broken-hearted troubadour,
       Whose mind's æsthetic and whose tastes are pure !
ANG.   Æsthetic ! He is æsthetic !
GROS.   Yes, yes — I am æsthetic
                   And poetic !
ALL THE LADIES. Then, we love you !

(*The Girls leave Dragoons and group, kneeling, around* GROSVENOR.
    Fury of BUNTHORNE, *who recognizes a rival.*)

DRAGOONS. They love him ! Horror !
BUN. *and* PA. They love him ! Horror !
GROS. They love me ! Horror ! Horror ! Horror !

ENSEMBLE — Tutti.

GIRLS.	GROSVENOR.
Oh, list while we a love confess That words imperfectly express. Those shell-like ears, ah, do not close To blighted love's distracting woes !	Again my cursed comeliness Spreads hopeless anguish and distress ! Thine ears, oh Fortune, do not close To my intolerable woes.

PATIENCE.	BUNTHORNE.
List, Reginald, while I confess A love that's all unselfishness; That it's unselfish, goodness knows, You won't dispute it, I suppose?	My jealousy I can't express, Their love they openly confess; His shell-like ears he does not close To their recital of their woes.

DRAGOONS. Now is not this ridiculous, etc.

END OF ACT I

G

ACT II

SCENE. — *A glade.* JANE *is discovered leaning on a violoncello, upon which she presently accompanies herself. Chorus of Maidens are heard singing in the distance.*

JANE. The fickle crew have deserted Reginald and sworn allegiance to his rival, and all, forsooth, because he has glanced with passing favour on a puling milkmaid ! Fools ! of that fancy he will soon weary — and then I, who alone am faithful to him, shall reap my reward. But do not dally too long, Reginald, for my charms are ripe, Reginald, and already they are decaying. Better secure me ere I have gone too far !

RECIT. — JANE.

Sad is that woman's lot who, year by year,
Sees, one by one, her beauties disappear,
When Time, grown weary of her heart-drawn sighs,
Impatiently begins to 'dim her eyes' !
Compelled, at last, in life's uncertain gloamings,
To wreathe her wrinkled brow with well-saved 'combings',
Reduced, with rouge, lip-salve, and pearly grey,
To 'make up' for lost time as best she may !

SONG — JANE.

Silvered is the raven hair,
    Spreading is the parting straight,
Mottled the complexion fair,
    Halting is the youthful gait,
Hollow is the laughter free,
    Spectacled the limpid eye —
Little will be left of me
    In the coming by and by !

Fading is the taper waist,
  Shapeless grows the shapely limb,
And although severely laced,
  Spreading is the figure trim !
Stouter than I used to be,
  Still more corpulent grow I —
There will be too much of me
  In the coming by and by !

[*Exit* JANE.

Enter GROSVENOR, *followed by Maidens, two and two, each playing
on an archaic instrument, as in Act I. He is reading abstractedly,
as* BUNTHORNE *did in Act I., and pays no attention to them.*

CHORUS OF MAIDENS.

Turn, oh, turn in this direction,
  Shed, oh, shed a gentle smile,
With a glance of sad perfection
  Our poor fainting hearts beguile !
On such eyes as maidens cherish
  Let thy fond adorers gaze,
Or incontinently perish
  In their all-consuming rays !

(*He sits — they group around him.*)

GROS. (*aside*). The old, old tale. How rapturously these maidens
love me, and how hopelessly ! Oh, Patience, Patience, with the love
of thee in my heart, what have I for these poor mad maidens but an
unvalued pity ? Alas, they will die of hopeless love for me, as I
shall die of hopeless love for thee !

ANG. Sir, will it please you read to us ?

GROS. (*sighing*). Yes, child, if you will. What shall I read ?

ANG. One of your own poems.

GROS. One of my own poems ? Better not, my child. *They* will
not cure thee of thy love.

ELLA. Mr. Bunthorne used to read us a poem of his own every
day.

SAPH. And, to do him justice, he read them extremely well.

GROS. Oh, did he so ? Well, who am I that I should take upon myself to withhold my gifts from you ? What am I but a trustee ? Here is a decalet — a pure and simple thing, a very daisy — a babe might understand it. To appreciate it, it is not necessary to think of anything at all.

ANG. Let us think of nothing at all !

GROSVENOR *recites.*

> Gentle Jane was as good as gold,
> She always did as she was told;
> She never spoke when her mouth was full,
> Or caught bluebottles their legs to pull,
> Or spilt plum jam on her nice new frock,
> Or put white mice in the eight-day clock,
> Or vivisected her last new doll,
> Or fostered a passion for alcohol.
> And when she grew up she was given in marriage
> To a first-class earl who keeps his carriage !

GROS. I believe I am right in saying that there is not one word in that decalet which is calculated to bring the blush of shame to the cheek of modesty.

ANG. Not one; it is purity itself.

GROS. Here's another.

> Teasing Tom was a very bad boy,
> A great big squirt was his favourite toy;
> He put live shrimps in his father's boots,
> And sewed up the sleeves of his Sunday suits;
> He punched his poor little sisters' heads,
> And cayenne-peppered their four-post beds,
> He plastered their hair with cobbler's wax,
> And dropped hot halfpennies down their backs.
> The consequence was he was lost totally,
> And married a girl in the *corps de bally* !

ANG. Marked you how grandly — how relentlessly — the damning catalogue of crime strode on, till Retribution, like a poisèd hawk, came swooping down upon the Wrong-Doer? Oh, it was terrible!

ELLA. Oh, sir, you are indeed a true poet, for you touch our hearts, and they go out to you!

GROS. (*aside*). This is simply cloying. (*Aloud.*) Ladies, I am sorry to appear ungallant, but this is Saturday, and you have been following me about ever since Monday. I should like the usual half-holiday. I shall take it as a personal favour if you will kindly allow me to close early to-day.

SAPH. Oh, sir, do not send us from you!

GROS. Poor, poor girls! It is best to speak plainly. I know that I am loved by you, but I never can love you in return, for my heart is fixed elsewhere! Remember the fable of the Magnet and the Churn.

ANG. (*wildly*). But we don't know the fable of the Magnet and the Churn!

GROS. Don't you? Then I will sing it to you.

SONG — GROSVENOR.

A magnet hung in a hardware shop,
    And all around was a loving crop
Of scissors and needles, nails and knives,
    Offering love for all their lives;
But for iron the magnet felt no whim,
Though he charmed iron, it charmed not him;
From needles and nails and knives he'd turn,
For he'd set his love on a Silver Churn!

ALL.   A Silver Churn?
GROS.   A Silver Churn!

        His most æsthetic,
        Very magnetic
    Fancy took this turn —
        'If I can wheedle
        A knife or a needle,
    Why not a Silver Churn?'

CHORUS.   His most æsthetic, etc.

GROS.   And Iron and Steel expressed surprise,
           The needles opened their well-drilled eyes,
           The penknives felt 'shut up', no doubt,
           The scissors declared themselves 'cut out',
           The kettles they boiled with rage, 'tis said,
           While every nail went off its head,
           And hither and thither began to roam,
           Till a hammer came up — and drove them home.

ALL.   It drove them home?
GROS.   It drove them home!

               While this magnetic,
               Peripatetic
           Lover he lived to learn,
               By no endeavour
               Can magnet ever
           Attract a Silver Churn!

ALL.   While this magnetic, etc.

    [*They go off in low spirits, gazing back at him from time to time.*

GROS. At last they are gone! What is this mysterious fascination that I seem to exercise over all I come across? A curse on my fatal beauty, for I am sick of conquests!

PATIENCE appears.

PA. Archibald!
GROS. (*turns and sees her*). Patience!
PA. I have escaped with difficulty from my Reginald. I wanted to see you so much that I might ask you if you still love me as fondly as ever?
GROS. Love you? If the devotion of a lifetime—— (*Seizes her hand.*)
PA. (*indignantly*). Hold! Unhand me, or I scream! (*He releases her.*) If you are a gentleman, pray remember that I am another's! (*Very tenderly.*) But you *do* love me, don't you?

GROS. Madly, hopelessly, despairingly !

PA. That's right ! I never can be yours; but that's right !

GROS. And you love this Bunthorne ?

PA. With a heart-whole ecstasy that withers, and scorches, and burns, and stings ! (*Sadly.*) It is my duty.

GROS. Admirable girl ! But you are not happy with him ?

PA. Happy ? I am miserable beyond description !

GROS. That's right ! I never can be yours; but that's right !

PA. But go now. I see dear Reginald approaching. Farewell, dear Archibald; I cannot tell you how happy it has made me to know that you still love me.

GROS. Ah, if I only dared—— (*Advances towards her.*)

PA. Sir ! this language to one who is promised to another ! (*Tenderly.*) Oh, Archibald, think of me sometimes, for my heart is breaking ! He is so unkind to me, and you would be so loving !

GROS. Loving ! (*Advances towards her.*)

PA. Advance one step, and as I am a good and pure woman, I scream ! (*Tenderly.*) Farewell, Archibald ! (*Sternly.*) Stop there ! (*Tenderly.*) Think of me sometimes ! (*Angrily.*) Advance at your peril ! Once more, adieu !

> [GROSVENOR *sighs, gazes sorrowfully at her, sighs deeply, and exit. She bursts into tears.*

Enter BUNTHORNE, *followed by* JANE. *He is moody and preoccupied.*

JANE *sings.*

> In a doleful train,
>   One and one I walk all day;
> For I love in vain —
>   None so sorrowful as they
>   Who can only sigh and say,
>   Woe is me, alackaday !

BUN. (*seeing* PATIENCE). Crying, eh ? What are you crying about ?

PA. I've only been thinking how dearly I love you !

BUN. Love me ! Bah !

JANE. Love him ! Bah !

BUN. (*to* JANE). Don't you interfere.

JANE. He always crushes me !

PA. (*going to him*). What is the matter, dear Reginald ? If you have any sorrow, tell it to me, that I may share it with you. (*Sighing.*) It is my duty !

BUN. (*snappishly*). Whom were you talking with just now ?

PA. With dear Archibald.

BUN. (*furiously*). With dear Archibald ! Upon my honour, this is too much !

JANE. A great deal too much !

BUN. (*angrily to* JANE). Do be quiet !

JANE. Crushed again !

PA. I think he is the noblest, purest, and most perfect being I have ever met. But I don't love him. It is true that he is devotedly attached to me, but indeed I don't love *him*. Whenever he grows affectionate, I scream. It is my duty ! (*Sighing.*)

BUN. I dare say !

JANE. So do I ! *I* dare say !

PA. Why, how could I love him and love you too ? You can't love two people at once !

BUN. Oh, can't you, though !

PA. No, you can't; I only wish you could.

BUN. I don't believe you know what love is !

PA. (*sighing*). Yes, I do. There was a happy time when I didn't, but a bitter experience has taught me.

[*Exeunt* BUNTHORNE *and* JANE.

BALLAD — PATIENCE.

Love is a plaintive song,
    Sung by a suffering maid,
Telling a tale of wrong,
    Telling of hope betrayed;
Tuned to each changing note,
    Sorry when *he* is sad,
Blind to his every mote,
    Merry when he is glad !
        Love that no wrong can cure,
            Love that is always new,

That is the love that's pure,
That is the love that's true !

Rendering good for ill,
   Smiling at every frown,
Yielding your own self-will,
   Laughing your tear-drops down;
Never a selfish whim,
   Trouble, or pain to stir;
Everything for him,
   Nothing at all for her !
      Love that will aye endure,
         Though the rewards be few,
      That is the love that's pure,
         That is the love that's true !

[*At the end of ballad exit* PATIENCE, *weeping.*

Enter BUNTHORNE *and* JANE.

BUN. Everything has gone wrong with me since that smug-faced idiot came here. Before that I was admired — I may say, loved.

JANE. Too mild — adored !

BUN. Do let a poet soliloquize ! The damozels used to follow me wherever I went; now they all follow him !

JANE. Not all ! *I* am still faithful to you.

BUN. Yes, and a pretty damozel *you* are !

JANE. No, not pretty. Massive. Cheer up ! I will never leave you, I swear it !

BUN. Oh, thank you ! I know what it is; it's his confounded mildness. They find me too highly spiced, if you please ! And no doubt I *am* highly spiced.

JANE. Not for my taste !

BUN. (*savagely*). No, but I am for theirs. But I will show the world I can be as mild as he. If they want insipidity, they shall have it. I'll meet this fellow on his own ground and beat him on it.

JANE. You shall. And I will help you.

BUN. You will ? Jane, there's a good deal of good in you, after all !

DUET — Bunthorne *and* Jane.

JANE.   So go to him and say to him, with compliment ironical —
BUN.   Sing 'Hey to you —
                     Good day to you' —
              And that's what I shall say !

JANE.   'Your style is much too sanctified — your cut is too
                  canonical' —
BUN.   Sing 'Bah to you —
                     Ha ! ha ! to you' —
              And that's what I shall say !

JANE.   'I was the beau ideal of the morbid young æsthetical —
        To doubt my inspiration was regarded as heretical —
        Until you cut me out with your placidity emetical.' —
BUN.   Sing 'Booh to you —
                     Pooh, pooh to you' —
              And that's what I shall say !

BOTH.   Sing 'Hey to you — good day to you' —
         Sing 'Bah to you — ha ! ha ! to you' —
         Sing 'Booh to you — pooh, pooh to you' —
         And that's what $\left\{ \begin{matrix} you \\ I \end{matrix} \right\}$ shall say !

BUN.   I'll tell him that unless he will consent to be more
                  jocular —
JANE.   Sing 'Booh to you —
                     Pooh, pooh to you' —
              And that's what you should say !

BUN.   To cut his curly hair, and stick an eyeglass in his ocular —
JANE.   Sing 'Bah to you —
                     Ha ! ha ! to you' —
              And that's what you should say !

BUN.   To stuff his conversation full of quibble and of quiddity —
        To dine on chops and roly-poly pudding with avidity —
        He'd better clear away with all convenient rapidity.

JANE.   Sing 'Hey to you —
                   Good day to you' —
           And that's what you should say !

BOTH.   Sing 'Booh to you — pooh, pooh to you' —
                   Sing 'Bah to you — ha ! ha ! to you' —
                   Sing 'Hey to you — good day to you' —
            And that's what $\left\{\begin{array}{c} \text{I} \\ \text{you} \end{array}\right\}$ shall say !

[Exeunt JANE *and* BUNTHORNE *together.*

Enter DUKE, COLONEL, *and* MAJOR. *They have abandoned their uniforms, and are dressed and made up in imitation of Æsthetics. They have long hair, and other outward signs of attachment to the brotherhood. As they sing they walk in stiff, constrained, and angular attitudes — a grotesque exaggeration of the attitudes adopted by* BUNTHORNE *and the young Ladies in Act I.*

TRIO — DUKE, COLONEL, *and* MAJOR.

It's clear that mediæval art alone retains its zest,
To charm and please its devotees we've done our little best.
We're not quite sure if all we do has the Early English ring;
But, as far as we can judge, it's something like this sort of thing:
         You hold yourself like this (*attitude*),
         You hold yourself like that (*attitude*),
By hook and crook you try to look both angular and flat (*attitude*).
         We venture to expect
         That what we recollect,
Though but a part of true High Art, will have its due effect.

If this is not exactly right, we hope you won't upbraid;
You can't get high Æsthetic tastes, like trousers, ready made.
True views on Mediævalism Time alone will bring,
But, as far as we can judge, it's something like this sort of thing:
         You hold yourself like this (*attitude*),
         You hold yourself like that (*attitude*),
By hook and crook you try to look both angular and flat (*attitude*).
         To cultivate the trim
         Rigidity of limb,
You ought to get a Marionette, and form your style on him (*attitude*).

COL. (*attitude*). Yes, it's quite clear that our only chance of making a lasting impression on these young ladies is to become as æsthetic as they are.

MAJ. (*attitude*). No doubt. The only question is how far we've succeeded in doing so. I don't know why, but I've an idea that this is not quite right.

DUKE. (*attitude*). *I* don't like it. I never did. I don't see what it means. I do it, but I don't like it.

COL. My good friend, the question is not whether we like it, but whether they do. They understand these things — we don't. Now I shouldn't be surprised if this is effective enough — at a distance.

MAJ. I can't help thinking we're a little stiff at it. It would be extremely awkward if we were to be 'struck' so !

COL. I don't think we shall be struck so. Perhaps we're a little awkward at first — but everything must have a beginning. Oh, here they come ! 'Tention !

They strike fresh attitudes, as ANGELA *and* SAPHIR *enter.*

ANG. (*seeing them*). Oh, Saphir — see — see ! The immortal fire has descended on them, and they are of the Inner Brotherhood — perceptively intense and consummately utter. (*The Officers have some difficulty in maintaining their constrained attitudes.*)

SAPH. (*in admiration*). How Botticellian ! How Fra Angelican ! Oh, Art, we thank thee for this boon !

COL. (*apologetically*). I'm afraid we're not quite right.

ANG. Not supremely, perhaps, but oh, so all-but ! (*To* SAPHIR.) Oh, Saphir, are they not quite too all-but ?

SAPH. They are indeed jolly utter !

MAJ. (*in agony*). I wonder what the Inner Brotherhood usually recommend for cramp ?

COL. Ladies, we will not deceive you. We are doing this at some personal inconvenience with a view of expressing the extremity of our devotion to you. We trust that it is not without its effect.

ANG. We will not deny that we are much moved by this proof of your attachment.

SAPH. Yes, your conversion to the principles of Æsthetic Art in its highest development has touched us deeply.

ANG. And if Mr. Grosvenor should remain obdurate —

SAPH. Which we have every reason to believe he will —

MAJ. (*aside, in agony*). I wish they'd make haste.

ANG. We are not prepared to say that our yearning hearts will not go out to you.

COL. (*as giving a word of command*). By sections of threes — Rapture ! (*All strike a fresh attitude, expressive of æsthetic rapture.*)

SAPH. Oh, it's extremely good — for beginners it's admirable.

MAJ. The only question is, who will take who ?

COL. Oh, the Duke chooses first, as a matter of course.

DUKE. Oh, I couldn't think of it — you are really too good !

COL. Nothing of the kind. You are a great matrimonial fish, and it's only fair that each of these ladies should have a chance of hooking you. It's perfectly simple. Observe, suppose you choose Angela, I take Saphir, Major takes nobody. Suppose you choose Saphir, Major takes Angela, I take nobody. Suppose you choose neither, I take Angela, Major takes Saphir. Clear as day !

QUINTET.

DUKE, COLONEL, MAJOR, ANGELA, *and* SAPHIR.

DUKE (*taking* SAPHIR).

If Saphir I choose to marry,
    I shall be fixed up for life;
Then the Colonel need not tarry,
    Angela can be his wife.

(DUKE *dances with* SAPHIR, COLONEL *with* ANGELA,
MAJOR *dances alone.*)

MAJOR (*dancing alone*).

In that case unprecedented,
    Single I shall live and die —
I shall have to be contented
    With their heartfelt sympathy !

ALL (*dancing as before*).

He will have to be contented
    With our heartfelt sympathy !

DUKE (*taking* ANGELA).

If on Angy I determine,
    At my wedding she'll appear
Decked in diamonds and in ermine,
    Major then can take Saphir !

(DUKE *dances with* ANGELA, MAJOR *with* SAPHIR,
        COLONEL *dances alone.*)

COLONEL (*dancing*).

In that case unprecedented,
    Single I shall live and die —
I shall have to be contented
    With their heartfelt sympathy !

ALL (*dancing as before*).

He will have to be contented
    With our heartfelt sympathy !

DUKE (*taking both* ANGELA *and* SAPHIR).

After some debate internal,
    If on neither I decide,
Saphir then can take the Colonel,
            (*Handing* SAPHIR *to* COLONEL.)
    Angy be the Major's bride !
            (*Handing* ANGELA *to* MAJOR.)

(COLONEL *dances with* SAPHIR, MAJOR *with* ANGELA,
        DUKE *dances alone.*)

DUKE (*dancing*).

In that case unprecedented,
    Single I must live and die —

I shall have to be contented
With their heartfelt sympathy !

ALL (*dancing as before*).

He will have to be contented
With our heartfelt sympathy.

[*At the end,* DUKE, COLONEL, *and* MAJOR, *and two girls
dance off arm-in-arm.*

Enter GROSVENOR.

GROS. It is very pleasant to be alone. It is pleasant to be able to
gaze at leisure upon those features which all others may gaze upon
at their good will ! (*Looking at his reflection in hand-mirror.*) Ah,
I am a very Narcissus !

Enter BUNTHORNE, *moodily.*

BUN. It's no use; I can't live without admiration. Since Gros-
venor came here, insipidity has been at a premium. Ah, he is there !
GROS. Ah, Bunthorne ! come here — look ! Very graceful, isn't
it !
BUN. (*taking hand-mirror*). Allow me; I haven't seen it. Yes, it
is graceful.
GROS. (*re-taking hand-mirror*). Oh, good gracious ! not that —
this——
BUN. You don't mean that ! Bah ! I am in no mood for trifling.
GROS. And what is amiss ?
BUN. Ever since you came here, you have entirely monopolized
the attentions of the young ladies. I don't like it, sir !
GROS. My dear sir, how can I help it ? They are the plague of
my life. My dear Mr. Bunthorne, with your personal disadvantages,
you can have no idea of the inconvenience of being madly loved, at
first sight, by every woman you meet.
BUN. Sir, until you came here I was adored !
GROS. Exactly — until I came here. That's my grievance. I cut
everybody out ! I assure you, if you could only suggest some means
whereby, consistently with my duty to society, I could escape these
inconvenient attentions, you would earn my everlasting gratitude.

BUN. I will do so at once. However popular it may be with the world at large, your personal appearance is highly objectionable to *me*.

GROS. It is? (*Shaking his hand.*) Oh, thank you! thank you! How can I express my gratitude?

BUN. By making a complete change at once. Your conversation must henceforth be perfectly matter-of-fact. You must cut your hair, and have a back parting. In appearance and costume you must be absolutely commonplace.

GROS. (*decidedly*). No. Pardon me, that's impossible.

BUN. Take care! When I am thwarted I am very terrible.

GROS. I can't help that. I am a man with a mission. And that mission must be fulfilled.

BUN. I don't think you quite appreciate the consequences of thwarting me.

GROS. I don't care what they are.

BUN. Suppose — I won't go so far as to say that I will do it — but suppose for one moment I were to curse you? (GROSVENOR *quails*.) Ah! Very well. Take care.

GROS. But surely you would never do that? (*In great alarm.*)

BUN. I don't know. It would be an extreme measure, no doubt. Still——

GROS. (*wildly*). But you would not do it — I am sure you would not. (*Throwing himself at* BUNTHORNE'S *knees, and clinging to him.*) Oh, reflect, reflect! You had a mother once.

BUN. Never!

GROS. Then you had an aunt! (BUNTHORNE *affected*.) Ah! I see you had! By the memory of that aunt, I implore you to pause ere you resort to this last fearful expedient. Oh, Mr. Bunthorne, reflect, reflect! (*Weeping.*)

BUN. (*aside, after a struggle with himself*). I must not allow myself to be unmanned! (*Aloud.*) It is useless. Consent at once, or may a nephew's curse——

GROS. Hold! Are you absolutely resolved?

BUN. Absolutely.

GROS. Will nothing shake you?

BUN. Nothing. I am adamant.

GROS. Very good. (*Rising.*) Then I yield.

BUN. Ha! You swear it?

Gros. I do, cheerfully. I have long wished for a reasonable pretext for such a change as you suggest. It has come at last. I do it on compulsion !

Bun. Victory ! I triumph !

DUET — Bunthorne *and* Grosvenor.

Bun.
When I go out of door,
Of damozels a score
 (All sighing and burning,
 And clinging and yearning)
Will follow me as before.
I shall, with cultured taste,
Distinguish gems from paste,
 And 'High diddle diddle'
 Will rank as an idyll,
If I pronounce it chaste !

Both.
 A most intense young man,
 A soulful-eyed young man,
An ultra-poetical, super-æsthetical,
 Out-of-the-way young man !

Gros.
Conceive me, if you can,
An every-day young man :
 A commonplace type,
 With a stick and a pipe,
And a half-bred black-and-tan ;
 Who thinks suburban 'hops'
 More fun than 'Monday Pops',
Who's fond of his dinner,
And doesn't get thinner
 On bottled beer and chops.

Both.
 A commonplace young man,
 A matter-of-fact young man,
A steady and stolid-y, jolly Bank-holiday
 Every-day young man !

BUN.   A Japanese young man,
                A blue-and-white young man,
            Francesca di Rimini, miminy, piminy,
                Je-ne-sais-quoi young man !

GROS.   A Chancery Lane young man,
                A Somerset House young man,
            A very delectable, highly respectable,
                Threepenny-bus young man !

BUN.   A pallid and thin young man,
                A haggard and lank young man,
            A greenery-yallery, Grosvenor Gallery,
                Foot-in-the-grave young man !

GROS.   A Sewell & Cross young man,
                A Howell & James young man,
            A pushing young particle — 'What's the next
                article ?' —
                Waterloo House young man !

ENSEMBLE.

BUN.	GROS.
Conceive me, if you can,	Conceive me, if you can,
A crotchety, cracked young man,	A matter-of-fact young man,
An ultra-poetical, super-aesthetical,	An alphabetical, arithmetical,
Out-of-the-way young man!	Every-day young man!

[*At the end*, GROSVENOR *dances off*. BUNTHORNE *remains*.

BUN. It is all right ! I have committed my last act of ill-nature, and henceforth I'm a changed character. (*Dances about stage, humming refrain of last air*.)

Enter PATIENCE. *She gazes in astonishment at him*.

PA. Reginald ! Dancing ! And — what in the world is the matter with you ?

BUN. Patience, I'm a changed man. Hitherto I've been gloomy, moody, fitful — uncertain in temper and selfish in disposition —

PA. You have, indeed ! (*Sighing.*)

BUN. All that is changed. I have reformed. I have modelled myself upon Mr. Grosvenor. Henceforth I am mildly cheerful. My conversation will blend amusement with instruction. I shall still be æsthetic ; but my æstheticism will be of the most pastoral kind.

PA. Oh, Reginald ! Is all this true ?

BUN. Quite true. Observe how amiable I am. (*Assuming a fixed smile.*)

PA. But, Reginald, how long will this last ?

BUN. With occasional intervals for rest and refreshment, as long as I do.

PA. Oh, Reginald, I'm so happy ! (*In his arms.*) Oh, dear, dear Reginald, I cannot express the joy I feel at this change. It will no longer be a duty to love you, but a pleasure — a rapture — an ecstasy !

BUN. My darling !

PA. But — oh, horror ! (*Recoiling from him.*)

BUN. What's the matter ?

PA. Is it quite certain that you have absolutely reformed — that you are henceforth a perfect being — utterly free from defect of any kind ?

BUN. It is quite certain. I have sworn it.

PA. Then I never can be yours !

BUN. Why not ?

PA. Love, to be pure, most be absolutely unselfish, and there can be nothing unselfish in loving so perfect a being as you have now become !

BUN. But, stop a bit ! I don't want to change — I'll relapse — I'll be as I was — interrupted !

Enter GROSVENOR, *followed by all the young Ladies, who are followed by Chorus of Dragoons. He has had his hair cut, and is dressed in an ordinary suit of dittoes and a pot hat. They all dance cheerfully round the stage in marked contrast to their former languor.*

CHORUS — Grosvenor *and* Girls.

Gros.	Girls.
I'm a Waterloo House young man,	We're Swears & Wells young girls,
A Sewell & Cross young man,	We're Madame Louise young girls,
A steady and stolid-y, jolly Bank-holiday,	We're prettily pattering, cheerily chattering,
Every-day young man!	Every-day young girls!

Bun. Angela — Ella — Saphir — what — what does this mean ?

Ang. It means that Archibald the All-Right cannot be all-wrong; and if the All-Right chooses to discard æstheticism, it proves that æstheticism ought to be discarded.

Pa. Oh, Archibald ! Archibald ! I'm shocked — surprised — horrified !

Gros. I can't help it. I'm not a free agent. I do it on compulsion.

Pa. This is terrible. Go ! I shall never set eyes on you again. But — oh, joy !

Gros. What is the matter ?

Pa. Is it quite, quite certain that you will always be a commonplace young man ?

Gros. Always — I've sworn it.

Pa. Why, then, there's nothing to prevent my loving you with all the fervour at my command !

Gros. Why, that's true.

Pa. My Archibald !

Gros. My Patience ! (*They embrace.*)

Bun. Crushed again !

Enter Jane.

Jane (*who is still æsthetic*). Cheer up ! I am still here. I have never left you, and I never will !

Bun. Thank you, Jane. After all, there is no denying it, you're a fine figure of a woman !

Jane. My Reginald !

Bun. My Jane !

Flourish. Enter Colonel, Duke, *and* Major.

COL. Ladies, the Duke has at length determined to select a bride ! (*General excitement.*)

DUKE. I have a great gift to bestow. Approach, such of you as are truly lovely. (*All come forward, bashfully, except* JANE *and* PATIENCE.) In personal appearance you have all that is necessary to make a woman happy. In common fairness, I think I ought to choose the only one among you who has the misfortune to be distinctly plain. (*Girls retire disappointed.*) Jane !

JANE (*leaving* BUNTHORNE'S *arms*). Duke ! (JANE *and* DUKE *embrace.* BUNTHORNE *is utterly disgusted.*)

BUN. Crushed again !

FINALE.

DUKE.
> After much debate internal,
> I on Lady Jane decide,
> Saphir now may take the Colonel,
> Angy be the Major's bride !

(SAPHIR *pairs off with* COLONEL, ANGELA *with* MAJOR,
ELLA *with* SOLICITOR.)

BUN.
> In that case unprecedented,
> Single I must live and die —
> I shall have to be contented
> With a tulip or li*ly* !

(*Takes a lily from button-hole and gazes affectionately at it.*)

ALL.
> He will have to be contented
> With a tulip or li*ly* !
>
> Greatly pleased with one another,
> To get married we decide.
> Each of us will wed the other,
> Nobody be Bunthorne's Bride !

DANCE.

CURTAIN

PRINCESS IDA
OR
CASTLE ADAMANT

DRAMATIS PERSONÆ

KING HILDEBRAND

HILARION (*his Son*)

CYRIL
FLORIAN } (*Hilarion's Friends*)

KING GAMA

ARAC
GURON } (*his Sons*)
SCYNTHIUS

PRINCESS IDA (*Gama's Daughter*)

LADY BLANCHE (*Professor of Abstract Science*)

LADY PSYCHE (*Professor of Humanities*)

MELISSA (*Lady Blanche's Daughter*)

SACHARISSA
CHLOE } (*Girl Graduates*)
ADA

Soldiers, Courtiers, 'Girl Graduates', 'Daughters of the Plough', etc.

———————

ACT I. — Pavilion in King Hildebrand's Palace.

ACT II. — Gardens of Castle Adamant.

ACT III. — Courtyard of Castle Adamant.

First produced at the Savoy Theatre, January 5, 1884.

PRINCESS IDA

OR

CASTLE ADAMANT

ACT I

SCENE. — *Pavilion attached to* KING HILDEBRAND'S *Palace. Soldiers and Courtiers discovered looking out through opera-glasses, telescopes, etc.,* FLORIAN *leading.*

CHORUS.

Search throughout the panorama
For a sign of royal Gama,
   Who to-day should cross the water
   With his fascinating daughter —
     Ida is her name.

Some misfortune evidently
Has detained them — consequently
   Search throughout the panorama
   For the daughter of King Gama,
     Prince Hilarion's flame !

SOLO.

FLOR.	Will Prince Hilarion's hopes be sadly blighted ?
ALL.	Who can tell ?
FLOR.	Will Ida break the vows that she has plighted ?
ALL.	Who can tell ?
FLOR.	Will she back out, and say she did not mean them ?

ALL.   Who can tell?
FLOR.   If so, there'll be the deuce to pay between them!

ALL.   No, no — we'll not despair,
                  For Gama would not dare
                  To make a deadly foe
                  Of Hildebrand, and so,
                     Search throughout, etc.

Enter KING HILDEBRAND, *with* CYRIL.

HILD.   See you no sign of Gama?
FLOR.   None, my liege!
HILD.   It's very odd indeed. If Gama fail
             To put in an appearance at our Court
             Before the sun has set in yonder west,
             And fail to bring the Princess Ida here
             To whom our son Hilarion was betrothed
             At the extremely early age of one,
             There's war between King Gama and ourselves!
             (*Aside to* CYRIL.) Oh, Cyril, how I dread this interview
             It's twenty years since he and I have met.
             He was a twisted monster — all awry —
             As though Dame Nature, angry with her work,
             Had crumpled it in fitful petulance!
CYR.   But, sir, a twisted and ungainly trunk
             Often bears goodly fruit. Perhaps he was
             A kind, well-spoken gentleman?
HILD.   Oh, no!
             For, adder-like, his sting lay in his tongue.
             (His 'sting' is present, though his 'stung' is past.)
FLOR. (*looking through glass*). But stay, my liege; o'er yonder
                  mountain's brow
             Comes a small body, bearing Gama's arms;
             And now I look more closely at it, sir,
             I see attached to it King Gama's legs;
             From which I gather this corollary
             That that small body must be Gama's own!
HILD.   Ha! Is the Princess with him?

FLOR.
                                Well, my liege,
Unless her highness is full six feet high,
And wears mustachios too — and smokes cigars —
And rides *en cavalier* in coat of steel —
I do not think she is.

HILD.
                           One never knows.
She's a strange girl, I've heard, and does odd things !
Come, bustle there !
For Gama place the richest robes we own —
For Gama place the coarsest prison dress —
For Gama let our best spare bed be aired —
For Gama let our deepest dungeon yawn —
For Gama lay the costliest banquet out —
For Gama place cold water and dry bread !
For as King Gama brings the Princess here,
Or brings her not, so shall King Gama have
Much more than everything — much less than nothing !

SONG AND CHORUS.

HILD.
    Now hearken to my strict command
    On every hand, on every hand —

CHORUS.

To your command,
On every hand,
We dutifully bow !

HILD.
    If Gama bring the Princess here,
    Give him good cheer, give him good cheer.

CHORUS.

If she come here
We'll give him a cheer,
And we will show you how.
Hip, hip, hurrah ! hip, hip, hurrah !
Hip, hip, hurrah ! hurrah ! hurrah !

We'll shout and sing
Long live the King,
And his daughter, too, I trow !
Then shout ha ! ha ! hip, hip, hurrah !
Hip, hip, hip, hip, hurrah !
For the fair Princess and her good papa,
Hurrah ! hurrah !

HILD.   But if he fail to keep his troth,
Upon our oath, we'll trounce them both !

CHORUS.

He'll trounce them both,
Upon his oath,
As sure as quarter-day !

HILD.   We'll shut him up in a dungeon cell,
And toll his knell on a funeral bell.

CHORUS.

From dungeon cell,
His funeral knell
Shall strike him with dismay !
Hip, hip, hurrah ! hip, hip, hurrah !
Hip, hip, hurrah ! hurrah ! hurrah !
As up we string
The faithless King,
In the old familiar way !
We'll shout ha ! ha ! hip, hip, hurrah !
Hip, hip, hip, hip, hurrah!
As we make an end of her false papa,
Hurrah ! hurrah !

                                        [*Exeunt all.*

Enter HILARION.

RECIT. — HILARION.

To-day we meet, my baby bride and I —
But ah, my hopes are balanced by my fears !

What transmutations have been conjured by
The silent alchemy of twenty years !

BALLAD — HILARION.

Ida was a twelvemonth old,
    Twenty years ago !
I was twice her age, I'm told,
    Twenty years ago !
Husband twice as old as wife
Argues ill for married life,
Baleful prophecies were rife,
    Twenty years ago !

Still, I was a tiny prince
    Twenty years ago.
She has gained upon me, since
    Twenty years ago.
Though she's twenty-one, it's true,
I am barely twenty-two —
False and foolish prophets you,
    Twenty years ago !

Enter HILDEBRAND.

HIL.   Well, father, is there news for me at last ?
HILD.   King Gama is in sight, but much I fear
    With no Princess !
HIL.   Alas, my liege, I've heard
    That Princess Ida has forsworn the world,
    And, with a band of women, shut herself
    Within a lonely country house, and there
    Devotes herself to stern philosophies !
HILD.   Then I should say the loss of such a wife
    Is one to which a reasonable man
    Would easily be reconciled.
HIL.   Oh, no !
    Or I am not a reasonable man.
    She *is* my wife — has been for twenty years !
    (*Holding glass.*) I think I see her now.

HILD.　　　　　　　　　　　　　　　　　　　Ha ! let me look !
HIL.　　In my mind's eye, I mean — a blushing bride,
　　　　All bib and tucker, frill and furbelow !
　　　　How exquisite she looked as she was borne,
　　　　Recumbent, in her foster-mother's arms !
　　　　How the bride wept — nor would be comforted
　　　　Until the hireling mother-for-the-nonce
　　　　Administered refreshment in the vestry.
　　　　And I remember feeling much annoyed
　　　　That she should weep at marrying with me.
　　　　But then I thought, 'These brides are all alike.
　　　　You cry at marrying me ? How much more cause
　　　　You'd have to cry if it were broken off !'
　　　　These were my thoughts ; I kept them to myself,
　　　　For at that age I had not learnt to speak.

　　　　　　　　　　　　　　　　　　　　　[Exeunt.

　　　　　　　Enter Courtiers.

CHORUS.

From the distant panorama
Come the sons of royal Gama.
　　They are heralds evidently,
　　And are sacred consequently,
　　　　Sons of Gama, hail ! oh, hail !

Enter ARAC, GURON, *and* SCYNTHIUS.

SONG — ARAC.

We are warriors three,
　　Sons of Gama, Rex.
Like most sons are we,
　　Masculine in sex.

ALL THREE.　　　　Yes, yes, yes,
　　　　　　　Masculine in sex.

ARAC.
> Politics we bar,
> > They are not our bent;
> On the whole we are
> > Not intelligent.

ALL THREE.
> > No, no, no,
> > Not intelligent.

ARAC.
> But with doughty heart,
> > And with trusty blade
> We can play our part —
> > Fighting is our trade.

ALL THREE.
> > Yes, yes, yes,
> > Fighting is our trade.

ALL THREE.
> Bold, and fierce, and strong, ha ! ha !
> > For a war we burn,
> With its right or wrong, ha ! ha !
> > We have no concern.
> Order comes to fight, ha ! ha !
> > Order is obeyed,
> We are men of might, ha ! ha !
> > Fighting is our trade.
> > Yes, yes, yes,
> Fighting is our trade, ha ! ha !

CHORUS.
> They are men of might, ha ! ha !
> Fighting is their trade.
> Order comes to fight, ha ! ha !
> Order is obeyed, ha ! ha !
> > Fighting is their trade !

Enter KING GAMA.

SONG — GAMA.

If you give me your attention, I will tell you what I am:
I'm a genuine philanthropist — all other kinds are sham.
Each little fault of temper and each social defect
In my erring fellow-creatures I endeavour to correct.
To all their little weaknesses I open people's eyes;
And little plans to snub the self-sufficient I devise;
I love my fellow-creatures — I do all the good I can —
Yet everybody says I'm such a disagreeable man !
        And I can't think why !

To compliments inflated I've a withering reply;
And vanity I always do my best to mortify;
A charitable action I can skilfully dissect;
And interested motives I'm delighted to detect;
I know everybody's income and what everybody earns;
And I carefully compare it with the income-tax returns;
But to benefit humanity however much I plan,
Yet everybody says I'm such a disagreeable man !
        And I can't think why !

I'm sure I'm no ascetic; I'm as pleasant as can be;
You'll always find me ready with a crushing repartee,
I've an irritating chuckle, I've a celebrated sneer,
I've an entertaining snigger, I've a fascinating leer.
To everybody's prejudice I know a thing or two;
I can tell a woman's age in half a minute — and I do.
But although I try to make myself as pleasant as I can,
Yet everybody says I am a disagreeable man !
        And I can't think why !

Enter HILDEBRAND, HILARION, CYRIL, *and* FLORIAN.

GAMA.   So this is Castle Hildebrand ? Well, well !
        Dame Rumour whispered that the place was grand;
        She told me that your taste was exquisite,
        Superb, unparalleled !

HILD. (*gratified*).   Oh, really, King !

GAMA.   But she's a liar ! Why, how old you've grown !
           Is this Hilarion ? Why, you've changed too —
           You were a singularly handsome child !

(*To* FLOR.)   Are you a courtier ? Come, then, ply your trade,
           Tell me some lies. How do you like your King ?
           Vile rumour says he's all but imbecile.
           Now, that's not true ?

FLOR.   My lord, we love our King.
           His wise remarks are valued by his court
           As precious stones.

GAMA.   And for the self-same cause.
           Like precious stones, his sensible remarks
           Derive their value from their scarcity !
           Come now, be honest, tell the truth for once !
           Tell it of me. Come, come, I'll harm you not.
           This leg is crooked — this foot is ill-designed —
           This shoulder wears a hump ! Come, out with it !
           Look, here's my face ! Now, am I not the worst
           Of Nature's blunders ?

CYR.   Nature never errs.
           To those who know the workings of your mind,
           Your face and figure, sir, suggest a book
           Appropriately bound.

GAMA (*enraged*).   Why, harkye, sir,
           How dare you bandy words with me ?

CYR.   No need
           To bandy aught that appertains to you.

GAMA (*furiously*).   Do you permit this, King ?

HILD.   We are in doubt
           Whether to treat you as an honoured guest,
           Or as a traitor knave who plights his word
           And breaks it.

GAMA (*quickly*).   If the casting vote's with me,
           I give it for the former !

HILD.   We shall see.
           By the terms of our contract, signed and sealed,
           You're bound to bring the Princess here to-day:
           Why is she not with you ?

H

GAMA.   Answer me this :
    What think you of a wealthy purse-proud man,
    Who, when he calls upon a starving friend,
    Pulls out his gold and flourishes his notes,
    And flashes diamonds in the pauper's eyes ?
    What name have you for such an one ?

HILD.   A snob.

GAMA. Just so. The girl has beauty, virtue, wit,
    Grace, humour, wisdom, charity, and pluck.
    Would it be kindly, think you, to parade
    These brilliant qualities before *your* eyes ?
    Oh no, King Hildebrand, I am no snob !

HILD. (*furiously*). Stop that tongue,
    Or you shall lose the monkey head that holds it !

GAMA. Bravo ! your King deprives me of my head,
    That he and I may meet on equal terms !

HILD. Where is she now ?

GAMA.   In Castle Adamant,
    One of my many country houses. There
    She rules a woman's University,
    With full a hundred girls, who learn of her.

CYR. A hundred girls ! A hundred ecstasies !

GAMA. But no mere girls, my good young gentleman;
    With all the college learning that you boast,
    The youngest there will prove a match for *you*.

CYR. With all my heart, if she's the prettiest !
(*To* FLOR.) Fancy, a hundred matches — all alight ! —
    That's if I strike them as I hope to do !

GAMA. Despair your hope; their hearts are dead to men.
    He who desires to gain their favour must
    Be qualified to strike their teeming brains,
    And not their hearts. They're safety matches, sir,
    And they light only on the knowledge box —
    So *you've* no chance !

FLOR. Are there no males whatever in those walls ?

GAMA. None, gentlemen, excepting letter mails —
    And they are driven (as males often are
    In other large communities) by women.
    Why, bless my heart, she's so particular

She'll scarcely suffer Dr. Watts's hymns —
And all the animals she owns are 'hers' !
The ladies rise at cockcrow every morn —

CYR.   Ah, then they have male poultry ?

GAMA.   Not at all,

(*Confidentially.*)   The crowing's done by an accomplished hen !

DUET — GAMA *and* HILDEBRAND.

GAMA.   Perhaps if you address the lady
                Most politely, most politely —
            Flatter and impress the lady,
                Most politely, most politely —
            Humbly beg and humbly sue —
            She may deign to look on you,
            But your doing you must do
                Most politely, most politely !

ALL.   Humbly beg and humbly sue, etc.

HILD.   Go you, and inform the lady,
                Most politely, most politely,
            If she don't, we'll storm the lady
                Most politely, most politely !

(*To* GAMA.)   You'll remain as hostage here;
            Should Hilarion disappear,
            We will hang you, never fear,
                Most politely, most politely !

            He'll ⎫

ALL.   I'll ⎬ remain as hostage here, etc.

            You'll ⎭

[GAMA, ARAC, GURON, *and* SCYNTHIUS *are marched off in custody,* HILDEBRAND *following.*

RECIT. — HILARION.

Come, Cyril, Florian, our course is plain,
     To-morrow morn fair Ida we'll engage;
But we will use no force her love to gain,
     Nature has armed us for the war we wage !

TRIO — HILARION, CYRIL, *and* FLORIAN.

HIL.
Expressive glances
Shall be our lances,
    And pops of Sillery
    Our light artillery.
We'll storm their bowers
With scented showers
Of fairest flowers
    That we can buy !

CHORUS.
    Oh, dainty triolet !
    Oh, fragrant violet !
    Oh, gentle heigho-let
      (Or little sigh).
On sweet urbanity,
Though mere inanity,
To touch their vanity
    We will rely !

CYR.
When day is fading,
With serenading
    And such frivolity
    We'll prove our quality.
A sweet profusion
Of soft allusion
This bold intrusion
    Shall justify.

CHORUS.
Oh, dainty triolet, etc.

FLOR.
We'll charm their senses
With verbal fences,
    With ballads amatory
    And declamatory.
Little heeding
Their pretty pleading,
Our love exceeding
    We'll justify !

CHORUS.   Oh, dainty triolet, etc.

Re-enter GAMA, ARAC, GURON, *and* SCYNTHIUS
heavily ironed.

RECIT.

GAMA.   Must we, till then, in prison cell be thrust ?
HILD.   You must !
GAMA.   This seems unnecessarily severe !
ARAC, GURON, *and* SCYNTHIUS.   Hear, hear !

TRIO — ARAC, GURON, *and* SCYNTHIUS.

> For a month to dwell
> In a dungeon cell;
>   Growing thin and wizen
>   In a solitary prison,
> Is a poor look-out
> For a soldier stout,
>   Who is longing for the rattle
>   Of a complicated battle —
> For the rum-tum-tum
> Of the military drum,
>   And the guns that go boom ! boom !

ALL.   The rum-tum-tum
            Of the military drum, etc.

HILD.   When Hilarion's bride
            Has at length complied
                With the just conditions
                Of our requisitions,
            You may go in haste
            And indulge your taste
                For the fascinating rattle
                Of a complicated battle —
            For the rum-tum-tum
            Of the military drum,
                And the guns that go boom ! boom !

ALL.   For the rum-tum-tum
                Of the military drum, etc.

ALL.   But till that time { we'll / you'll } here remain,

           And bail { they / we } will not entertain,

           Should she { his / our } mandate disobey,

           { Our / Your } lives the penalty will pay !

     [GAMA, ARAC, GURON, *and* SCYNTHIUS *are marched off.*

END OF ACT I

ACT II

Gardens in Castle Adamant. A river runs across the back of the stage, crossed by a rustic bridge. Castle Adamant in the distance.

Girl graduates discovered seated at the feet of LADY PSYCHE.

CHORUS.

Towards the empyrean heights
　　Of every kind of lore,
We've taken several easy flights,
　　And mean to take some more.
In trying to achieve success
　　No envy racks our heart,
And all the knowledge we possess,
　　We mutually impart.

SONG — MELISSA.

Pray, what authors should she read
Who in Classics would succeed?

PSYCHE.

If you'd climb the Helicon,
You should read Anacreon,
Ovid's *Metamorphoses*,
Likewise Aristophanes,
And the works of Juvenal:
These are worth attention, all;
But, if you will be advised,
You will get them Bowdlerized!

CHORUS.

Ah! we will get them Bowdlerized!

SOLO — SACHARISSA.

Pray you, tell us, if you can,
What's the thing that's known as Man?

PSYCHE.

Man will swear and Man will storm —
Man is not at all good form —
Man is of no kind of use —
Man's a donkey — Man's a goose —
Man is coarse and Man is plain —
Man is more or less insane —
Man's a ribald — Man's a rake,
Man is Nature's sole mistake!

CHORUS.

We'll a memorandum make —
Man is Nature's sole mistake!

And thus to empyrean height
    Of every kind of lore,
In search of wisdom's pure delight,
    Ambitiously we soar.
In trying to achieve success
    No envy racks our heart,
For all we know and all we guess,
    We mutually impart!

Enter LADY BLANCHE. *All stand up demurely.*

BLA.   Attention, ladies, while I read to you
        The Princess Ida's list of punishments.
        The first is Sacharissa. She's expelled!
ALL.   Expelled!
BLA.   Expelled, because although she knew
        No man of any kind may pass our walls,
        She dared to bring a set of chessmen here!
SACH. *(crying)*. I meant no harm; they're only men of wood!

BLA.　　They're men with whom you give each other mate,
　　　　　And that's enough ! The next is Chloe.
CHLOE.　　　　　　　　　　　　　　　　　Ah !
BLA.　　Chloe will lose three terms, for yesterday,
　　　　　When looking through her drawing-book, I found
　　　　　A sketch of a perambulator !
ALL (*horrified*).　　　　　　　　Oh !
BLA.　　*Double* perambulator, shameless girl !
　　　　　That's all at present. Now, attention, pray ;
　　　　　Your Principal the Princess comes to give
　　　　　Her usual inaugural address
　　　　　To those young ladies who joined yesterday.

CHORUS.

Mighty maiden with a mission,
　　Paragon of common sense,
Running fount of erudition,
　　Miracle of eloquence,
　　We are blind, and we would see ;
　　We are bound, and would be free ;
　　We are dumb, and we would talk ;
　　We are lame, and we would walk.

Enter the PRINCESS.

Mighty maiden with a mission —
　　Paragon of common sense ;
Running fount of erudition —
　　Miracle of eloquence !

PRIN. (*Recit.*)　　Minerva, oh, hear me !

ARIA.

Oh, goddess wise
　　That lovest light,
　　Endow with sight
Their unillumined eyes.

At this my call,
                A fervent few
                Have come to woo
        The rays that from thee fall.
Let fervent words and fervent thoughts be mine,
That I may lead them to thy sacred shrine !

Women of Adamant, fair Neophytes —
Who thirst for such instruction as we give,
Attend, while I unfold a parable.
The elephant is mightier than Man,
Yet Man subdues him. Why ? The elephant
Is elephantine everywhere but here (*tapping her forehead*),
And Man, whose brain is to the elephant's
As Woman's brain to Man's — (that's rule of three), —
Conquers the foolish giant of the woods,
As Woman, in her turn, shall conquer Man.
In Mathematics, Woman leads the way :
The narrow-minded pedant still believes
That two and two make four ! Why, we can prove,
We women — household drudges as we are —
That two and two make five — or three — or seven;
Or five-and-twenty, if the case demands !
Diplomacy ? The wiliest diplomat
Is absolutely helpless in our hands,
He wheedles monarchs — woman wheedles him !
Logic ? Why, tyrant Man himself admits
It's waste of time to argue with a woman !
Then we excel in social qualities :
Though Man professes that he holds our sex
In utter scorn, I venture to believe
He'd rather pass the day with one of you,
Than with five hundred of his fellow-men !
In all things we excel. Believing this,
A hundred maidens here have sworn to place
Their feet upon his neck. If we succeed,
We'll treat him better than he treated us :
But if we fail, why, then let hope fail too !
Let no one care a penny how she looks —

Let red be worn with yellow — blue with green —
Crimson with scarlet — violet with blue !
Let all your things misfit, and you yourselves
At inconvenient moments come undone !
Let hair-pins lose their virtue; let the hook
Disdain the fascination of the eye —
The bashful button modestly evade
The soft embraces of the button-hole !
Let old associations all dissolve,
Let Swan secede from Edgar — Gask from Gask,
Sewell from Cross — Lewis from Allenby !
In other words — let Chaos come again !

(*Coming down.*) Who lectures in the Hall of Arts to-day ?

BLA.   I, madam, on Abstract Philosophy.
There I propose considering, at length,
Three points — The Is, the Might Be, and the Must.
Whether the Is, from being actual fact,
Is more important than the vague Might Be,
Or the Might Be, from taking wider scope,
Is for that reason greater than the Is :
And lastly, how the Is and Might Be stand
Compared with the inevitable Must !

PRIN.   The subject's deep — how do you treat it, pray ?

BLA.   Madam, I take three possibilities,
And strike a balance, then, between the three :
As thus : The Princess Ida Is our head,
The Lady Psyche Might Be, — Lady Blanche,
Neglected Blanche, inevitably Must.
Given these three hypotheses — to find
The actual betting against each of them !

PRIN.   Your theme's ambitious : pray you, bear in mind
Who highest soar fall farthest. Fare you well,
You and your pupils ! Maidens, follow me.

[*Exeunt* PRINCESS *and Maidens singing refrain of chorus, 'And
thus to empyrean heights', etc. Manet* LADY BLANCHE.

BLA.   I should command here — I was born to rule,
But do I rule ? I don't. Why ? I don't know.

I shall some day. Not yet. I bide my time.
I once was Some One — and the Was Will Be.
The Present as we speak becomes the Past,
The Past repeats itself, and so is Future !
This sounds involved. It's not. It's right enough.

SONG — LADY BLANCHE.

Come, mighty Must !
    Inevitable Shall !
In thee I trust.
    Time weaves my coronal !
Go, mocking Is !
    Go, disappointing Was !
That I am this
    Ye are the cursèd cause !
Yet humble second shall be first,
        I ween;
And dead and buried be the curst
        Has Been !

Oh, weak Might Be !
    Oh, May, Might, Could, Would, Should !
How powerless ye
    For evil or for good !
In every sense
    Your moods I cheerless call,
Whate'er your tense
    Ye are Imperfect, all !
Ye have deceived the trust I've shown
        In ye !
Away ! The Mighty Must alone
        Shall be !

[*Exit* LADY BLANCHE.

Enter HILARION, CYRIL, *and* FLORIAN, *climbing over wall, and
    creeping cautiously among the trees and rocks at the back of
    the stage.*

TRIO — Hilarion, Cyril, Florian.

Gently, gently,
Evidently
  We are safe so far,
After scaling
Fence and paling,
  Here, at last, we are !
In this college
Useful knowledge
  Everywhere one finds,
And already,
Growing steady,
  We've enlarged our minds.

Cyr.	We've learnt that prickly cactus Has the power to attract us When we fall.
All.	When we fall !
Hil.	That nothing man unsettles Like a bed of stinging nettles, Short or tall.
All.	Short or tall !
Flor.	That bull-dogs feed on throttles — That we don't like broken bottles On a wall.
All.	On a wall !
Hil.	That spring-guns breathe defiance ! And that burglary's a science After all !
All.	After all !

RECIT. — Florian.

A Woman's college ! maddest folly going !
What can girls learn within its walls worth knowing ?
I'll lay a crown (the Princess shall decide it)
I'll teach them twice as much in half-an-hour outside it.

HILARION.

Hush, scoffer; ere you sound your puny thunder,
List to their aims, and bow your head in wonder !

> They intend to send a wire
>   To the moon — to the moon;
> And they'll set the Thames on fire
>   Very soon — very soon;
> Then they learn to make silk purses
>   With their rigs — with their rigs,
> From the ears of Lady Circe's
>   Piggy-wigs — piggy-wigs.
> And weasels at their slumbers
>   They trepan — they trepan;
> To get sunbeams from cu*cum*bers,
>   They've a plan — they've a plan.
> They've a firmly rooted notion
> They can cross the Polar Ocean,
> And they'll find Perpetual Motion,
>   If they can — if they can.

ALL.
> These are the phenomena
> That every pretty domina
>   Is hoping we shall see
>   At her Universitee !

CYR.
> As for fashion, they forswear it,
>   So they say — so they say;
> And the circle — they will square it
>   Some fine day — some fine day;
> Then the little pigs they're teaching
>   For to fly — for to fly;
> And the niggers they'll be bleaching,
>   By and by — by and by !
> Each newly-joined aspirant
>   To the clan — to the clan —
> Must repudiate the tyrant

Known as Man — known as Man.
They mock at him and flout him,
For they do not care about him,
And they're 'going to do without him'
If they can — if they can !

ALL.   These are the phenomena, etc.

In this college
Useful knowledge
Ev'rywhere one finds,
And already,
Growing steady,
We've enlarg'd our minds.

HIL.   So that's the Princess Ida's castle ! Well,
They must be lovely girls, indeed, if it requires
Such walls as those to keep intruders off !
CYR.   To keep men off is only half their charge,
And that the easier half. I much suspect
The object of these walls is not so much
To keep men off as keep the maidens in !
FLOR.   But what are these ? (*Examining some Collegiate robes.*)
HIL. (*looking at them*).   Why, Academic robes,
Worn by the lady undergraduates
When they matriculate. Let's try them on. (*They do so.*)
Why, see, — we're covered to the very toes.
Three lovely lady undergraduates
Who, weary of the world and all its wooing —
FLOR.   And penitent for deeds there's no undoing —
CYR.   Looked at askance by well-conducted maids —
ALL.   Seek sanctuary in these classic shades !

TRIO — HILARION, CYRIL, FLORIAN.

HIL.   I am a maiden, cold and stately,
Heartless I, with a face divine.
What do I want with a heart, innately ?
Every heart I meet is mine !

ALL.   Haughty, humble, coy, or free,
       Little care I what maid may be.
     So that a maid is fair to see,
       Every maid is the maid for me !

                    (*Dance.*)

CYR.   I am a maiden frank and simple,
       Brimming with joyous roguery;
   Merriment lurks in every dimple,
       Nobody breaks more hearts than I !

ALL.   Haughty, humble, coy, or free,
       Little care I what maid may be.
     So that a maid is fair to see,
       Every maid is the maid for me !

                    (*Dance.*)

FLOR.   I am a maiden coyly blushing,
       Timid am I as a startled hind;
   Every suitor sets me flushing:
       I am the maid that wins mankind !

ALL.   Haughty, humble, coy, or free,
       Little care I what maid may be.
     So that a maid is fair to see,
       Every maid is the maid for me !

Enter the PRINCESS *reading. She does not see them.*

FLOR. But who comes here ? The Princess, as I live !
     What shall we do ?
HIL. (*aside*).   Why, we must brave it out !
(*Aloud*). Madam, accept our humblest reverence.

 (*They bow, then, suddenly recollecting themselves, curtsey.*)

PRIN. (*surprised*). We greet you, ladies. What would you with us ?
HIL. (*aside*). What shall I say ? (*Aloud.*) We are three students,
      ma'am,
      Three well-born maids of liberal estate,
      Who wish to join this University.

(HILARION *and* FLORIAN *curtsey again.* CYRIL *bows extravagantly,
then, being recalled to himself by* FLORIAN, *curtseys.*)

PRIN.	If, as you say, you wish to join our ranks,
	And will subscribe to all our rules, 'tis well.
FLOR.	To all your rules we cheerfully subscribe.
PRIN.	You say you're noblewomen. Well, you'll find
	No sham degrees for noblewomen here.
	You'll find no sizars here, or servitors,
	Or other cruel distinctions, meant to draw
	A line 'twixt rich and poor: you'll find no tufts
	To mark nobility, except such tufts
	As indicate nobility of brain.
	As for your fellow-students, mark me well:
	There are a hundred maids within these walls,
	All good, all learned, and all beautiful;
	They are prepared to love you: will you swear
	To give the fullness of your love to them ?
HIL.	Upon our words and honours, ma'am, we will !
PRIN.	But we go further: will you undertake
	That you will never marry any man ?
FLOR.	Indeed we never will !
PRIN.	Consider well,
	You must prefer our maids to all mankind !
HIL.	To all mankind we much prefer your maids !
CYR.	We should be dolts indeed, if we did not,
	Seeing how fair——
HIL. (*aside to* CYRIL).	Take care — that's rather strong !
PRIN.	But have you left no lovers at your home
	Who may pursue you here ?
HIL.	No, madam, none.
	We're homely ladies, as no doubt you see,
	And we have never fished for lover's love.
	We smile at girls who deck themselves with gems,
	False hair, and meretricious ornament,
	To chain the fleeting fancy of a man,
	But do not imitate them. What we have
	Of hair, is all our own. Our colour, too,
	Unladylike, but not unwomanly,
	Is Nature's handiwork, and man has learnt
	To reckon Nature an impertinence.

PRIN.   Well, beauty counts for naught within these walls;
         If all you say is true, you'll pass with us
         A happy, happy time !

CYR.   If, as you say,
         A hundred lovely maidens wait within,
         To welcome us with smiles and open arms,
         I think there's very little doubt we shall !

QUARTETTE — PRINCESS, HILARION, CYRIL, FLORIAN.

PRIN.   The world is but a broken toy,
               Its pleasure hollow — false its joy,
                   Unreal its loveliest hue,
                           Alas !
                   Its pains alone are true,
                           Alas !
                   Its pains alone are true.

HIL.   The world is everything you say,
               The world we think has had its day.
                   Its merriment is slow,
                           Alas !
                   We've tried it, and we know,
                           Alas !
                   We've tried it and we know.

TUTTI.

PRINCESS.	HILARION, CYRIL, FLORIAN.
The world is but a broken toy,	The world is but a broken toy,
Its pleasure hollow — false its joy,	We freely give it up with joy,
Unreal its loveliest hue,	Unreal its loveliest hue,
Alas!	Alas!
Its pains alone are true,	Its pains alone are true,
Alas!	Alas!
Its pains alone are true!	Its pains alone are true!

[*Exit* PRINCESS. *The three gentlemen watch her off.* LADY
     PSYCHE *enters, and regards them with amazement.*

HIL.   I'faith, the plunge is taken, gentlemen !
         For, willy-nilly, we are maidens now,
         And maids against our will we must remain !
                           (*All laugh heartily.*)

Psy. (*aside*).　These ladies are unseemly in their mirth.

(*The gentlemen see her, and, in confusion, resume
　　　their modest demeanour.*)

Flor. (*aside*).　Here's a catastrophe, Hilarion !
　　　　　　This is my sister ! She'll remember me,
　　　　　　Though years have passed since she and I have met !

Hil. (*aside to* Florian).　Then make a virtue of necessity,
　　　　　And trust our secret to her gentle care.

Flor. (*to* Psyche, *who has watched* Cyril *in amazement*).　Psyche !
　　　　　Why, don't you know me ? Florian !

Psy. (*amazed*).　Why, Florian !

Flor.　　　　　　　　　　My sister ! (*embraces her*).

Psy.　　　　　　　　　　　Oh, my dear !
　　　　What are you doing here — and who are these ?

Hil.　　I am that Prince Hilarion to whom
　　　　Your Princess is betrothed. I come to claim
　　　　Her plighted love. Your brother Florian
　　　　And Cyril come to see me safely through.

Psy.　　The Prince Hilarion ? Cyril too ? How strange !
　　　　My earliest playfellows !

Hil.　　　　　　　　　　Why, let me look !
　　　　Are you that learned little Psyche who
　　　　At school alarmed her mates because she called
　　　　A buttercup 'ranunculus bulbosus' ?

Cyr.　　Are you indeed that Lady Psyche who
　　　　At children's parties drove the conjurer wild,
　　　　Explaining all his tricks before he did them ?

Hil.　　Are you that learned little Psyche who
　　　　At dinner parties, brought in to dessert,
　　　　Would tackle visitors with 'You don't know
　　　　Who first determined longitude — I do —
　　　　Hipparchus 'twas — B.C. one sixty-three !'
　　　　Are you indeed that small phenomenon ?

Psy.　　That small phenomenon indeed am I !
　　　　But, gentlemen, 'tis death to enter here :
　　　　We have all promised to renounce mankind !

Flor.　　Renounce mankind? On what ground do you base
　　　　This senseless resolution ?

PSY.   Senseless ? No.
    We are all taught, and, being taught, believe
    That Man, sprung from an Ape, is Ape at heart.
CYR.   That's rather strong.
PSY.   The truth is always strong !

SONG — LADY PSYCHE.

A Lady fair, of lineage high,
Was loved by an Ape, in the days gone by.
The Maid was radiant as the sun,
The Ape was a most unsightly one —
    So it would not do —
    His scheme fell through,
For the Maid, when his love took formal shape,
    Expressed such terror
    At his monstrous error,
That he stammered an apology and made his 'scape,
The picture of a disconcerted Ape.

With a view to rise in the social scale,
He shaved his bristles, and he docked his tail,
He grew moustachios, and he took his tub,
And he paid a guinea to a toilet club —
    But it would not do,
    The scheme fell through —
For the Maid was Beauty's fairest Queen,
    With golden tresses,
    Like a real princess's,
While the Ape, despite his razor keen,
Was the apiest Ape that ever was seen !

He bought white ties, and he bought dress suits,
He crammed his feet into bright tight boots —
And to start in life on a brand-new plan,
He christened himself Darwinian Man !
    But it would not do,
    The scheme fell through —
For the Maiden fair, whom the monkey craved,

               Was a radiant Being,
               With a brain far-seeing —
While Darwinian Man, though well-behaved,
At best is only a monkey shaved !

ALL.   While Darwinian Man, etc.

       During this MELISSA *has entered unobserved; she*
               looks on in amazement.

MEL. (*coming down*). Oh, Lady Psyche !
PSY. (*terrified*).   What ! you heard us then?
        Oh, all is lost !
MEL.   Not so ! I'll breathe no word !

            (*Advancing in astonishment to* FLORIAN.)

       How marvellously strange ! and are you then
       Indeed young men ?
FLOR.   Well, yes, just now we are —
       But hope by dint of study to become,
       In course of time, young women.
MEL. (*eagerly*).   No, no, no —
       Oh, don't do that ! Is this indeed a man ?
       I've often heard of them, but, till to-day,
       Never set eyes on one. They told me men
       Were hideous, idiotic, and deformed !
       They're quite as beautiful as women are !
       As beautiful, they're infinitely more so !
       Their cheeks have not that pulpy softness which
       One gets so weary of in womankind :
       Their features are more marked — and — oh, their chins !
       How curious ! (*Feeling his chin.*)
FLOR.   I fear it's rather rough.
MEL. (*eagerly*). Oh, don't apologize — I like it so !

QUINTETTE — PSYCHE, MELISSA, HILARION,
           CYRIL, FLORIAN.

PSY.   The woman of the wisest wit
        May sometimes be mistaken, O !
     In Ida's views, I must admit,
        My faith is somewhat shaken, O !

CYR.	On every other point than this
	    Her learning is untainted, O !
	But Man's a theme with which she is
	    Entirely unacquainted, O !
	        — acquainted, O !
	        — acquainted, O !
	    Entirely unacquainted, O !

ALL.	Then jump for joy and gaily bound, The truth is found — the truth is found ! Set bells a-ringing through the air — Ring here and there and everywhere — And echo forth the joyous sound, The truth is found — the truth is found !

(Dance.)

MEL.	My natural instinct teaches me
	    (And instinct is important, O !)
	You're everything you ought to be,
	    And nothing that you oughtn't, O !

HIL.	That fact was seen at once by you
	    In casual conversation, O !
	Which is most creditable to
	    Your powers of observation, O !
	        — servation, O !
	        — servation, O !
	    Your powers of observation, O !

ALL.	Then jump for joy, etc.

[*Exeunt* PSYCHE, HILARION, CYRIL, *and* FLORIAN.
    MELISSA *going*.

Enter LADY BLANCHE.

BLA.	Melissa !
MEL. (*returning*).	Mother !
BLA.	Here — a word with you. Those are the three new students ?
MEL. (*confused*).	Yes, they are. They're charming girls.
BLA.	Particularly so. So graceful, and so very womanly ! So skilled in all a girl's accomplishments !

MEL. (*confused*). Yes — very skilled.

BLA.   They sing so nicely too !

MEL. They *do* sing nicely !

BLA.   Humph ! It's very odd.
    Two are tenors, one is a baritone !

MEL. (*much agitated*). They've all got colds !

BLA.   Colds ! Bah ! D'ye think I'm blind ?
    These 'girls' are men disguised !

MEL.   Oh no — indeed !
    You wrong these gentlemen — I mean — why, see,
    Here is an *étui* dropped by one of them (*picking up an étui*).
    Containing scissors, needles, and——

BLA. (*opening it*).   Cigars !
    Why, these *are* men ! And you knew this, you minx !

MEL. Oh, spare them — they are gentlemen indeed.
    The Prince Hilarion (married years ago
    To Princess Ida) with two trusted friends !
    Consider, mother, he's her husband now,
    And has been, twenty years ! Consider, too,
    You're only second here — you should be first.
    Assist the Prince's plan, and when he gains
    The Princess Ida, why, you *will* be first.
    You will design the fashions — think of that —
    And always serve out all the punishments !
    The scheme is harmless, mother — wink at it !

BLA. (*aside*). The prospect's tempting ! Well, well, well, I'll try —
    Though I've not winked at anything for years !
    'Tis but one step towards my destiny —
    The mighty Must ! the inevitable Shall !

DUET — MELISSA *and* LADY BLANCHE.

MEL. Now wouldn't you like to rule the roast,
        And guide this University ?

BLA.   I must agree
        'Twould pleasant be.
          (Sing hey, a Proper Pride !)

MEL. And wouldn't you like to clear the coast
        Of malice and perversity ?

BLA.   Without a doubt
                       I'll bundle 'em out,
                          Sing hey, when I preside !

BOTH. Sing, hoity, toity ! Sorry for some !

       Sing, marry come up and $\begin{Bmatrix} my \\ her \end{Bmatrix}$ day will come !

                       Sing, Proper Pride
                       Is the horse to ride,
                    And Happy-go-lucky, my Lady, O !

BLA.   For years I've writhed beneath her sneers,
             Although a born Plantagenet !

MEL.   You're much too meek,
                       Or you would speak.
                          (Sing hey, I'll say no more !)

BLA.   Her elder I, by several years,
             Although you'd ne'er imagine it.

MEL.   Sing, so I've heard
                       But never a word
                          Have I e'er believed before !

BOTH. Sing, hoity, toity ! Sorry for some !

       Sing, marry come up and $\begin{Bmatrix} my \\ her \end{Bmatrix}$ day will come !

                       Sing, she shall learn
                       That a worm will turn.
                    Sing Happy-go-lucky, my Lady, O !

                                        [*Exit* LADY BLANCHE.

MEL.   Saved for a time, at least !

                    Enter FLORIAN, *on tiptoe.*

FLOR. (*whispering*).   Melissa — come !
MEL.   Oh, sir ! you must away from this at once —
       My mother guessed your sex ! It was my fault —
       I blushed and stammered so that she exclaimed,
       'Can these be men ?' Then, seeing this, 'Why, these——'
       '*Are men*', she would have added, but '*are men*'
       Stuck in her throat ! She keeps your secret, sir,
       For reasons of her own — but fly from this
       And take me with you — that is — no — not that !

FLOR. I'll go, but not without you ! (*Bell.*) Why, what's that ?
MEL. The luncheon bell.
FLOR. I'll wait for luncheon then !

Enter HILARION *with* PRINCESS, CYRIL *with* PSYCHE, LADY BLANCHE *and* LADIES. *Also 'Daughters of the Plough' bearing luncheon.*

CHORUS.

Merrily ring the luncheon bell !
Here in meadow of asphodel,
Feast we body and mind as well,
So merrily ring the luncheon bell !

SOLO — BLANCHE.

Hunger, I beg to state,
Is highly indelicate,
This is a fact profoundly true,
So learn your appetites to subdue.

ALL. Yes, yes,
We'll learn our appetites to subdue !

SOLO — CYRIL (*eating*).

Madam, your words so wise,
Nobody should despise,
Cursed with an appetite keen I am
And I'll subdue it —
And I'll subdue it —
And I'll subdue it with cold roast lamb !

ALL. Yes — yes —
We'll subdue it with cold roast lamb !

CHORUS. Merrily ring, etc.

PRIN. You say you know the court of Hildebrand ?
There is a Prince there — I forget his name —
HIL. Hilarion ?
PRIN. Exactly — is he well ?

HIL.   If it be well to droop and pine and mope,
        To sigh 'Oh, Ida ! Ida !' all day long,
        'Ida ! my love ! my life ! Oh, come to me !'
        If it be well, I say, to do all this,
        Then Prince Hilarion is very well.

PRIN.   He breathes *our* name ? Well, it's a common one !
        And is the booby comely ?

HIL.   Pretty well.
        I've heard it said that if I dressed myself
        In Prince Hilarion's clothes (supposing this
        Consisted with my maiden modesty),
        I might be taken for Hilarion's self.
        But what is this to you or me, who think
        Of all mankind with undisguised contempt ?

PRIN.   Contempt ? Why, damsel, when I think of man,
        Contempt is not the word.

CYR. (*getting tipsy*).   I'm sure of that,
        Or if it is, it surely should not be !

HIL. (*aside to* CYRIL). Be quiet, idiot, or they'll find us out.

CYR.   The Prince Hilarion's a goodly lad !

PRIN.   *You* know him then ?

CYR. (*tipsily*).   I rather think I do !
        We are inseparables !

PRIN.   Why, what's this ?
        You love him then ?

CYR.   We do indeed — all three !

HIL.   Madam, she jests ! (*Aside to* CYRIL.) Remember where you
            are !

CYR.   Jests ? Not at all ! Why, bless my heart alive,
        You and Hilarion, when at the Court,
        Rode the same horse !

PRIN. (*horrified*).   Astride ?

CYR.   Of course ! Why not ?
        Wore the same clothes — and once or twice, I think,
        Got tipsy in the same good company !

PRIN.   Well, these are nice young ladies, on my word !

CYR. (*tipsy*). Don't you remember that old kissing-song
        He'd sing to blushing Mistress Lalage,
        The hostess of the Pigeons ? Thus it ran:

SONG — CYRIL.

(During symphony HILARION *and* FLORIAN *try to stop* CYRIL. *He shakes them off angrily.)*

> Would you know the kind of maid
>   Sets my heart aflame-a ?
> Eyes must be downcast and staid,
>   Cheeks must flush for shame-a !
>   She may neither dance nor sing,
>   But, demure in everything,
>   Hang her head in modest way,
>   With pouting lips that seem to say,
> 'Oh, kiss me, kiss me, kiss me, kiss me,
>   Though I die of shame-a !'
> Please you, that's the kind of maid
>   Sets my heart aflame-a !

> When a maid is bold and gay
>   With a tongue goes clang-a,
> Flaunting it in brave array,
>   Maiden may go hang-a !
>   Sunflower gay and hollyhock
>   Never shall my garden stock;
>   Mine the blushing rose of May,
>   With pouting lips that seem to say,
> 'Oh, kiss me, kiss me, kiss me, kiss me,
>   Though I die for shame-a !'
> Please you, that's the kind of maid
>   Sets my heart aflame-a !

PRIN.   Infamous creature, get you hence away !

*(*HILARION, *who has been with difficulty restrained by* FLORIAN *during this song, breaks from him and strikes* CYRIL *furiously on the breast.)*

HIL.   Dog ! there is something more to sing about !

CYR. *(sobered).* Hilarion, are you mad ?

PRIN. *(horrified).*   Hilarion ? Help !
    Why, these are men ! Lost ! lost ! betrayed ! undone !

                                  (Running on to bridge.)

Girls, get you hence ! Man-monsters, if you dare
Approach one step, I—— Ah !

> (*Loses her balance, and falls into the stream.*)

PSY. Oh ! save her, sir !

BLA. It's useless, sir, — you'll only catch your death !

> (HILARION *springs in.*)

SACH. He catches her !

MEL. And now he lets her go !
Again she's in his grasp——

PSY. And now she's not.
He seizes her back hair !

BLA. (*not looking*). And it comes off !

PSY. No, no ! She's saved ! — she's saved ! — she's saved ! —
she's saved !

FINALE.

CHORUS OF LADIES.

Oh ! joy, our chief is saved,
And by Hilarion's hand;
The torrent fierce he braved,
And brought her safe to land !
For his intrusion we must own
This doughty deed may well atone !

PRIN. Stand forth ye three,
Whoe'er ye be,
And hearken to our stern decree !

HIL., CYR., *and* FLOR. Have mercy, lady, — disregard your oaths !

PRIN. I know not mercy, men in women's clothes !
The man whose sacrilegious eyes
Invade our strict seclusion, dies.
Arrest these coarse intruding spies !

(*They are arrested by the 'Daughters of the Plough'.*)

FLOR., CYR., *and* LADIES. Have mercy, lady, — disregard your oaths !

PRIN. I know not mercy, men in women's clothes !

> (CYRIL *and* FLORIAN *are bound.*)

SONG — HILARION.

Whom thou hast chained must wear his chain,
 Thou canst not set him free,
He wrestles with his bonds in vain
 Who lives by loving thee !
If heart of stone for heart of fire,
 Be all thou hast to give,
If dead to me my heart's desire,
 Why should I wish to live ?

FLOR., CYR., *and* LADIES. Have mercy, O lady !

No word of thine — no stern command
 Can teach my heart to rove,
Then rather perish by thy hand,
 Than live without thy love !
A loveless life apart from thee
 Were hopeless slavery,
If kindly death will set me free,
 Why should I fear to die ?

 [*He is bound by two of the attendants, and the three gentle-men are marched off.*

Enter MELISSA.

MEL.   Madam, without the castle walls
      An armèd band
    Demand admittance to our halls
      For Hildebrand !

ALL.   Oh, horror !

PRIN.   Deny them !
      We will defy them !

ALL.   Too late — too late !
      The castle gate
    Is battered by them !

(*The gate yields.* SOLDIERS *rush in.* ARAC, GURON, *and* SCYNTHIUS *are with them, but with their hands handcuffed.*)

ENSEMBLE.

GIRLS.	MEN.
Rend the air with wailing,	Walls and fences scaling,
Shed the shameful tear!	Promptly we appear;
Walls are unavailing,	Walls are unavailing,
Man has entered here!	We have entered here.
Shame and desecration	Female execration
Are his staunch allies,	Stifle if you're wise,
Let your lamentation	Stop your lamentation,
Echo to the skies!	Dry your pretty eyes!

Enter HILDEBRAND.

RECIT.

PRIN.   Audacious tyrant, do you dare
              To beard a maiden in her lair?

HILD.   Since you inquire,
                We've no desire
           To beard a maiden here, or anywhere!

SOL.   No, no — we've no desire
           To beard a maiden here, or anywhere!

SOLO — HILDEBRAND.

Some years ago
No doubt you know
(And if you don't I'll tell you so)
You gave your troth
Upon your oath
To Hilarion my son.
A vow you make
You must not break,
(If you think you may, it's a great mistake),
For a bride's a bride
Though the knot were tied
At the early age of one!
And I'm a peppery kind of King,
Who's indisposed for parleying
To fit the wit of a bit of a chit,
And that's the long and the short of it!

SOL.   For he's a peppery kind of King, etc.

If you decide
To pocket your pride
And let Hilarion claim his bride,
Why, well and good,
It's understood
We'll let bygones go by —
But if you choose
To sulk in the blues
I'll make the whole of you shake in your shoes.
I'll storm your walls,
And level your halls,
In the twinkling of an eye !
For I'm a peppery Potentate,
Who's little inclined his claim to bate,
To fit the wit of a bit of a chit,
And that's the long and the short of it !

SOL.   For he's a peppery kind of King, etc.

TRIO — ARAC, GURON, *and* SCYNTHIUS.

We may remark, though nothing can
Dismay us,
That if you thwart this gentleman,
He'll slay us.
We don't fear death, of course — we're taught
To shame it ;
But still upon the whole we thought
We'd name it.
(*To each other.*) Yes, yes, yes, better perhaps to name it.

Our interests we would not press
With chatter,
Three hulking brothers more or less
Don't matter ;
If you'd pooh-pooh this monarch's plan,
Pooh-pooh it,
But when he says he'll hang a man,
He'll do it.
(*To each other.*) Yes, yes, yes, devil doubt he'll do it.

PRIN. (*Recit.*) Be reassured, nor fear his anger blind,
                His menaces are idle as the wind.
                He dares not kill you — vengeance lurks behind !

AR., GUR., SCYN. *We* rather think he dares, but never mind !
                        No, no, — never, never mind !

HILD.   I rather think I dare, but never, never mind !
             Enough of parley — as a special boon,
             We give you till to-morrow afternoon ;
             Release Hilarion, then, and be his bride,
             Or you'll incur the guilt of fratricide !

ENSEMBLE.

PRINCESS.	THE OTHERS.

To yield at once to such a foe
  With shame were rife;
So quick ! away with him, although
    He saved my life !
That he is fair, and strong, and
      tall,
Is very evident to all,
Yet I will die before I call
    Myself his wife !
	Oh ! yield at once, 'twere better so
	  Than risk a strife !
	And let the Prince Hilarion go —
	    He saved thy life !
	Hilarion's fair, and strong, and
	      tall —
	A worse misfortune might befall —
	It's not so dreadful, after all,
	    To be his wife !

SOLO — PRINCESS.

Though I am but a girl,
Defiance thus I hurl,
    Our banners all
    On outer wall
We fearlessly unfurl.

ALL.   Though she is but a girl, etc.

PRINCESS.	THE OTHERS.
That he is fair, etc.	Hilarion's fair, etc.

(*The* PRINCESS *stands, surrounded by girls kneeling.* HILDEBRAND
   *and soldiers stand on built rocks at back and sides of stage.
   Picture.*)

END OF ACT II

ACT III

SCENE. — *Outer Walls and Courtyard of Castle Adamant.* MELISSA, SACHARISSA, *and ladies discovered, armed with battleaxes.*

CHORUS.

Death to the invader !
　Strike a deadly blow,
As an old Crusader
　Struck his Paynim foe !
Let our martial thunder
Fill his soul with wonder,
Tear his ranks asunder,
　Lay the tyrant low !

SOLO — MELISSA.

Thus our courage, all untarnished,
　We're instructed to display :
But to tell the truth unvarnished,
　We are more inclined to say,
'Please you, do not hurt us.'

ALL.　　　'Do not hurt us, if it please you !'
MEL.　　'Please you let us be.'
ALL.　　　'Let us be — let us be !'
MEL.　　'Soldiers disconcert us.'
ALL.　　　'Disconcert us, if it please you !'
MEL.　　'Frightened maids are we.'
ALL.　　　'Maids are we — maids are we !'

MELISSA.

But 'twould be an error
To confess our terror,

So, in Ida's name,
Boldly we exclaim :

CHORUS.

Death to the invader !
    Strike a deadly blow,
As an old Crusader
    Struck his Paynim foe !

Flourish. Enter PRINCESS, *armed, attended by*
BLANCHE *and* PSYCHE.

PRIN.   I like your spirit, girls! We have to meet
    Stern bearded warriors in fight to-day:
    Wear naught but what is necessary to
    Preserve your dignity before their eyes,
    And give your limbs full play.

BLA.   One moment, ma'am,
    Here is a paradox we should not pass
    Without inquiry. We are prone to say,
    'This thing is Needful — that, Superfluous' —
    Yet they invariably co-exist !
    We find the Needful comprehended in
    The circle of the grand Superfluous,
    Yet the Superfluous cannot be bought
    Unless you're amply furnished with the Needful.
    These singular considerations are —

PRIN.   Superfluous, yet not Needful — so you see
    The terms may independently exist.

(*To Ladies.*) Women of Adamant, we have to show
    That Women, educated to the task,
    Can meet Man, face to face, on his own ground,
    And beat him there. Now let us set to work:
    Where is our lady surgeon ?

SAC.   Madam, here !

PRIN.   We shall require your skill to heal the wounds
    Of those that fall.

SAC. (*alarmed*).   What, heal the wounded ?

PRIN.   Yes !

SAC.   And cut off real live legs and arms ?

PRIN.   Of course !

SAC.   I wouldn't do it for a thousand pounds !

PRIN.   Why, how is this ? Are you faint-hearted, girl ?
You've often cut them off in theory !

SAC.   In theory I'll cut them off again
With pleasure, and as often as you like,
But not in practice.

PRIN.   Coward ! get you hence,
I've craft enough for that, and courage too,
I'll do your work ! My fusiliers, advance !
Why, you are armed with axes ! Gilded toys !
Where are your rifles, pray ?

CHLOE.   Why, please you, ma'am,
We left them in the armoury, for fear
That in the heat and turmoil of the fight,
They might go off !

PRIN.   'They might !' Oh, craven souls !
Go off yourselves ! Thank heaven, I have a heart
That quails not at the thought of meeting men ;
I will discharge your rifles ! Off with you !
Where's my bandmistress ?

ADA.   Please you, ma'am, the band
Do not feel well, and can't come out to-day !

PRIN.   Why, this is flat rebellion ! I've no time
To talk to them just now. But, happily,
I can play several instruments at once,
And I will drown the shrieks of those that fall
With trumpet music, such as soldiers love !
How stand we with respect to gunpowder ?
My Lady Psyche — you who superintend
Our lab'ratory — are you well prepared
To blow these bearded rascals into shreds ?

PSY.   Why, madam —

PRIN.   Well ?

PSY.   Let us try gentler means.
We can dispense with fulminating grains
While we have eyes with which to flash our rage !
We can dispense with villainous saltpetre
While we have tongues with which to blow them up !

We can dispense, in short, with all the arts
That brutalize the practical polemist !

PRIN. (*contemptuously*). I never knew a more dispensing chemist !
Away, away — I'll meet these men alone
Since all my women have deserted me !

[*Exeunt all but* PRINCESS, *singing refrain of* '*Please you,
do not hurt us*', *pianissimo.*

PRIN.   So fail my cherished plans — so fails my faith —
And with it hope, and all that comes of hope !

SONG — PRINCESS.

I built upon a rock,
    But ere Destruction's hand
        Dealt equal lot
        To Court and cot,
    My rock had turned to sand !
I leant upon an oak,
    But in the hour of need,
        Alack-a-day,
        My trusted stay
    Was but a bruisèd reed !
        Ah, faithless rock,
        My simple faith to mock !
        Ah, trait'rous oak,
        Thy worthlessness to cloak.

I drew a sword of steel,
    But when to home and hearth
        The battle's breath
        Bore fire and death,
    My sword was but a lath !
I lit a beacon fire,
    But on a stormy day
        Of frost and rime,
        In wintertime,
    My fire had died away !
        Ah, coward steel,
        That fear can unanneal !

> False fire indeed,
> To fail me in my need !

She sinks on a seat. Enter CHLOE *and all the ladies.*

CHLOE.   Madam, your father and your brothers claim
An audience !

PRIN.   What do they do here ?

CHLOE.   They come
To fight for you !

PRIN.   Admit them !

BLA.   Infamous !
One's brothers, ma'am, are men !

PRIN.   So I have heard.
But all my women seem to fail me when
I need them most. In this emergency,
Even one's brothers may be turned to use.

Enter GAMA, *quite pale and unnerved.*

GAMA.   My daughter !

PRIN.   Father ! thou art free !

GAMA.   Aye, free !
Free as a tethered ass ! I come to thee
With words from Hildebrand. Those duly given
I must return to blank captivity.
I'm free so far.

PRIN.   Your message.

GAMA.   Hildebrand
Is loth to war with women. Pit my sons,
My three brave sons, against these popinjays,
These tufted jack-a-dandy featherheads,
And on the issue let thy hand depend !

PRIN.   Insult on insult's head ! Are we a stake
For fighting men ? What fiend possesses thee,
That thou hast come with offers such as these
From such as he to such an one as I ?

GAMA.   I am possessed
By the pale devil of a shaking heart !
My stubborn will is bent. I dare not face
That devilish monarch's black malignity !

He tortures me with torments worse than death,
I haven't anything to grumble at !
He finds out what particular meats I love,
And gives me them. The very choicest wines,
The costliest robes — the richest rooms are mine:
He suffers none to thwart my simplest plan,
And gives strict orders none should contradict me !
He's made my life a curse ! (*weeps*).

PRIN.   My tortured father !

SONG — GAMA.

Whene'er I poke
Sarcastic joke
    Replete with malice spiteful,
This people mild
Politely smiled,
    And voted me delightful !
Now when a wight
Sits up all night
    Ill-natured jokes devising,
And all his wiles
Are met with smiles,
    It's hard, there's no disguising !

Oh, don't the days seem lank and long
When all goes right and nothing goes wrong,
And isn't your life extremely flat
With nothing whatever to grumble at !

When German bands
From music stands
Played Wagner imper*fect*ly —
I bade them go —
They didn't say no,
But off they went directly !
The organ boys
They stopped their noise

With readiness surprising,
  And grinning herds
  Of hurdy-gurds
Retired apologising !

Oh, don't the days seem lank and long, etc.

   I offered gold
   In sums untold
To all who'd contradict me —
   I said I'd pay
   A pound a day
To anyone who kicked me —
   I bribed with toys
   Great vulgar boys
To utter something spiteful,
   But, bless you, no !
   They *would* be so
Confoundedly politeful !

 In short, these aggravating lads,
 They tickle my tastes, they feed my fads,
 They give me this and they give me that,
 And I've nothing whatever to grumble at !

He bursts into tears, and falls sobbing on a seat.

PRIN. My poor old father ! How he must have suffered !
   Well, well, I yield !
GAMA (*hysterically*). She yields ! I'm saved, I'm saved !

                [*Exit.*

PRIN. Open the gates — admit these warriors,
   Then get you all within the castle walls.   [*Exit.*

*The gates are opened, and the girls mount the battlements as soldiers
 enter. Also* ARAC, GURON, *and* SCYNTHIUS.

     CHORUS OF SOLDIERS.

  When anger spreads his wing,
   And all seems dark as night for it,
   There's nothing but to fight for it,

But ere you pitch your ring,
   Select a pretty site for it,
   (This spot is suited quite for it),
And then you gaily sing,

'Oh, I love the jolly rattle
Of an ordeal by battle,
There's an end of tittle-tattle,
   When your enemy is dead.
It's an arrant molly-coddle
Fears a crack upon his noddle
And he's only fit to swaddle
   In a downy feather-bed !' —

ALL.   For a fight's a kind of thing
That I love to look upon,
    So let us sing,
    Long live the King,
And his son Hilarion !

During this, HILARION, FLORIAN, *and* CYRIL *are brought out by the*
   'Daughters of the Plough'. *They are still bound and wear the*
   robes. Enter GAMA.

GAMA.   Hilarion ! Cyril ! Florian ! dressed as women !
      Is this indeed Hilarion ?
HIL.   Yes, it is !
GAMA.   Why, you look handsome in your women's clothes !
      Stick to 'em ! men's attire becomes you not !
(*To* CYRIL *and* FLORIAN.) And you, young ladies, will you please
      to pray
      King Hildebrand to set me free again ?
      Hang on his neck and gaze into his eyes,
      He never could resist a pretty face !
HIL.   You dog, you'll find, though I wear woman's garb,
      My sword is long and sharp !
GAMA.   Hush, pretty one !
      Here's a virago ! Here's a termagant !
      If length and sharpness go for anything,
      You'll want no sword while you can wag your tongue !

CYR.   What need to waste your words on such as he ?
        He's old and crippled.

GAMA.   Aye, but I've three sons,
        Fine fellows, young, and muscular, and brave,
        They're well worth talking to ! Come, what d'ye say ?

ARAC.   Aye, pretty ones, engage yourselves with us,
        If three rude warriors affright you not !

HIL.   Old as you are, I'd wring your shrivelled neck
        If you were not the Princess Ida's father.

GAMA.   If I were not the Princess Ida's father,
        And so had not her brothers for my sons,
        No doubt you'd wring my neck — in safety too !
        Come, come, Hilarion, begin, begin !
        Give them no quarter — they will give you none.
        You've this advantage over warriors
        Who kill their country's enemies for pay, —
        You know what you are fighting for — look there!
        (*Pointing to Ladies on the battlements.*)

[*Exit* GAMA. HILARION, FLORIAN, *and* CYRIL *are led off.*

SONG — ARAC.

            This helmet, I suppose,
            Was meant to ward off blows,
                    It's very hot,
                    And weighs a lot,
            As many a guardsman knows,
            So off that helmet goes.

ALL.   Yes, yes, yes,
            So off that helmet goes !

                        (*Giving their helmets to attendants.*)

ARAC.   This tight-fitting cuirass
            Is but a useless mass,
                    It's made of steel,
                    And weighs a deal,
            A man is but an ass
            Who fights in a cuirass,
            So off goes that cuirass.

ALL.   Yes, yes, yes,
                        So off goes that cuirass !

                                    (*Removing cuirasses.*)

ARAC.   These brassets, truth to tell,
                        May look uncommon well,
                                    But in a fight
                                    They're much too tight,
                        They're like a lobster shell !

ALL.   Yes, yes, yes,
                        They're like a lobster shell.

                                    (*Removing their brassets.*)

ARAC.   These things I treat the same (*indicating leg pieces*).
                        (I quite forget their name)
                                    They turn one's legs
                                    To cribbage pegs —
                        Their aid I thus disclaim,
                        Though I forget their name !

ALL.   Yes, yes, yes,
                        Their aid $\left\{\begin{array}{c} \text{we} \\ \text{they} \end{array}\right\}$ thus disclaim !

(*They remove their leg pieces and wear close-fitting
                        shape suits.*)

Enter HILARION, FLORIAN, *and* CYRIL.

(*Desperate fight between the three Princes and the three Knights,
during which the Ladies on the battlements and the Soldiers on
the stage sing the following chorus.*)

                        This is our duty plain towards
                                    Our Princess all immaculate,
                        We ought to bless her brothers' swords
                                    And piously ejaculate:
                                    Oh, Hungary !
                                    Oh, Hungary !
                        Oh, doughty sons of Hungary !

                    May all success
                    Attend and bless
                    Your warlike ironmongery !
                    Hilarion ! Hilarion ! Hilarion !

(*By this time*, ARAC, GURON, *and* SCYNTHIUS *are on the ground,
    wounded* — HILARION, CYRIL, *and* FLORIAN *stand over them.*)

PRIN. (*entering through gate and followed by Ladies*, HILDEBRAND,
and GAMA). Hold ! stay your hands ! — we yield ourselves to
you !

                    Ladies, my brothers all lie bleeding there !
                    Bind up their wounds — but look the other way.
(*Coming down.*) Is this the end ? (*bitterly to* LADY BLANCHE). How
                    say you, Lady Blanche —
                    Can I with dignity my post resign ?
                    And if I do, will you then take my place ?
BLA.   To answer this, it's meet that we consult
            The great Potential Mysteries ; I mean
            The five Subjunctive Possibilities —
            The May, the Might, the Would, the Could, the Should.
            Can you resign ? The prince May claim you ; if
            He Might, you Could — and if you Should, I Would !
PRIN.   I thought as much ! Then, to my fate I yield —
            So ends my cherished scheme ! Oh, I had hoped
            To band all women with my maiden throng,
            And make them all abjure tyrannic Man !
HILD.   A noble aim !
PRIN.   You ridicule it now ;
            But if I carried out this glorious scheme,
            At my exalted name Posterity
            Would bow in gratitude !
HILD.   But pray reflect —
            If you enlist all women in your cause,
            And make them all abjure tyrannic Man,
            The obvious question then arises, 'How
            Is this Posterity to be provided ?'
PRIN.   I never thought of that ! My Lady Blanche,
            How do you solve the riddle ?

BLA.   Don't ask me —
Abstract Philosophy won't answer it.
Take him — he is your Shall. Give in to Fate !

PRIN.   And you desert me. I alone am staunch !

HIL.   Madam, you placed your trust in Woman — well,
Woman has failed you utterly — try Man,
Give him one chance, it's only fair — besides,
Women are far too precious, too divine,
To try unproven theories upon.
Experiments, the proverb says, are made
On humble subjects — try our grosser clay,
And mould it as you will !

CYR.   Remember, too,
Dear Madam, if at any time you feel
A-weary of the Prince, you can return
To Castle Adamant, and rule your girls
As heretofore, you know.

PRIN.   And shall I find
The Lady Psyche here ?

PSY.   If Cyril, ma'am,
Does not behave himself, I think you will.

PRIN.   And you, Melissa, shall I find *you* here ?

MEL.   Madam, however Florian turns out,
Unhesitatingly I answer, No !

GAMA.   Consider this, my love, if your mamma
Had looked on matters from your point of view
(I wish she had), why, where would you have been ?

BLA.   There's an unbounded field of speculation,
On which I could discourse for hours !

PRIN.   No doubt !
We will not trouble you. Hilarion,
I have been wrong — I see my error now.
Take me, Hilarion — 'We will walk the world
Yoked in all exercise of noble end !
And so through those dark gates across the wild
That no man knows ! Indeed, I love thee — Come !'

FINALE.

PRIN.

With joy abiding,
Together gliding
   Through life's variety,
   In sweet society,
And thus enthroning
The love I'm owning,
On this atoning
   I will rely !

CHORUS.

It were profanity
For poor humanity
To treat as vanity
   The sway of Love.
In no locality
Or principality
Is our mortality
   Its sway above !

HILARION.

When day is fading,
With serenading
   And such frivolity
   Of tender quality —
With scented showers
Of fairest flowers,
The happy hours
   Will gaily fly !

CHORUS.

It were profanity, etc.

CURTAIN

THE GRAND DUKE

OR

THE STATUTORY DUEL

DRAMATIS PERSONÆ

RUDOLPH (*Grand Duke of Pfennig Halbpfennig*)
ERNEST DUMMKOPF (*a Theatrical Manager*)
LUDWIG (*his Leading Comedian*)
DR. TANNHÄUSER (*a Notary*)
THE PRINCE OF MONTE CARLO
VISCOUNT MENTONE
BEN HASHBAZ (*a Costumier*)
HERALD

THE PRINCESS OF MONTE CARLO (*betrothed to* RUDOLPH)
THE BARONESS VON KRAKENFELDT (*betrothed to* RUDOLPH)
JULIA JELLICOE (*an English Comédienne*)
LISA (*a Soubrette*)

OLGA
GRETCHEN
BERTHA ⎬ (*Members of Ernest Dummkopf's Company*)
ELSA
MARTHA

Chamberlains, Nobles, Actors, Actresses, etc.

———————

ACT I. — Scene. Public Square of Speisesaal.

ACT II. — Scene. Hall in the Grand Ducal Palace.

Date 1750.

First produced at the Savoy Theatre on March 7, 1896.

THE GRAND DUKE

OR

THE STATUTORY DUEL

ACT I

SCENE. — *Market-place of Speisesaal, in the Grand Duchy of Pfennig Halbpfennig. A well, with decorated ironwork, up* L.C. GRETCHEN, BERTHA, OLGA, MARTHA, *and other members of* ERNEST DUMMKOPF'S *theatrical company are discovered, seated at several small tables, enjoying a repast in honour of the nuptials of* LUDWIG, *his leading comedian, and* LISA, *his soubrette.*

CHORUS.

Won't it be a pretty wedding?
 Will not Lisa look delightful?
Smiles and tears in plenty shedding —
 Which in brides of course is rightful.
 One could say, if one were spiteful,]
Contradiction little dreading,
 Her bouquet is simply frightful —
Still, 'twill be a pretty wedding!
Oh, it is a pretty wedding!
 Such a pretty, pretty wedding!

ELSA.   If her dress *is* badly fitting,
     Theirs the fault who made her *trousseau.*

BERTHA. If her gloves *are* always splitting,
     Cheap kid gloves, we know, will do so.

OLGA.   If upon her train she stumbled,
   On one's train one's always treading.

GRET.   If her hair *is* rather tumbled,
   Still, 'twill be a pretty wedding !

CHORUS.   Such a pretty, pretty wedding !

CHORUS.

Here they come, the couple plighted —
   On life's journey gaily start them.
Soon to be for aye united,
   Till divorce or death shall part them.

(LUDWIG *and* LISA *come forward.*)

DUET — LUDWIG *and* LISA.

LUD.   Pretty Lisa, fair and tasty,
   Tell me now, and tell me truly,
Haven't you been rather hasty ?
   Haven't you been rash unduly ?
Am I quite the dashing *sposo*
   That your fancy could depict you ?
Perhaps you think I'm only so-so ?
      (*She expresses admiration.*)
   Well, I will not contradict you !

CHORUS.   No, he will not contradict you !

LISA.   Who am I to raise objection ?
   I'm a child, untaught and homely —
When you tell me you're perfection,
   Tender, truthful, true, and comely —
That in quarrel no one's bolder,
   Though dissensions always grieve you —
Why, my love, you're so much older
   That, of course, I must believe you !

CHORUS.   Yes, of course, she must believe you !

CHORUS.

If he ever acts unkindly,
Shut your eyes and love him blindly —
Should he call you names uncomely,
Shut your mouth and love him dumbly —
Should he rate you, rightly — leftly —
Shut your ears and love him deafly.
Ha ! ha ! ha ! ha ! ha ! ha ! ha !
Thus and thus and thus alone
Ludwig's wife may hold her own !

(LUDWIG *and* LISA *sit at table.*)

Enter NOTARY TANNHÄUSER.

NOT. Hallo ! Surely I'm not late ? (*All chatter unintelligibly in reply.*)

NOT. But, dear me, you're all at breakfast ! Has the wedding taken place ? (*All chatter unintelligibly in reply.*)

NOT. My good girls, one at a time, I beg. Let me understand the situation. As solicitor to the conspiracy to dethrone the Grand Duke — a conspiracy in which the members of this company are deeply involved — I am invited to the marriage of two of its members. I present myself in due course, and I find, not only that the ceremony has taken place — which is not of the least consequence — but the wedding breakfast is half eaten — which is a consideration of the most serious importance.

(LUDWIG *and* LISA *come down.*)

LUD. But the ceremony has *not* taken place. We can't get a parson !

NOT. Can't get a parson ! Why, how's that ? They're three a penny !

LUD. Oh, it's the old story — the Grand Duke !

ALL. Ugh !

LUD. It seems that the little imp has selected this, our wedding day, for a convocation of all the clergy in the town to settle the details of his approaching marriage with the enormously wealthy

Baroness von Krakenfeldt, and there won't be a parson to be had for love or money until six o'clock this evening !

LISA. And as we produce our magnificent classical revival of *Troilus and Cressida* to-night at seven, we have no alternative but to eat our wedding breakfast before we've earned it. So sit down, and make the best of it.

GRET. Oh, I should like to pull his Grand Ducal ears for him, that I should ! He's the meanest, the cruellest, the most spiteful little ape in Christendom !

OLGA. Well, we shall soon be freed from his tyranny. To-morrow the Despot is to be dethroned !

LUD. Hush, rash girl ! You know not what you say.

OLGA. Don't be absurd ! We're all in it — we're all tiled, here.

LUD. That has nothing to do with it. Know ye not that in alluding to our conspiracy without having first given and received the secret sign, you are violating a fundamental principle of our Association ?

SONG — LUDWIG.

By the mystic regulation
Of our dark Association,
Ere you open conversation
    With another kindred soul,
    You must eat a sausage-roll ! (*Producing one.*)

ALL.   You must eat a sausage-roll !

LUD.   If, in turn, he eats another,
      That's a sign that he's a brother —
      Each may fully trust the other.
         It is quaint and it is droll,
         But it's bilious on the whole.

ALL.   Very bilious on the whole.

LUD.   It's a greasy kind of pasty,
      Which, perhaps, a judgement hasty
      Might consider rather tasty:
         Once (to speak without disguise)
         It found favour in our eyes.

ALL.   It found favour in our eyes.

LUD.   But when you've been six months feeding
                   (As we have) on this exceeding
                   Bilious food, it's no ill-breeding
                      If at these repulsive pies
                      Our offended gorges rise !

ALL.   Our offended gorges rise !

MARTHA. Oh, bother the secret sign ! I've eaten it until I'm quite uncomfortable ! I've given it six times already to-day — and (*whimpering*) I can't eat any breakfast !

BERTHA. And it's so unwholesome. Why, we should all be as yellow as frogs if it wasn't for the make-up !

LUD. All this is rank treason to the cause. I suffer as much as any of you. I loathe the repulsive thing — I can't contemplate it without a shudder — but I'm a conscientious conspirator, and if you won't give the sign I will. (*Eats sausage-roll with an effort.*)

LISA. Poor martyr ! He's always at it, and it's a wonder where he puts it !

NOT. Well now, about *Troilus and Cressida*. What do *you* play ?

LUD. (*struggling with his feelings*). If you'll be so obliging as to wait until I've got rid of this feeling of warm oil at the bottom of my throat, I'll tell you all about it. (LISA *gives him some brandy.*) Thank you, my love; it's gone. Well, the piece will be produced upon a scale of unexampled magnificence. It is confidently predicted that my appearance as King Agamemnon, in a Louis Quatorze wig, will mark an epoch in the theatrical annals of Pfennig Halbpfennig. I endeavoured to persuade Ernest Dummkopf, our manager, to lend us the classical dresses for our marriage. Think of the effect of a real Athenian wedding procession cavorting through the streets of Speisesaal ! Torches burning — cymbals banging — flutes tootling — citharæ twanging — and a throng of fifty lovely Spartan virgins capering before us, all down the High Street, singing 'Eloia ! Eloia ! Opoponax, Eloia !' It would have been tremendous !

NOT. And he declined ?

LUD. He did, on the prosaic ground that it might rain, and the ancient Greeks didn't carry umbrellas ! If, as is confidently expected, Ernest Dummkopf is elected to succeed the dethroned one, mark my words, he will make a mess of it.

[*Exit* LUDWIG *with* LISA.

OLGA. He's sure to be elected. His entire company has promised to plump for him on the understanding that all the places about the Court are filled by members of his troupe, according to professional precedence.

ERNEST *enters in great excitement.*

BERTHA (*looking off*). Here comes Ernest Dummkopf. Now we shall know all about it !

ALL. Well — what's the news ? How is the election going ?

ERN. Oh, it's a certainty — a practical certainty ! Two of the candidates have been arrested for debt, and the third is a baby in arms — so, if you keep your promises, and vote solid, I'm cocksure of election !

OLGA. Trust to us. But you remember the conditions ?

ERN. Yes — all of you shall be provided for, for life. Every man shall be ennobled — every lady shall have unlimited credit at the Court Milliner's, and all salaries shall be paid weekly in advance !

GRET. Oh, it's quite clear he knows how to rule a Grand Duchy !

ERN. Rule a Grand Duchy ? Why, my good girl, for ten years past I've ruled a theatrical company ! A man who can do that **can** rule anything !

SONG — ERNEST.

Were I a king in very truth,
And had a son — a guileless youth —
    In probable succession ;
To teach him patience, teach him tact,
How promptly in a fix to act,
He should adopt, in point of fact,
    A manager's profession.
To that condition he should stoop
    (Despite a too fond mother),
With eight or ten 'stars' in his troupe,
    All jealous of each other !

Oh, the man who can rule a theatrical crew,
Each member a genius (and some of them two),
And manage to humour them, little and great,
    Can govern this tuppenny State !

ALL.   Oh, the man, etc.

    Both A and B rehearsal slight —
    They say they'll be 'all right at night'
        (They've both to go to school yet);
    C in each act *must* change her dress,
    D *will* attempt to 'square the press';
    E won't play Romeo unless
        His grandmother plays Juliet;
    F claims all hoydens as her rights
        (She's played them thirty seasons);
    And G must show herself in tights
        For two convincing reasons —
        Two very well-shaped reasons !
Oh, the man who can drive a theatrical team,
With wheelers and leaders in order supreme,
Can govern and rule, with a wave of his fin,
    All Europe — with Ireland thrown in !

ALL.   Oh, the man, etc.

                     [*Exeunt all but* ERNEST.

ERN. Elected by my fellow-conspirators to be Grand Duke of
Pfennig Halbpfennig as soon as the contemptible little occupant of
the historical throne is deposed — here is promotion indeed !
Why, instead of playing Troilus of Troy for a month, I shall play
Grand Duke of Pfennig Halbpfennig for a lifetime ! Yet, am I
happy ? No — far from happy ! The lovely English *comédienne* —
the beautiful Julia, whose dramatic ability is so overwhelming that
our audiences forgive even her strong English accent — that rare
and radiant being treats my respectful advances with disdain unutterable ! And yet, who knows ? She is haughty and ambitious,
and it may be that the splendid change in my fortunes may work
a corresponding change in her feelings towards me !

Enter JULIA JELLICOE.

JULIA. Herr Dummkopf, a word with you, if you please.

ERN. Beautiful English maiden——

JULIA. No compliments, I beg. I desire to speak with you on a purely professional matter, so we will, if you please, dispense with allusions to my personal appearance, which can only tend to widen the breach which already exists between us.

ERN. (*aside*). My only hope shattered ! The haughty Londoner still despises me ! (*Aloud.*) It shall be as you will.

JULIA. I understand that the conspiracy in which we are all concerned is to develop to-morrow, and that the company is likely to elect you to the throne on the understanding that the posts about the Court are to be filled by members of your theatrical troupe, according to their professional importance.

ERN. That is so.

JULIA. Then all I can say is that it places me in an extremely awkward position.

ERN. (*very depressed*). I don't see how it concerns you.

JULIA. Why, bless my heart, don't you see that, as your leading lady, I am bound under a serious penalty to play the leading part in all your productions ?

ERN. Well ?

JULIA. Why, of course, the leading part in this production will be the Grand Duchess !

ERN. My wife ?

JULIA. That is another way of expressing the same idea.

ERN. (*aside — delighted*). I scarcely dared even to hope for this !

JULIA. Of course, as your leading lady, you'll be mean enough to hold me to the terms of my agreement. Oh, that's so like a man ! Well, I suppose there's no help for it — I shall have to do it !

ERN. (*aside*). She's mine ! (*Aloud.*) But — do you really think you would care to play that part ? (*Taking her hand.*)

JULIA (*withdrawing it*). Care to play it ? Certainly not — but what am I to do ? Business is business, and I am bound by the terms of my agreement.

ERN. It's for a long run, mind — a run that may last many, many years — no understudy — and once embarked upon there's no throwing it up.

JULIA. Oh, we're used to these long runs in England: they are the curse of the stage — but, you see, I've no option.

ERN. You think the part of Grand Duchess will be good enough for you ?

JULIA. Oh, I think so. It's a very good part in Gerolstein, and oughtn't to be a bad one in Pfennig Halbpfennig. Why, what did you suppose I was going to play ?

ERN. (*keeping up a show of reluctance*). But, considering your strong personal dislike to me and your persistent rejection of my repeated offers, won't you find it difficult to throw yourself into the part with all the impassioned enthusiasm that the character seems to demand ? Remember, it's a strongly emotional part, involving long and repeated scenes of rapture, tenderness, adoration, devotion — all in luxuriant excess, and all of the most demonstrative description.

JULIA. My good sir, throughout my career I have made it a rule never to allow private feeling to interfere with my professional duties. You may be quite sure that (however distasteful the part may be) if I undertake it, I shall consider myself professionally bound to throw myself into it with all the ardour at my command.

ERN. (*aside — with effusion*). I'm the happiest fellow alive ! (*Aloud.*) Now — would you have any objection — to — to give me some idea — if it's only a mere sketch — as to how you would play it ? It would be really interesting — to me — to know your conception of — of — the part of my wife.

JULIA. How would I play it ? Now, let me see — let me see. (*Considering.*) Ah, I have it !

BALLAD — JULIA.

How would I play this part —
    The Grand Duke's Bride ?
All rancour in my heart
    I'd duly hide —
I'd drive it from my recollection
And 'whelm you with a mock affection,
Well calculated to defy detection —
That's how I'd play this part —
    The Grand Duke's Bride.

With many a winsome smile
     I'd witch and woo;
With gay and girlish guile
     I'd frenzy you —
    I'd madden you with my caressing,
    Like turtle, her first love confessing —
    That it was 'mock', no mortal would be guessing,
With so much winsome wile
     I'd witch and woo !

Did any other maid
     With you succeed,
I'd pinch the forward jade —
     I would indeed !
    With jealous frenzy agitated
    (Which would, of course, be simulated),
    I'd make her wish she'd never been created —
Did any other maid
     With you succeed !

And should there come to me,
     Some summers hence,
In all the childish glee
     Of innocence,
    Fair babes, aglow with beauty vernal,
    My heart would bound with joy diurnal !
    This sweet display of sympathy maternal,
Well, that would also be
     A mere pretence !

My histrionic art
     Though you deride,
That's how I'd play that part —
     The Grand Duke's Bride !

ENSEMBLE.

ERNEST.	JULIA.
Oh joy! when two glowing young hearts,	My boy, when two glowing young hearts,
From the rise of the curtain,	From the rise of the curtain,
Thus throw themselves into their parts,	Thus throw themselves into their parts,
Success is most certain!	Success is most certain!
If the *rôle* you're prepared to endow	The *rôle* I'm prepared to endow
With such delicate touches,	With most delicate touches,
By the heaven above us, I vow	By the heaven above us, I vow
You shall be my Grand Duchess!	I will be your Grand Duchess!

(Dance.)

Enter all the Chorus with LUDWIG, NOTARY,
and LISA — *all greatly agitated.*

EXCITED CHORUS.

My goodness me! what shall we do? Why, what a dreadful
   situation!
(*To* LUD.) It's all your fault, you booby you — you lump of indis-
   crimination!
I'm sure I don't know where to go — it's put me into such a
   tetter —
But this at all events I know — the sooner we are off, the
   better!

ERN.   What means this *agitato*? What d'ye seek?
       As your Grand Duke elect I bid you speak!

SONG — LUDWIG.

Ten minutes since I met a chap
   Who bowed an easy salutation —
Thinks I, 'This gentleman, mayhap,
   Belongs to our Association.'
      But, on the whole,
      Uncertain yet,
      A sausage-roll
      I took and eat —
That chap replied (I don't embellish)
By eating *three* with obvious relish.

CHORUS (*angrily*).   Why, gracious powers,
          No chum of ours
     Could eat three sausage-rolls with relish !

LUD.   Quite reassured, I let him know
        Our plot — each incident explaining;
  That stranger chuckled much, as though
      He thought me highly entertaining.
       I told him all,
        Both bad and good;
       I bade him call —
        He said he would :
  I added much — the more I muckled,
  The more that chuckling chummy chuckled !

ALL (*angrily*).   A bat could see
         He couldn't be
     A chum of ours if he chuckled !

LUD.   Well, as I bowed to his applause,
        Down dropped he with hysteric bellow —
  And *that* seemed right enough, because
    I *am* a devilish funny fellow.
       Then suddenly,
        As still he squealed,
     It flashed on me
       That I'd revealed
  Our plot, with all details effective,
  To Grand Duke Rudolph's own detective !

ALL.   What folly fell,
        To go and tell
    Our plot to any one's detective !

CHORUS.

(*Attacking* LUDWIG.)   You booby dense —
        You oaf immense,
       With no pretence
      To common sense !

A stupid muff
Who's made of stuff
Not worth a puff
Of candle-snuff !

Pack up at once and off we go, unless we're anxious to exhibit
Our fairy forms all in a row, strung up upon the Castle gibbet !

[*Exeunt Chorus. Manent* LUGWIG, LISA, ERNEST, JULIA,
and NOTARY.

JULIA. Well, a nice mess you've got us into ! There's an end of
our precious plot ! All up — pop — fizzle — bang — done for !

LUD. Yes, but — ha ! ha ! — fancy my choosing the Grand
Duke's private detective, of all men, to make a confidant of ! When
you come to think of it, it's really devilish funny !

ERN. (*angrily*). When you come to think of it, it's extremely
injudicious to admit into a conspiracy every pudding-headed
baboon who presents himself !

LUD. Yes — I should never do that. If I were chairman of this
gang, I should hesitate to enrol *any* baboon who couldn't produce
satisfactory credentials from his last Zoological Gardens.

LISA. Ludwig is far from being a baboon. Poor boy, he could
not help giving us away — it's his trusting nature — he was deceived.

JULIA (*furiously*). His trusting nature ! (*To* LUDWIG.) Oh, I
should like to talk to you in my own language for five minutes —
only five minutes ! I know some good, strong, energetic English
remarks that would shrivel your trusting nature into raisins — only
you wouldn't understand them !

LUD. Here we perceive one of the disadvantages of a neglected
education !

ERN. (*to* JULIA). And I suppose you'll never be my Grand
Duchess now !

JULIA. Grand Duchess ? My good friend, if you don't produce
the piece how can I play the part ?

ERN. True. (*To* LUDWIG.) You see what you've done.

LUD. But, my dear sir, you don't seem to understand that the
man ate three sausage-rolls. Keep that fact steadily before you.
Three large sausage-rolls.

JULIA. Bah ! — Lots of people eat sausage-rolls who are not conspirators.

LUD. Then they shouldn't. It's bad form. It's not the game. When one of the Human Family proposes to eat a sausage-roll, it is his duty to ask himself, 'Am I a conspirator?' And if, on examination, he finds that he is *not* a conspirator, he is bound in honour to select some other form of refreshment.

LISA. Of course he is. One should always play the game. (*To* NOTARY, *who has been smiling placidly through this.*) What are you grinning at, you greedy old man?

NOT. Nothing — don't mind me. It is always amusing to the legal mind to see a parcel of laymen bothering themselves about a matter which to a trained lawyer presents no difficulty whatever.

ALL. No difficulty !

NOT. None whatever ! The way out of it is quite simple.

ALL. Simple ?

NOT. Certainly ! Now attend. In the first place, you two men fight a Statutory Duel.

ERN. A Statutory Duel ?

JULIA. A Stat-tat-tatutory Duel ! Ach ! what a crack-jaw language this German is !

LUD. Never heard of such a thing.

NOT. It is true that the practice has fallen into abeyance through disuse. But all the laws of Pfennig Halbpfennig run for a hundred years, when they die a natural death, unless, in the meantime, they have been revived for another century. The Act that institutes the Statutory Duel was passed a hundred years ago, and as it has never been revived, it expires to-morrow. So you're just in time.

JULIA. But what is the use of talking to us about Statutory Duels when we none of us know what a Statutory Duel is?

NOT. Don't you? Then I'll explain.

SONG — NOTARY.

About a century since,
    The code of the duello
      To sudden death
      For want of breath
    Sent many a strapping fellow.

The then presiding Prince
　　(Who useless bloodshed hated),
　　　　He passed an Act,
　　　　Short and compact,
　　Which may be briefly stated.
Unlike the complicated laws
A Parliamentary draftsman draws,
　　　　It may be briefly stated.

ALL.　　We know that complicated laws,
　　　　Such as a legal draftsman draws,
　　　　　　Cannot be briefly stated.

NOT.　　By this ingenious law,
　　　　　　If any two shall quarrel,
　　　　　　　　They may not fight
　　　　　　　　With falchions bright
　　　　　　(Which seemed to him immoral);
　　　　But each a card shall draw,
　　　　And he who draws the lowest
　　　　　　　　Shall (so 'twas said)
　　　　　　　　Be thenceforth dead —
　　　　In fact, a legal 'ghoest'
　　　　(When exigence of rhyme compels,
　　　　Orthography forgoes her spells,
　　　　　　And 'ghost' is written 'ghoest').

ALL (*aside*).　　With what an emphasis he dwells
　　　　　　Upon 'orthography' and 'spells' !
　　　　　　　　That kind of fun's the lowest.

NOT.　　When off the loser's popped
　　　　　　(By pleasing legal fiction),
　　　　　　　　And friend and foe
　　　　　　　　Have wept their woe
　　　　　　In counterfeit affliction,
　　　　The winner must adopt
　　　　　　The loser's poor relations —
　　　　　　　　Discharge his debts,
　　　　　　　　Pay all his bets,

                    And take his obligations.
                 In short, to briefly sum the case,
                 The winner takes the loser's place,
                    With all its obligations.

ALL.   How neatly lawyers state a case !
                 The winner takes the loser's place,
                    With all its obligations !

LUD. I see. The man who draws the lowest card——

NOT. Dies, *ipso facto*, a social death. He loses all his civil rights — his identity disappears — the Revising Barrister expunges his name from the list of voters, and the winner takes his place, whatever it may be, discharges all his functions, and adopts all his responsibilities.

ERN. This is all very well, as far as it goes, but it only protects one of us. What's to become of the survivor ?

LUD. Yes, that's an interesting point, because *I* might be the survivor.

NOT. The survivor goes at once to the Grand Duke, and, in a burst of remorse, denounces the dead man as the moving spirit of the plot. He is accepted as King's evidence, and, as a matter of course, receives a free pardon. To-morrow, when the law expires, the dead man will, *ipso facto*, come to life again — the Revising Barrister will restore his name to the list of voters, and he will resume all his obligations as though nothing unusual had happened.

JULIA. When he will be at once arrested, tried, and executed on the evidence of the informer ! Candidly, my friend, I don't think much of your plot !

NOT. Dear, dear, dear, the ignorance of the laity ! My good young lady, it is a beautiful maxim of our glorious Constitution that a man can only die once. Death expunges crime, and when he comes to life again, it will be with a clean slate.

ERN. It's really very ingenious.

LUD. (*to* NOTARY). My dear sir, we owe you our lives !

LISA (*aside to* LUDWIG). May I kiss him ?

LUD. Certainly not: you're a big girl now. (*To* ERNEST.) Well, miscreant, are you prepared to meet me on the field of honour ?

ERN. At once. By Jove, what a couple of fire-eaters we are !

LISA. Ludwig doesn't know what fear is.

LUD. Oh, I don't mind this sort of duel !

ERN. It's not like a duel with swords. I hate a duel with swords. It's not the blade I mind — it's the blood.

LUD. And I hate a duel with pistols. It's not the ball I mind — it's the bang.

NOT. Altogether it is a great improvement on the old method of giving satisfaction.

QUINTET.

LUDWIG, LISA, NOTARY, ERNEST, JULIA.

Strange the views some people hold !
    Two young fellows quarrel —
Then they fight, for both are bold —
Rage of both is uncontrolled —
Both are stretched out, stark and cold !
    Prithee, where's the moral ?
       Ding dong ! Ding dong !
There's an end to further action,
And this barbarous transaction
Is described as 'satisfaction' !
    Ha ! ha ! ha ! ha ! satisfaction !
       Ding dong ! Ding dong !
Each is laid in churchyard mould —
Strange the views some people hold !

Better than the method old,
    Which was coarse and cruel,
Is the plan that we've extolled.
Sing thy virtues manifold
(Better than refinèd gold),
    Statutory Duel !
       Sing song ! Sing song !
Sword or pistol neither uses —
Playing card he lightly chooses,
And the loser simply loses !
    Ha ! ha ! ha ! ha ! simply loses.
       Sing song ! Sing song !

K

Some prefer the churchyard mould !
Strange the views some people hold !

NOT. (*offering a card to* ERNEST).
Now take a card and gaily sing
How little you care for Fortune's rubs —

ERN. (*drawing a card*).
Hurrah, hurrah ! — I've drawn a King !

ALL.   He's drawn a King !
He's drawn a King !
Sing Hearts and Diamonds, Spades and Clubs !

ALL (*dancing*).   He's drawn a King !
How strange a thing !
An excellent card — his chance it aids —
Sing Hearts and Diamonds, Spades and Clubs —
Sing Diamonds, Hearts and Clubs and Spades !

NOT. (*to* LUDWIG).
Now take a card with heart of grace —
(Whatever our fate, let's play our parts).

LUD. (*drawing card*).
Hurrah, hurrah ! — I've drawn an Ace !

ALL.   He's drawn an Ace !
He's drawn an Ace !
Sing Clubs and Diamonds, Spades and Hearts !

ALL (*dancing*).
He's drawn an Ace !
Observe his face —
Such very good fortune falls to few —
Sing Clubs and Diamonds, Spades and Hearts —
Sing Clubs, Spades, Hearts and Diamonds too !

NOT.   That both these maids may keep their troth,
And never misfortune them befall,
I'll hold 'em as trustee for both —

ALL.

> He'll hold 'em both !
> He'll hold 'em both !
> Sing Hearts, Clubs, Diamonds, Spades and all !

ALL (*dancing*).

> By joint decree
> As $\left\{\begin{array}{c}\text{our}\\\text{your}\end{array}\right\}$ trustee
> This Notary $\left\{\begin{array}{c}\text{we}\\\text{you}\end{array}\right\}$ will now install —
> In custody let him keep $\left\{\begin{array}{c}\text{their}\\\text{our}\end{array}\right\}$ hearts,
> Sing Hearts, Clubs, Diamonds, Spades and all !

[*Dance and exeunt* LUDWIG, ERNEST, *and* NOTARY *with the two Girls.*

March. Enter the seven Chamberlains of the
GRAND DUKE RUDOLPH.

CHORUS OF CHAMBERLAINS.

> The good Grand Duke of Pfennig Halbpfennig,
> Though, in his own opinion, very very big,
> In point of fact he's nothing but a miserable prig
> Is the good Grand Duke of Pfennig Halbpfennig !

> Though quite contemptible, as every one agrees,
> We must dissemble if we want our bread and cheese,
> So hail him in a chorus, with enthusiasm big,
> The good Grand Duke of Pfennig Halbpfennig !

Enter the GRAND DUKE RUDOLPH. *He is meanly and miserably dressed in old and patched clothes, but blazes with a profusion of orders and decorations. He is very weak and ill, from low living.*

SONG — RUDOLPH.

> A pattern to professors of monarchical autonomy,
> I don't indulge in levity or compromising *bonhomie*,
> But dignified formality, consistent with economy,
>   Above all other virtues I particularly prize.

I never join in merriment — I don't see joke or jape any —
I never tolerate familiarity in shape any —
This, joined with an extravagant respect for tuppence-ha'penny,
    A keynote to my character sufficiently supplies.

(*Speaking.*) Observe. (*To Chamberlains.*) My snuff-box !

(*The snuff-box is passed with much ceremony from the Junior Cham-*
    berlain, through all the others, until it is presented by the Senior
    Chamberlain to RUDOLPH, *who uses it.*)

       That incident a keynote to my character supplies.

RUD.   I weigh out tea and sugar with precision mathematical —
    Instead of beer, a penny each — my orders are emphatical —
    (Extravagance unpardonable, any more than that I call),
      But, on the other hand, my Ducal dignity to keep —
    All Courtly ceremonial — to put it comprehensively —
    I rigidly insist upon (but not, I hope, offensively)
    Whenever ceremonial can be practised inexpensively —
      And, when you come to think of it, it's really very cheap !

(*Speaking.*) Observe. (*To Chamberlains.*) My handkerchief !

(*Handkerchief is handed by Junior Chamberlain to the next in order,*
    and so on until it reaches RUDOLPH, *who is much inconvenienced*
    by the delay.)

      It's sometimes inconvenient, but it's always very cheap !

RUD. My Lord Chamberlain, as you are aware, my marriage with
the wealthy Baroness von Krakenfeldt will take place to-morrow,
and you will be good enough to see that the rejoicings are on a scale
of unusual liberality. Pass that on. (*Chamberlain whispers to Vice-
Chamberlain, who whispers to the next, and so on.*) The sports will
begin with a Wedding Breakfast Bee. The leading pastry-cooks of
the town will be invited to compete, and the winner will not only
enjoy the satisfaction of seeing his breakfast devoured by the
Grand Ducal pair, but he will also be entitled to have the Arms of
Pfennig Halbpfennig tattoo'd between his shoulder-blades. The

Vice-Chamberlain will see to this. All the public fountains of Speisesaal will run with Gingerbierheim and Currantweinmilch at the public expense. The Assistant Vice-Chamberlain will see to this. At night, everybody will illuminate; and as I have no desire to tax the public funds unduly, this will be done at the inhabitants' private expense. The Deputy Assistant Vice-Chamberlain will see to this. All my Grand Ducal subjects will wear new clothes, and the Sub-Deputy Assistant Vice-Chamberlain will collect the usual commission on all sales. Wedding presents (which, on this occasion, should be on a scale of extraordinary magnificence) will be received at the Palace at any hour of the twenty-four, and the Temporary Sub-Deputy Assistant Vice-Chamberlain will sit up all night for this purpose. The entire population will be commanded to enjoy themselves, and with this view the Acting Temporary Sub-Deputy Assistant Vice-Chamberlain will sing comic songs in the Market-place from noon to nightfall. Finally, we have composed a Wedding Anthem, with which the entire population are required to provide themselves. It can be obtained from our Grand Ducal publishers at the usual discount price, and all the Chamberlains will be expected to push the sale. (*Chamberlains bow and exeunt.*) I don't feel at all comfortable. I hope I'm not doing a foolish thing in getting married. After all, it's a poor heart that never rejoices, and this wedding of mine is the first little treat I've allowed myself since my christening. Besides, Caroline's income is very considerable, and as her ideas of economy are quite on a par with mine, it ought to turn out well. Bless her tough old heart, she's a mean little darling! Oh, here she is, punctual to her appointment!

Enter BARONESS VON KRAKENFELDT.

BAR. Rudolph! Why, what's the matter?

RUD. Why, I'm not quite myself, my pet. I'm a little worried and upset. I want a tonic. It's the low diet, I think. I am afraid, after all, I shall have to take the bull by the horns and have an egg with my breakfast.

BAR. I shouldn't do anything rash, dear. Begin with a jujube. (*Gives him one.*)

RUD. (*about to eat it, but changes his mind*). I'll keep it for supper. (*He sits by her and tries to put his arm round her waist.*)

BAR. Rudolph, don't ! What in the world are you thinking of ?

RUD. I was thinking of embracing you, my sugar-plum. Just as a little cheap treat.

BAR. What, here ? In public ? Really, you appear to have no sense of delicacy.

RUD. No sense of delicacy, Bon-bon !

BAR. No. I can't make you out. When you courted me, all your courting was done publicly in the Market-place. When you proposed to me, you proposed in the Market-place. And now that we're engaged you seem to desire that our first *tête-à-tête* shall occur in the Market-place ! Surely you've a room in your Palace — with blinds — that would do ?

RUD. But, my own, I can't help myself. I'm bound by my own decree.

BAR. Your own decree ?

RUD. Yes. You see, all the houses that give on the Market-place belong to me, but the drains (which date back to the reign of Charlemagne) want attending to, and the houses wouldn't let — so, with a view to increasing the value of the property, I decreed that all love-episodes between affectionate couples should take place, in public, on this spot, every Monday, Wednesday, and Friday, when the band doesn't play.

BAR. Bless me, what a happy idea ! So moral too ! And have you found it answer ?

RUD. Answer ? The rents have gone up fifty per cent, and the sale of opera-glasses (which is a Grand Ducal monopoly) has received an extraordinary stimulus ! So, under the circumstances, *would* you allow me to put my arm round your waist ? As a source of income. Just once !

BAR. But it's so very embarrassing. Think of the opera-glasses !

RUD. My good girl, that's just what I *am* thinking of. Hang it all, we must give them *something* for their money ! What's that ?

BAR. (*unfolding paper, which contains a large letter, which she hands to him*). It's a letter which your detective asked me to hand to you. I wrapped it up in yesterday's paper to keep it clean.

RUD. Oh, it's only his report ! That'll keep. But, I say, you've never been and bought a newspaper ?

BAR. My dear Rudolph, do you think I'm mad ? It came wrapped round my breakfast.

Rud. (*relieved*). I thought you were not the sort of girl to go and buy a newspaper ! Well, as we've got it, we may as well read it. What does it say ?

Bar. Why — dear me — here's your biography ! 'Our Detested Despot !'

Rud. Yes — I fancy that refers to me.

Bar. And it says — Oh, it can't be !

Rud. What can't be ?

Bar. Why, it says that although you're going to marry me to-morrow, you were betrothed in infancy to the Princess of Monte Carlo !

Rud. Oh yes — that's quite right. Didn't I mention it ?

Bar. Mention it ! You never said a word about it !

Rud. Well, it doesn't matter, because, you see, it's practically off.

Bar. Practically off ?

Rud. Yes. By the terms of the contract the betrothal is void unless the Princess marries before she is of age. Now, her father, the Prince, is stony-broke, and hasn't left his house for years for fear of arrest. Over and over again he has implored me to come to him to be married — but in vain. Over and over again he has implored me to advance him the money to enable the Princess to come to me — but in vain. I am very young, but not as young as that; and as the Princess comes of age at two to-morrow, why, at two to-morrow I'm a free man, so I appointed that hour for our wedding, as I shall like to have as much marriage as I can get for my money.

Bar. I see. Of course, if the married state is a happy state, it's a pity to waste any of it.

Rud. Why, every hour we delayed I should lose a lot of you and you'd lose a lot of me !

Bar. My thoughtful darling ! Oh, Rudolph, we ought to be very happy !

Rud. If I'm not, it'll be my first bad investment. Still, there *is* such a thing as a slump even in Matrimonials.

Bar. I often picture us in the long, cold, dark December evenings, sitting close to each other and singing impassioned duets to keep us warm, and thinking of all the lovely things we could afford to buy if we chose, and, at the same time, planning out our lives in a spirit of the most rigid and exacting economy !

RUD. It's a most beautiful and touching picture of connubial bliss in its highest and most rarefied development !

DUET — BARONESS *and* RUDOLPH.

BAR. As o'er our penny roll we sing,
    It is not reprehensive
To think what joys our wealth would bring
Were we disposed to do the thing
    Upon a scale extensive.
There's rich mock-turtle — thick and clear —

RUD. (*confidentially*). Perhaps we'll have it once a year !
BAR. (*delighted*). You *are* an open-handed dear !
RUD. Though, mind you, it's expensive.
BAR. No doubt it *is* expensive.
BOTH. How fleeting are the glutton's joys !
With fish and fowl he lightly toys,

RUD. And pays for such expensive tricks
Sometimes as much as two-and-six !

BAR.   As two-and-six ?

RUD.   As two-and-six —

BOTH. Sometimes as much as two-and-six !

BAR. It gives him no advantage mind —
For you and he have only dined,
And you remain when once it's down
A better man by half-a-crown.

RUD.   By half-a-crown ?
BAR.   By half-a-crown.
BOTH. Yes, two-and-six is half-a-crown.
  Then let us be modestly merry,
  And rejoice with a derry down derry,
    For to laugh and to sing
    No extravagance bring —
  It's a joy economical, very !

BAR.   Although as you're of course aware
        (I never tried to hide it)
        I moisten my insipid fare
        With water — which I can't abear —

RUD.   Nor I — I can't abide it.

BAR.   This pleasing fact our souls will cheer,
        With fifty thousand pounds a year
        We *could* indulge in table beer !

RUD.   Get out !

BAR.   We could — I've tried it !

RUD.   Yes, yes, of course you've tried it !

BOTH.   Oh, he who has an income clear
        Of fifty thousand pounds a year —

BAR.   Can purchase all his fancy loves,
        Conspicuous hats —

RUD.   Two-shilling gloves —

BAR. (*doubtfully*).   Two-shilling gloves ?

RUD. (*positively*).   Two-shilling gloves —

BOTH.   Yes, think of that, two-shilling gloves !

BAR.   Cheap shoes and ties of gaudy hue,
        And Waterbury watches, too —
        And think that he could buy the lot
        Were he a donkey —

RUD.   Which he's *not* !

BAR.   Oh no, he's *not* !

RUD.   Oh no, he's *not* !

BOTH (*dancing*).
        That kind of donkey he is *not* !
            Then let us be modestly merry,
            And rejoice with a derry down derry,
                For to laugh and to sing
                Is a rational thing —
            It's a joy economical, very !

                            [*Exit* BARONESS.

RUD. Oh, now for my detective's report. (*Opens letter.*) What's
this ! Another conspiracy ! A conspiracy to depose *me* ! And my
private detective was so convulsed with laughter at the notion of a
conspirator selecting him for a confidant that he was physically

unable to arrest the malefactor ! Why, it'll come off ! This comes of
engaging a detective with a keen sense of the ridiculous ! For the
future I'll employ none but Scotchmen. And the plot is to explode
to-morrow ! My wedding day ! Oh, Caroline, Caroline ! (*Weeps.*)
This is perfectly frightful ! What's to be done ? I don't know ! I
ought to keep cool and think, but you *can't* think when your veins
are full of hot soda-water, and your brain's fizzing like a firework,
and all your faculties are jumbled in a perfect whirlpool of tumbli-
cation ! And I'm going to be ill ! I know I am ! I've been living
too low, and I'm going to be very ill indeed !

SONG — RUDOLPH.

When you find you're a broken-down critter,
Who is all of a trimmle and twitter,
With your palate unpleasantly bitter,
 As if you'd just eaten a pill —
When your legs are as thin as dividers,
And you're plagued with unruly insiders,
And your spine is all creepy with spiders,
 And you're highly gamboge in the gill —
When you've got a beehive in your head,
 And a sewing machine in each ear,
And you feel that you've eaten your bed,
 And you've got a bad headache *down here* —
  When such facts are about,
   And these symptoms you find
    In your body or crown —
  Well, you'd better look out,
   You may make up your mind
    You had better lie down !

When your lips are all smeary — like tallow,
And your tongue is decidedly yallow,
With a pint of warm oil in your swallow,
 And a pound of tin-tacks in your chest —
When you're down in the mouth with the vapours,
And all over your Morris wall-papers
Black-beetles are cutting their capers,
 And crawly things never at rest —

When you doubt if your head is your own,
    And you jump when an open door slams —
Then you've got to a state which is known
    To the medical world as 'jim-jams'.
        If such symptoms you find
        In your body or head,
            They're not easy to quell —
        You may make up your mind
        You are better in bed,
            For you're not at all well !

(*Sinks exhausted and weeping at foot of well.*)

Enter LUDWIG.

LUD. Now for my confession and full pardon. They told me the Grand Duke was dancing duets in the Market-place, but I don't see him. (*Sees* RUDOLPH.) Hallo ! Who's this ? (*Aside.*) Why, it *is* the Grand Duke !

RUD. (*sobbing*). Who are you, sir, who presume to address me in person ? If you've anything to communicate, you must fling yourself at the feet of my Acting Temporary Sub-Deputy Assistant Vice-Chamberlain, who will fling himself at the feet of his immediate superior, and so on, with successive foot-flingings through the various grades — your communication will, in course of time, come to my august knowledge.

LUD. But when I inform your Highness that in me you see the most unhappy, the most unfortunate, the most completely miserable man in your whole dominion——

RUD. (*still sobbing*). *You* the most miserable man in my whole dominion ? How can you have the face to stand there and say such a thing ? Why, look at me ! Look at me ! (*Bursts into tears.*)

LUD. Well, I wouldn't be a cry-baby.

RUD. A cry-baby ? If you had just been told that you were going to be deposed to-morrow, and perhaps blown up with dynamite for all I know, wouldn't *you* be a cry-baby ? I do declare if I could only hit upon some cheap and painless method of putting an end to an existence which has become insupportable, I would unhesitatingly adopt it !

LUD. You would ? (*Aside.*) I see a magnificent way out of this ! By Jupiter, I'll try it ! (*Aloud.*) Are you, by any chance, in earnest ?

RUD. In earnest ? Why, look at me !

LUD. If you are really in earnest — if you really desire to escape scot-free from this impending — this unspeakably horrible catastrophe — without trouble, danger, pain, or expense — why not resort to a Statutory Duel ?

RUD. A Statutory Duel ?

LUD. Yes. The Act is still in force, but it will expire to-morrow afternoon. You fight — you lose — you are dead for a day. To-morrow, when the Act expires, you will come to life again and resume your Grand Duchy as though nothing had happened. In the meantime, the explosion will have taken place and the survivor will have had to bear the brunt of it.

RUD. Yes, that's all very well, but who'll be fool enough to *be* the survivor ?

LUD. (*kneeling*). Actuated by an overwhelming sense of attachment to your Grand Ducal person, I unhesitatingly offer myself as the victim of your subjects' fury.

RUD. You do ? Well, really that's very handsome. I daresay being blown up is not nearly as unpleasant as one would think.

LUD. Oh, yes it is. It mixes one up, awfully !

RUD. But suppose I were to lose ?

LUD. Oh, that's easily arranged. (*Producing cards.*) I'll put an Ace up my sleeve — you'll put a King up yours. When the drawing takes place, I shall seem to draw the higher card and you the lower. And there you are !

RUD. Oh, but that's cheating.

LUD. So it is. I never thought of that. (*Going.*)

RUD. (*hastily*). Not that I mind. But I say — you won't take an unfair advantage of your day of office ? You won't go tipping people, or squandering my little savings in fireworks, or any nonsense of that sort ?

LUD. I am hurt — really hurt — by the suggestion.

RUD. You — you wouldn't like to put down a deposit, perhaps ?

LUD. No. I don't think I should like to put down a deposit.

RUD. Or give a guarantee ?

LUD. A guarantee would be equally open to objection.

RUD. It would be more regular. Very well, I suppose you must have your own way.

LUD. Good. I say — we must have a devil of a quarrel !

RUD. Oh, a devil of a quarrel !

LUD. Just to give colour to the thing. Shall I give you a sound thrashing before all the people ? Say the word — it's no trouble.

RUD. No, I think not, though it would be very convincing and it's extremely good and thoughtful of you to suggest it. Still, a devil of a quarrel !

LUD. Oh, a devil of a quarrel !

RUD. No half measures. Big words — strong language — rude remarks. Oh, a devil of a quarrel !

LUD. Now the question is, how shall we summon the people ?

RUD. Oh, there's no difficulty about that. Bless your heart, they've been staring at us through those windows for the last half-hour !

FINALE.

RUD.   Come hither, all you people —
    When you hear the fearful news,
   All the pretty women weep'll,
    Men will shiver in their shoes.

LUD.   And they'll all cry 'Lord, defend us !'
    When they learn the fact tremendous
    That to give this man his gruel
    In a Statutory Duel —

BOTH.   This plebeian man of shoddy —
    This contemptible nobody —
    Your Grand Duke does not refuse !

(During this, Chorus of men and women have entered, all trembling with apprehension under the impression that they are to be arrested for their complicity in the conspiracy.)

CHORUS.

With faltering feet,
    And our muscles in a quiver,
Our fate we meet
    With our feelings all unstrung !

              If our plot complete
                                    He has managed to diskiver,
              There is no retreat —
                                    We shall certainly be hung !

RUD. (*aside to* LUDWIG).

    Now *you* begin and pitch it strong — walk into me abusively —

LUD. (*aside to* RUDOLPH).

    I've several epithets that I've reserved for you exclusively.

    A choice selection I have here when you are ready *to* begin.

RUD.   Now *you* begin——

LUD.   No, *you* begin——

RUD.   No, *you* begin——

LUD.   No, *you* begin !

CHORUS (*trembling*).

              Has it happed as we expected ?
              Is our little plot detected ?

              DUET — RUDOLPH *and* LUDWIG.

RUD. (*furiously*).

        Big bombs, small bombs, great guns and little ones !
                      Put him in a pillory !
                      Rack him with artillery !

LUD. (*furiously*).

    Long swords, short swords, tough swords and brittle ones !
                      Fright him into fits !
                      Blow him into bits !

RUD.   You muff, sir !

LUD.   You lout, sir !

RUD.   Enough, sir !

LUD.   Get out, sir !   (*Pushes him.*)

RUD.   A hit, sir ?

LUD.   Take that, sir !   (*Slaps him.*)

RUD.   It's tit, sir,

LUD.   For tat, sir !

CHORUS (*appalled*).

              When two doughty heroes thunder,
              All the world is lost in wonder;
                  When such men their temper lose,
                  Awful are the words they use !

LUD. Tall snobs, small snobs, rich snobs and needy ones !

RUD. (*jostling him*). Whom are you alluding to ?

LUD. (*jostling him*). Where are you intruding to ?

RUD. Fat snobs, thin snobs, swell snobs and seedy ones !

LUD.   I rather think you err.
                        To whom do you refer ?

RUD.   To you, sir !

LUD.   To me, sir ?

RUD.   I do, sir !

LUD.   We'll see, sir !

RUD.   I jeer, sir !

(*Makes a face at* LUDWIG.) Grimace, sir !

LUD.   Look here, sir —

(*Makes a face at* RUDOLPH.) A face, sir !

CHORUS (*appalled*).

          When two heroes, once pacific,
          Quarrel, the effect's terrific !
             What a horrible grimace !
             What a paralysing face !

ALL.   Big bombs, small bombs, etc.

LUD. *and* RUD. (*recit.*).

          He has insulted me, and, in a breath,
          This day we fight a duel to the death !

NOT. (*checking them*).

          You mean, of course, by duel (*verbum sat.*),
          A Statutory Duel.

ALL.   Why, what's that ?

NOT.   According to established legal uses,
          A card apiece each bold disputant chooses —
          Dead as a doornail is the dog who loses —
          The winner steps into the dead man's shoeses !

ALL.   The winner steps into the dead man's shoeses !

RUD. *and* LUD.   Agreed !   Agreed !

RUD.   Come, come — the pack !

LUD. (*producing one*).   Behold it here !

RUD.   I'm on the rack !

LUD.   I quake with fear !

      (NOTARY *offers card to* LUDWIG.)

LUD.   First draw to you !

Rud.   If that's the case,
         Behold the King ! (*Drawing card from his sleeve.*)
Lud. (*same business*).   Behold the Ace !
Chorus.   Hurrah, hurrah ! Our Ludwig's won,
             And wicked Rudolph's course is run —
             So Ludwig will as Grand Duke reign
             Till Rudolph comes to life again —
Rud.   Which will occur to-morrow !
             I come to life to-morrow !
Gret. (*with mocking curtsey*).
             My Lord Grand Duke, farewell !
                 A pleasant journey, very,
             To your convenient cell
                 In yonder cemetery !
Lisa (*curtseying*).
             Though malcontents abuse you,
             We're much distressed to lose you !
             You were, when you were living,
             So liberal, so forgiving !
Bertha.   So merciful, so gentle !
             So highly ornamental !
Olga.   And now that you've departed,
             You leave us broken-hearted !
All (*pretending to weep*).   Yes, truly, truly, truly, truly —
                 Truly broken-hearted !
             Ha ! ha ! ha ! ha ! ha ! ha ! (*Mocking him.*)
Rud. (*furious*).   Rapscallions, in penitential fires,
                 You'll rue the ribaldry that from you falls !
             To-morrow afternoon the law expires,
                 And then — look out for squalls !
                         [*Exit* Rudolph, *amid general ridicule.*
Chorus.   Give thanks, give thanks to wayward fate —
                 By mystic fortune's sway,
             Our Ludwig guides the helm of State
                 For one delightful day !
(*To* Ludwig.)   We hail you, sir !
                 We greet you, sir !
                 Regale you, sir !
                 We treat you, sir !

Our ruler be
By fate's decree
For one delightful day !

Not.   You've done it neatly ! Pity that your powers
        Are limited to four-and-twenty hours !

Lud.   No matter, though the time will quickly run,
        In hours twenty-four much may be done !

SONG — Ludwig.

Oh, a Monarch who boasts intellectual graces
     Can do, if he likes, a good deal in a day —
He can put all his friends in conspicuous places,
     With plenty to eat and with nothing to pay !
You'll tell me, no doubt, with unpleasant grimaces,
To-morrow, deprived of your ribbons and laces,
You'll get your dismissal — with very long faces —
     But wait ! on that topic I've something to say !

(*Dancing.*)   I've something to say — I've something to say — I've
        something to say !
     Oh, our rule shall be merry — I'm not an ascetic —
       And while the sun shines we will get up our hay —
     By a pushing young Monarch, of turn energetic,
       A very great deal may be done in a day !

Chorus.   Oh, his rule will be merry, etc.

(*During this*, Ludwig *whispers to* Notary, *who writes*.)

For instance, this measure (his ancestor drew it),
               (*alluding to* Notary)
     This law against duels — to-morrow will die —
The Duke will revive, and you'll certainly rue it —
     He'll give you 'what for' and he'll let you know why !
But in twenty-four hours there's time to renew it —
With a century's life I've the right to imbue it —
It's easy to do — and, by Jingo, I'll do it !

(*Signing paper, which* Notary *presents*.)

It's done ! Till I perish your Monarch am I !
Your Monarch am I — your Monarch am I — your Monarch
        am I !

> Though I do not pretend to be very prophetic,
>   I fancy I know what you're going to say —
> By a pushing young Monarch, of turn energetic,
>   A very great deal may be done in a day !

ALL (*astonished*).
> Oh, it's simply uncanny, his power prophetic —
>   It's perfectly right — we *were* going to say,
>   By a pushing, etc.

Enter JULIA, *at back.*

LUD. (*recit.*).   This very afternoon — at two (about) —
>   The Court appointments will be given out.
>   To each and all (for that was the condition)
>   According to professional position !

ALL.   Hurrah !

JULIA (*coming forward*).
>   According to professional position ?

LUD.   According to professional position !

JULIA.   Then, horror !

ALL.   Why, what's the matter ? What's the matter ?
>   What's the matter ?

SONG — JULIA. (LISA *clinging to her.*)

>   Ah, pity me, my comrades true,
>   Who love, as well I know you do,
>   This gentle child,
>   To me so fondly dear !

ALL.   Why, what's the matter ?

JULIA.   Our sister love so true and deep
>   From many an eye unused to weep
>   Hath oft beguiled
>   The coy reluctant tear !

ALL.   Why, what's the matter ?

JULIA.   Each sympathetic heart 'twill bruise
>   When you have heard the frightful news
>   (O will it not ?)
>   That I must now impart !

ALL.   Why, what's the matter ?

JULIA.	Her love for him is all in all !
	Ah, cursed fate ! that it should fall
	Unto *my* lot
	To break my darling's heart !
ALL.	Why, what's the matter ?
LUD.	What means our Julia by those fateful looks ?
	Please do not keep us all on tenter-hooks —
	Now, what's the matter ?
JULIA.	Our duty, if we're wise,
	We never shun.
	This Spartan rule applies
	To every one.
	In theatres, as in life,
	Each has her line —
	This part — the Grand Duke's wife
	(Oh agony !) is mine !
	A maxim new I do not start —
	The canons of dramatic art
	Decree that this repulsive part
	(The Grand Duke's wife)
	Is mine !
ALL.	Oh, *that's* the matter !
LISA (*appalled, to* LUDWIG).	Can that be so ?
LUD.	I do not know —
	But time will show
	If that be so.
CHORUS.	Can that be so ? etc.
LISA (*recit.*).	Be merciful !

DUET — LISA *and* JULIA.

LISA.	Oh, listen to me, dear —
	I love him only, darling !
	Remember, oh, my pet,
	On him my heart is set !
	This kindness do me, dear —
	Nor leave me lonely, darling !
	Be merciful, my pet,
	Our love do not forget !

JULIA.   Now don't be foolish, dear —
            You couldn't play it, darling !
            It's 'leading business', pet,
            And you're but a soubrette.
      So don't be mulish, dear —
            Although I say it, darling,
            It's not your line, my pet —
            I play that part, you bet !
             I play that part —
            I play that part, you bet !

          (LISA *overwhelmed with grief.*)

NOT.   The lady's right. Though Julia's engagement
              Was for the stage meant —
      It certainly frees Ludwig from his
              Connubial promise.
      Though marriage contracts — or whate'er you call 'em —
              Are very solemn,
      Dramatic contracts (which you all adore so)
              Are even more so !

ALL.   That's very true !
      Though marriage contracts, etc.

              SONG — LISA.

      The die is cast,
            My hope has perished !
            Farewell, O Past,
            Too bright to last,
            Yet fondly cherished !
            My light has fled,
            My hope is dead,
      Its doom is spoken —
            My day is night,
            My wrong is right
            In all men's sight —
      My heart is broken !

                        [Exit, weeping.

LUD. (*recit.*). Poor child, where will she go ? What will she do ?

JULIA. *That* isn't in your part, you know.

LUD. (*sighing*). Quite true !
(*With an effort.*) Depressing topics we'll not touch upon —
    Let us begin as we are going on !
    For this will be a jolly Court, for little and for big !

ALL. Sing hey, the jolly jinks of Pfennig Halbpfennig !

LUD. From morn to night our lives shall be as merry as a grig !

ALL. Sing hey, the jolly jinks of Pfennig Halbpfennig !

LUD. All state and ceremony we'll eternally abolish —
    We don't mean to insist upon unnecessary polish —
    And, on the whole, I rather think you'll find our rule
      tollolish !

ALL. Sing hey, the jolly jinks of Pfennig Halbpfennig !

JULIA. But stay — your new-made Court
    Without a courtly coat is —
      We shall require
      Some Court attire,
    And at a moment's notice.
    In clothes of common sort
      Your courtiers must not grovel —
      Your new *noblesse*
      Must have a dress
    Original and novel !

LUD. Old Athens we'll exhume !
    The necessary dresses,
      Correct and true
      And all brand-new,
    The company possesses :
    Henceforth our Court costume
      Shall live in song and story,
      For we'll upraise
      The dead old days
    Of Athens in her glory !

ALL.   Yes, let's upraise
                         The dead old days
                         Of Athens in her glory !

ALL.   Agreed !   Agreed !
     For this will be a jolly Court for little and for big ! etc.

(*They carry* LUDWIG *round stage and deposit him on the ironwork
     of well.* JULIA *stands by him, and the rest group round them.*)

END OF ACT I

ACT II

(The Next Morning.)

Scene. — *Entrance Hall of the Grand Ducal Palace.*

Enter a procession of the members of the theatrical company (now dressed in the costumes of Troilus and Cressida), *carrying garlands, playing on pipes, citharæ, and cymbals, and heralding the return of* Ludwig *and* Julia *from the marriage ceremony, which has just taken place.*

Chorus.

As before you we defile,
   Eloia ! Eloia !
Pray you, gentles, do not smile
If we shout, in classic style,
   Eloia !
Ludwig and his Julia true
Wedded are each other to —
So we sing, till all is blue,
   Eloia ! Eloia !
    Opoponax ! Eloia !

Wreaths of bay and ivy twine,
   Eloia ! Eloia !
Fill the bowl with Lesbian wine,
And to revelry incline —
   Eloia !
For as gaily we pass on
Probably we shall, anon,
Sing a Diergeticon —
   Eloia ! Eloia !
    Opoponax ! Eloia !

RECIT. — LUDWIG.

Your loyalty our Ducal heartstrings touches:
Allow me to present your new Grand Duchess.
Should she offend, you'll graciously excuse her —
And kindly recollect *I* didn't choose her !

SONG — LUDWIG.

At the outset I may mention it's my sovereign intention
    To revive the classic memories of Athens at its best,
For the company possesses all the necessary dresses
    And a course of quiet cramming will supply us with the rest.
We've a choir hyporchematic (that is, ballet-operatic)
    Who respond to the *choreutæ* of that cultivated age,
And our clever chorus-master, all but captious criticaster
    Would accept as the *choregus* of the early Attic stage.
This return to classic ages is considered in their wages,
    Which are always calculated by the day or by the week —
And I'll pay 'em (if they'll back me) all in *oboloi* and *drachmæ*,
        Which they'll get (if they prefer it) at the Kalends that are
        Greek !

(*Confidentially to audience.*)

At this juncture I may mention
    That this erudition sham
Is but classical pretension,
    The result of steady 'cram.':
Periphrastic methods spurning,
    To this audience discerning
I admit this show of learning
    Is the fruit of steady 'cram.' !

CHORUS.   Periphrastic methods, etc.

In the period Socratic every dining-room was Attic
    (Which suggests an architecture of a topsy-turvy kind),
There they'd satisfy their thirst on a *recherché* cold ἄριστον,
    Which is what they called their lunch — and so may you, if you're
        inclined.

As they gradually got on, they'd τρέπεσθαι πρὸς τὸν πότον
  (Which is Attic for a steady and a conscientious drink).
But they mixed their wine with water — which I'm sure they didn't
      oughter —
  And we modern Saxons know a trick worth two of that, I think !
Then came rather risky dances (under certain circumstances)
  Which would shock that worthy gentleman, the Licenser of Plays,
Corybantian maniac kick — Dionysiac or Bacchic —
  And the Dithyrambic revels of those undecorous days.

(*Confidentially to audience.*)

> And perhaps I'd better mention,
>   Lest alarming you I am,
> That it isn't our intention
>   To perform a Dithyramb —
> It displays a lot of stocking,
> Which is always very shocking,
> And of course I'm only mocking
>   At the prevalence of 'cram.'!

CHORUS.   It displays a lot, etc.

Yes, on reconsideration, there are customs of that nation
  Which are not in strict accordance with the habits of our day,
And when I come to codify, their rules I mean to modify,
  Or Mrs. Grundy, p'r'aps, may have a word or two to say.
For they hadn't macintoshes or umbrellas or goloshes —
  And a shower with their dresses must have played the very deuce,
And it must have been unpleasing when they caught a fit of sneezing,
  For, it seems, of pocket-handkerchiefs they didn't know the use.
They wore little underclothing — scarcely anything — or nothing —
  And their dress of Coan silk was quite transparent in design —
Well, in fact, in summer weather, something like the 'altogether'.
  And it's *there*, I rather fancy, I shall have to draw the line !

(*Confidentially to audience.*)

> And again I wish to mention
>   That this erudition sham
> Is but classical pretension,
>   The result of steady 'cram.'

> Yet my classic lore aggressive
> (If you'll pardon the possessive)
> Is exceedingly impressive
>   When you're passing an exam.

CHORUS.   Yet his classic lore, etc.
                    [*Exeunt Chorus. Manent* LUDWIG, JULIA, *and* LISA.

LUD. (*recit.*).
> Yes, Ludwig and his Julia are mated !
> For when an obscure comedian, whom the law backs,
> To sovereign rank is promptly elevated,
> He takes it with its incidental drawbacks !
>   So Julia and I are duly mated !

(LISA, *through this, has expressed intense distress at
            having to surrender* LUDWIG.)

SONG — LISA.

> Take care of him — he's much too good to live,
>   With him you must be very gentle :
> Poor fellow, he's so highly sensitive,
>   And O, so sentimental !
> Be sure you never let him sit up late
>   In chilly open air conversing —
> Poor darling, he's extremely delicate,
>   And wants a deal of nursing !

LUD.   I want a deal of nursing !

LISA.   And O, remember this —
>   When he is cross with pain,
> A flower and a kiss —
> A simple flower — a tender kiss
>   Will bring him round again !

> His moods you must assiduously watch :
>   When he succumbs to sorrow tragic,
> Some hardbake or a bit of butter-scotch
>   Will work on him like magic.

To contradict a character so rich
        In trusting love were simple blindness —
He's one of those exalted natures which
        Will only yield to kindness !

LUD.   I only yield to kindness !

LISA.   And O, the bygone bliss !
                And O, the present pain !
            That flower and that kiss —
            That simple flower — that tender kiss
                I ne'er shall give again !

[*Exit, weeping.*

JULIA. And now that everybody has gone, and we're happily and comfortably married, I want to have a few words with my new-born husband.

LUD. (*aside*). Yes, I expect you'll often have a few words with your new-born husband ! (*Aloud.*) Well, what is it ?

JULIA. Why, I've been thinking that as you and I have to play our parts for life, it is most essential that we should come to a definite understanding as to how they shall be rendered. Now, I've been considering how I can make the most of the Grand Duchess.

LUD. Have you ? Well, if you'll take my advice, you'll make a very fine part of it.

JULIA. Why, that's quite *my* idea.

LUD. I shouldn't make it one of your hoity-toity vixenish viragoes.

JULIA. You think not ?

LUD. Oh, I'm quite clear about that. I should make her a tender, gentle, submissive, affectionate (but not too affectionate) child-wife — timidly anxious to coil herself into her husband's heart, but kept in check by an awestruck reverence for his exalted intellectual qualities and his majestic personal appearance.

JULIA. Oh, that is your idea of a good part ?

LUD. Yes — a wife who regards her husband's slightest wish as an inflexible law, and who ventures but rarely into his august presence, unless (which would happen seldom) he should summon her to appear before him. A crushed, despairing violet, whose blighted existence would culminate (all too soon) in a lonely and pathetic death-scene ! A fine part, my dear.

JULIA. Yes. There's a good deal to be said for your view of it. Now there are some actresses whom it would fit like a glove.

LUD. (*aside*). I wish I'd married one of 'em !

JULIA. But, you see, I *must* consider my temperament. For instance, my temperament would demand some strong scenes of justifiable jealousy.

LUD. Oh, there's no difficulty about that. You shall have *them*.

JULIA. With a lovely but detested rival——

LUD. Oh, *I'll* provide the rival.

JULIA. Whom I should stab — stab — stab !

LUD. Oh, I wouldn't stab her. It's been done to death. I should treat her with a silent and contemptuous disdain, and delicately withdraw from a position which, to one of your sensitive nature, would be absolutely untenable. Dear me, I can see you delicately withdrawing, up centre and off !

JULIA. *Can* you ?

LUD. Yes. It's a fine situation — and in your hands, full of quiet pathos !

DUET — LUDWIG *and* JULIA.

LUD.   Now, Julia, come,
          Consider it from
                This dainty point of view —
          A timid tender
          Feminine gender,
                Prompt to coyly coo —
          Yet silence seeking,
          Seldom speaking
                Till she's spoken to —
          A comfy, cosy,
          Rosy-posy
                Innocent *ingenoo* !
                     The part you're suited to —
                     (To give the deuce her due)
                A sweet (O, jiminy !)
                Miminy-piminy,
                     Innocent inge*noo* !

ENSEMBLE.

LUD.	JULIA
The part you're suited to —	I'm much obliged to you,
(To give the deuce her due)	I don't think that would do —
A sweet (O, jiminy!)	To play (O, jiminy!)
Miminy-piminy,	Miminy-piminy,
Innocent inge*noo*!	Innocent inge*noo*!

JULIA.   You forget my special magic
　　　　　　　　(In a high dramatic sense)
　　　　　Lies in situations tragic —
　　　　　　　　Undeniably intense.
　　　　　As I've justified promotion
　　　　　　　In the histrionic art,
　　　　　I'll submit to you my notion
　　　　　　Of a first-rate part.

LUD.   Well, let us see your notion
　　　　　　Of a first-rate part.

JULIA (*dramatically*).
　　　　　I have a rival ! Frenzy-thrilled,
　　　　　　　I find you both together !
　　　　　My heart stands still — with horror chilled —
　　　　　　Hard as the millstone nether !
　　　　　Then softly, slyly, snaily, snaky —
　　　　　Crawly, creepy, quaily, quaky —
　　　　　　　I track her on her homeward way,
　　　　　　　As panther tracks her fated prey !

(*Furiously*.)   I fly at her soft white throat —
　　　　　　　The lily-white laughing leman !
　　　　　On her agonized gaze I gloat
　　　　　　With the glee of a dancing demon !
　　　　　My rival she — I have no doubt of her —
　　　　　So I hold on — till the breath is out of her !
　　　　　　　— till the breath is out of her !

And then — Remorse ! Remorse !
O cold unpleasant corse,
     Avaunt ! Avaunt !
That lifeless form
    I gaze upon —
That face, still warm
    But weirdly wan —
Those eyes of glass
    I contemplate —
And then, alas,
    Too late — too late !
I find she is — your Aunt !
(*Shuddering.*)   Remorse ! Remorse !
Then, mad — mad — mad !
    With fancies wild — chimerical —
Now sorrowful — silent — sad —
    Now hullaballoo hysterical !
      Ha ! ha ! ha ! ha !
But whether I'm sad or whether I'm glad,
    Mad ! mad ! mad ! mad !

This calls for the resources of a high-class art,
And satisfies my notion of a first-rate part !

                    [*Exit* JULIA.

Enter all the Chorus, hurriedly, and in great excitement.

CHORUS.

Your Highness, there's a party at the door —
    Your Highness, at the door there is a party —
      She says that we expect her,
      But we do not recollect her,
For we never saw her countenance before !

With rage and indignation she is rife,
    Because our welcome wasn't very hearty —
      She's as sulky as a super,
      And she's swearing like a trooper,
O, you never heard such language in your life !

Enter BARONESS VON KRAKENFELDT, *in a fury.*

With fury indescribable I burn !
   With rage I'm nearly ready to explode !
There'll be grief and tribulation when I learn
   To whom this slight unbearable is owed !
For whatever may be due I'll pay it double —
   There'll be terror indescribable and trouble !
With a hurly-burly and a hubble-bubble
   I'll pay you for this pretty episode !

ALL.   Oh, whatever may be due she'll pay it double ! —
   It's very good of her to take the trouble —
   But we don't know what she means by 'hubble-bubble' —
   No doubt it's an expression *à la mode.*

BAR. (*to* LUDWIG).
   Do you know who I am ?
LUD. (*examining her*).   I don't;
   Your countenance I can't fix, my dear.
BAR.   This proves I'm not a sham.

          (*Showing pocket-handkerchief.*)

LUD. (*examining it*).   It won't;
   It only says 'Krakenfeldt, Six,' my dear.
BAR.   Express your grief profound !
LUD.   I shan't !
   This tone I never allow, my love.
BAR.   Rudolph at once produce !
LUD.   I can't;
   He isn't at home just now, my love.
BAR. (*astonished*).   He isn't at home just now !
ALL.   He isn't at home just now,
(*Dancing derisively.*) He has an appointment particular, very —
   You'll find him, I think, in the town cemetery;
   And that's how we come to be making so merry,
      For he isn't at home just now !
BAR.   But bless my heart and soul alive, it's impudence personified !
   I've come here to be matrimonially matrimonified !

Lud.   For any disappointment I am sorry unaffectedly,
        But yesterday that nobleman expired quite unexpectedly
ALL (*sobbing*).   Tol the riddle lol !
                              Tol the riddle lol !
        Tol the riddle, lol the riddle, lol lol lay !
(*Then laughing wildly*.)   Tol the riddle, lol the riddle, lol lol lay !

BAR. But this is most unexpected. He was well enough at a quarter to twelve yesterday.

LUD. Yes. He died at half-past eleven.

BAR. Bless me, how very sudden !

LUD. It *was* sudden.

BAR. But what in the world am I to do ? I was to have been married to him to-day !

ALL (*singing and dancing*).
        For any disappointment we are sorry unaffectedly,
        But yesterday that nobleman expired quite unexpectedly —
                Tol the riddle lol !

BAR. Is this Court Mourning or a Fancy Ball ?

LUD. Well, it's a delicate combination of both effects. It is intended to express inconsolable grief for the decease of the late Duke and ebullient joy at the accession of his successor. *I* am his successor. Permit me to present you to my Grand Duchess. (*Indicating* JULIA.)

BAR. Your Grand Duchess ? Oh, your Highness ! (*Curtseying profoundly*.)

JULIA (*sneering at her*). Old frump !

BAR. Humph ! A recent creation, probably ?

LUD. We were married only half an hour ago.

BAR. Exactly. I thought she seemed new to the position.

JULIA. Ma'am, I don't know who you are, but I flatter myself I can do justice to *any* part on the very shortest notice.

BAR. My dear, under the circumstances you are doing admirably — and you'll improve with practice. It's so difficult to be a lady when one isn't born to it.

JULIA (*in a rage, to* LUDWIG). Am I to stand this ? Am I not to be allowed to pull her to pieces ?

LUD. (*aside to* JULIA). No, no — it isn't Greek. Be a violet, I beg.

BAR. And now tell me all about this distressing circumstance. How did the Grand Duke die?

LUD. He perished nobly — in a Statutory Duel.

BAR. In a Statutory Duel? But that's only a civil death! — and the Act expires to-night, and then he will come to life again!

LUD. Well, no. Anxious to inaugurate my reign by conferring some inestimable boon on my people, I signalized this occasion by reviving the law for another hundred years.

BAR. For another hundred years? Then set the merry joybells ringing! Let festive epithalamia resound through these ancient halls! Cut the satisfying sandwich — broach the exhilarating Marsala — and let us rejoice to-day, if we never rejoice again!

LUD. But I don't think I quite understand. We have already rejoiced a good deal.

BAR. Happy man, you little reck of the extent of the good things you are in for. When you killed Rudolph you adopted all his over-whelming responsibilities. Know then that I, Caroline von Kraken-feldt, am the most overwhelming of them all!

LUD. But stop, stop — I've just been married to somebody else!

JULIA. Yes, ma'am, to somebody else, ma'am! Do you under-stand, ma'am? To somebody else!

BAR. Do keep this young woman quiet: she fidgets me!

JULIA. Fidgets you!

LUD. (*aside to* JULIA). Be a violet — a crushed, despairing violet.

JULIA. Do you suppose I intend to give up a magnificent part without a struggle?

LUD. My good girl, she has the law on her side. Let us both bear this calamity with resignation. If you must struggle, go away and struggle in the seclusion of your chamber.

SONG — BARONESS *and* CHORUS.

Now away to the wedding we go,
So summon the charioteers —
No kind of reluctance they show
To embark on their married careers.

L

Though Julia's emotion may flow
        For the rest of her maidenly years,
ALL.   To the wedding we eagerly go,
            So summon the charioteers !

Now away, etc.

(*All dance off to wedding except* JULIA.)

RECIT. — JULIA.

So ends my dream — so fades my vision fair !
Of hope no gleam — distraction and despair !
My cherished dream, the Ducal throne to share,
That aim supreme has vanished into air !

SONG — JULIA.

Broken every promise plighted —
        All is darksome — all is dreary.
Every new-born hope is blighted !
        Sad and sorry — weak and weary !
Death the Friend or Death the Foe,
Shall I call upon thee ? No !
I will go on living, though
        Sad and sorry — weak and weary !

No, no ! Let the bygone go by !
        No good ever came of repining :
If to-day there are clouds o'er the sky,
        To-morrow the sun may be shining !
            To-morrow, be kind,
            To-morrow, to me !
            With loyalty blind
            I curtsey to thee !
To-day is a day of illusion and sorrow,
So *viva* To-morrow, To-morrow, To-morrow !
        God save you, To-morrow !
        Your servant, To-morrow !
God save you, To-morrow, To-morrow, To-morrow !
                                        [*Exit* JULIA.

Enter ERNEST.

ERN. It's of no use — I can't wait any longer. At any risk I must gratify my urgent desire to know what is going on. (*Looking off.*) Why, what's that ? Surely I see a wedding procession winding down the hill, dressed in my *Troilus and Cressida* costumes ! That's Ludwig's doing ! I see how it is — he found the time hang heavy on his hands, and is amusing himself by getting married to Lisa. No — it can't be to Lisa, for here she is !

Enter LISA.

LISA (*not seeing him*). I really cannot stand seeing my Ludwig married twice in one day to somebody else !

ERN. Lisa !

(LISA *sees him, and stands as if transfixed with horror.*)

ERN. Come here — don't be a little fool — I want you.

(LISA *suddenly turns and bolts off.*)

ERN. Why, what's the matter with the little donkey ? One would think she saw a ghost ! But if he's not marrying Lisa, whom *is* he marrying ? (*Suddenly.*) Julia ! (*Much overcome.*) I see it all ! The scoundrel ! He had to adopt all my responsibilities, and he's shabbily taken advantage of the situation to marry the girl I'm engaged to ! But no, it can't be Julia, for here *she* is !

Enter JULIA.

JULIA (*not seeing him*). I've made up my mind. I won't stand it ! I'll send in my notice at once !

ERN. Julia ! Oh, what a relief !

(JULIA *gazes at him as if transfixed.*)

ERN. Then you've not married Ludwig ? You are still true to me ?

(JULIA *turns and bolts in grotesque horror.*

ERNEST *follows and stops her.*)

ERN. Don't run away ! Listen to me. Are you all crazy ?

JULIA (*in affected terror*). What would you with me, spectre ? Oh, ain't his eyes sepulchral ! And ain't his voice hollow ! What are you doing out of your tomb at this time of day — apparition ?

ERN. I do wish I could make you girls understand that I'm only technically dead, and that physically I'm as much alive as ever I was in my life !

JULIA. Oh, but it's an awful thing to be haunted by a technical bogy !

ERN. You won't be haunted much longer. The law must be on its last legs, and in a few hours I shall come to life again — resume all my social and civil functions, and claim my darling as my blushing bride !

JULIA. Oh — then you haven't heard ?

ERN. My love, I've heard nothing. How could I ? There are no daily papers where I come from.

JULIA. Why, Ludwig challenged Rudolph and won, and now *he's* Grand Duke, and he's revived the law for another century !

ERN. What ! But you're not serious — you're only joking !

JULIA. My good sir, I'm a light-hearted girl, but I don't chaff bogies.

ERN. Well, that's the meanest dodge I ever heard of !

JULIA. Shabby trick, *I* call it.

ERN. But you don't mean to say that you're going to cry off !

JULIA. I really can't afford to wait until your time is up. You know, I've always set my face against long engagements.

ERN. Then defy the law and marry me now. We will fly to your native country, and I'll play broken-English in London as you play broken-German here !

JULIA. No. These legal technicalities cannot be defied. Situated as you are, you have no power to make me your wife. At best you could only make me your widow.

ERN. Then be my widow — my little, dainty, winning, winsome widow !

JULIA. Now what would be the good of that ? Why, you goose, I should marry again within a month !

DUET — ERNEST *and* JULIA.

ERN.　　　If the light of love's lingering ember
　　　　　　Has faded in gloom,
　　　　You cannot neglect, O remember,
　　　　　　A voice from the tomb !

> That stern supernatural diction
> Should act as a solemn restriction,
> Although by a mere legal fiction
> A voice from the tomb !

JULIA (*in affected terror*).

> I own that utterance chills me —
>   It withers my bloom !
> With awful emotion it thrills me —
>   That voice from the tomb !
> Oh, spectre, won't anything lay thee ?
> Though pained to deny or gainsay thee,
> In this case I cannot obey thee,
>   Thou voice from the tomb !

(*Dancing.*)

> So, spectre appalling,
>   I bid you good-day —
> Perhaps you'll be calling
>   When passing this way.
> Your bogydom scorning,
> And all your love-lorning,
> I bid you good-morning,
>   I bid you good-day.

ERN. (*furious*).

> My offer recalling,
>   Your words I obey —
> Your fate is appalling,
>   And full of dismay.
> To pay for this scorning
> I give you fair warning
> I'll haunt you each morning,
>   Each night, and each day !

(*Repeat Ensemble, and exeunt in opposite directions.*)

(*Re-enter the Wedding Procession dancing.*)

CHORUS.

Now bridegroom and bride let us toast
In a magnum of merry champagne —

Let us make of this moment the most,
    We may not be so lucky again.
So drink to our sovereign host
    And his highly intelligent reign —
His health and his bride's let us toast
    In a magnum of merry champagne !

SONG — Baroness *with* Chorus.

I once gave an evening party
    (A sandwich and cut-orange ball),
But my guests had such appetites hearty
    That I couldn't enjoy it, enjoy it at all !
I made a heroic endeavour
    To look unconcerned, but in vain,
And I vow'd that I never — oh never —
    Would ask anybody again !
But there's a distinction decided —
    A difference truly immense —
When the wine that you drink is provided, provided,
    At somebody else's expense.
So bumpers — aye, ever so many —
    The cost we may safely ignore !
For the wine doesn't cost us a penny,
    Tho' it's Pomméry seventy-four !

Chorus.   So bumpers — aye, ever so many — etc.

Come, bumpers — aye, ever so many —
    And then, if you will, many more !
This wine doesn't cost us a penny,
    Tho' it's Pomméry, Pomméry seventy-four !
Old wine is a true panacea
    For ev'ry conceivable ill,
When you cherish the soothing idea
    That somebody else pays the bill !
Old wine is a pleasure that's hollow
    When at your own table you sit,
For you're thinking each mouthful you swallow
    Has cost you, has cost you a threepenny-bit !

So bumpers — aye, ever so many —
And then, if you will, many more !
This wine doesn't cost us a penny,
Tho' it's Pomméry seventy-four !

CHORUS. So, bumpers — aye, ever so many — etc.

(March heard.)

LUD. (*recit.*). Why, who is this approaching,
Upon our joy encroaching ?
Some rascal come a-poaching
Who's heard that wine we're broaching ?

ALL. Who may this be ?
Who may this be ?
Who is he ? Who is he ? Who is he ?

Enter HERALD.

HER. The Prince of Monte Car*lo*,
From Mediterranean water,
Has come here to bestow
On you his beautiful daughter.
They've paid off all they owe,
As every statesman oughter —
That Prince of Monte Car*lo*
And his be-eautiful daughter !

CHORUS. The Prince of Monte Car*lo*, etc.

HER. The Prince of Monte Car*lo*,
Who is so very partickler,
Has heard that you're also
For ceremony a stickler —
Therefore he lets you know
By word of mouth auric'lar —
(That Prince of Monte Car*lo*
Who is so very particklar) —

CHORUS. The Prince of Monte Car*lo*, etc.

HER.   That Prince of Monte Car*lo*,
                    From Mediterranean water,
                Has come here to bestow
                    On you his be-eautiful daughter !

LUD. (*recit.*).   His Highness we know not — nor the locality
                    In which is situate his Principality;
                But, as he guesses by some odd fatality,
                This *is* the shop for cut and dried formality !
                    Let him appear —
                    He'll find that we're
                Remarkable for cut and dried formality.

                    (*Reprise of March. Exit* HERALD.
                        LUDWIG *beckons his Court.*)

LUD.   I have a plan — I'll tell you all the plot of it —
                He wants formality — he shall have a lot of it !

                    (*Whispers to them, through symphony.*)

                Conceal yourselves, and when I give the cue,
                Spring out on him — you all know what to do !

                    (*All conceal themselves behind the draperies that
                            enclose the stage.*)

Pompous March. Enter the PRINCE *and* PRINCESS OF MONTE CARLO,
attended by six theatrical-looking nobles and the Court Costumier.

                    DUET — PRINCE *and* PRINCESS.

PRINCE.   We're rigged out in magnificent array
                    (Our own clothes are much gloomier)
                In costumes which we've hired by the day
                    From a very well-known costumier.

COST. (*bowing*).   *I* am the well-known costumier.

PRINCESS.   With a brilliant staff a Prince should make a show
                    (It's a rule that never varies),
                So we've engaged from the Theatre Monaco
                    Six supernumeraries.

NOBLES.   We're the supernumeraries.

ALL.   At a salary immense,
Quite regardless of expense,
Six supernumeraries !

PRINCE.   They do not speak, for they break our grammar's laws,
And their language is lamentable —
And they never take off their gloves, because
Their nails are not presentable.

NOBLES.   Our nails are not presentable !

PRINCESS.   To account for their shortcomings manifest
We explain, in a whisper bated,
They are wealthy members of the brewing interest
To the Peerage elevated.

NOBLES.   To the Peerage elevated.

ALL.   They're $\Big\}$ very, very rich,
We're
And accordingly, as sich,
To the Peerage elevated.

PRINCE. Well, my dear, here we are at last — just in time to compel Duke Rudolph to fulfil the terms of his marriage contract. Another hour and we should have been too late.

PRINCESS. Yes, papa, and if you hadn't fortunately discovered a means of making an income by honest industry, we should never have got here at all.

PRINCE. Very true. Confined for the last two years within the precincts of my palace by an obdurate bootmaker who held a warrant for my arrest, I devoted my enforced leisure to a study of the doctrine of chances — mainly with the view of ascertaining whether there was the remotest chance of my ever going out for a walk again — and this led to the discovery of a singularly fascinating little round game which I have called Roulette, and by which, in one sitting, I won no less than five thousand francs ! My first act was to pay my bootmaker — my second, to engage a good useful working set of second-hand nobles — and my third, to hurry you off to Pfennig Halbpfennig as fast as a *train de luxe* could carry us !

PRINCESS. Yes, and a pretty job-lot of second-hand nobles you've scraped together !

PRINCE (*doubtfully*). Pretty, you think ? Humph ! I don't know. I should say tol-lol, my love — only tol-lol. They are not wholly satisfactory. There is a certain air of unreality about them — they are not convincing.

COST. But, my goot friend, vhat can you expect for eighteen-pence a day !

PRINCE. Now take this Peer, for instance. What the deuce do you call *him* ?

COST. Him ? Oh, he's a swell — he's the Duke of Riviera.

PRINCE. Oh, he's a Duke, is he ? Well, that's no reason why he should look so confoundedly haughty. (*To Noble.*) Be affable, sir ! (*Noble takes attitude of affability.*) That's better. (*Passing to another.*) Now, who's this with his moustache coming off ?

COST. Vhy, you're Viscount Mentone, ain't you ?

NOBLE. Blest if I know. (*Turning up sword-belt.*) It's wrote here — yes, Viscount Mentone.

COST. Then vhy don't you say so ? 'Old yerself up — you ain't carryin' sandwich boards now. (*Adjusts his moustache.*)

PRINCE. Now, once for all, you Peers — when His Highness arrives, don't stand like sticks, but appear to take an intelligent and sympathetic interest in what is going on. You needn't say anything, but let your gestures be in accordance with the spirit of the conversation. Now take the word from me. Affability ! (*attitude*). Submission ! (*attitude*). Surprise ! (*attitude*). Shame ! (*attitude*). Grief ! (*attitude*). Joy ! (*attitude*). That's better ! You can do it if you like !

PRINCESS. But, papa, where in the world is the Court ? There is positively no one here to receive us ! I can't help feeling that Rudolph wants to get out of it because I'm poor. He's a miserly little wretch — that's what he is.

PRINCE. Well, I shouldn't go so far as to say that. I should rather describe him as an enthusiastic collector of coins — of the realm — and we must not be too hard upon a numismatist if he feels a certain disinclination to part with some of his really very valuable specimens. It's a pretty hobby: I've often thought I should like to collect some coins myself.

PRINCESS. Papa, I'm sure there's some one behind that curtain. I saw it move !

PRINCE. Then no doubt they are coming. Now mind, you Peers — haughty affability combined with a sense of what is due to your exalted ranks, or I'll fine you half a franc each — upon my soul I will !

(*Gong. The curtains fly back and the Court are discovered. They give a wild yell and rush on to the stage dancing wildly, with* PRINCE, PRINCESS, *and Nobles, who are taken by surprise at first, but eventually join in a reckless dance. At the end all fall down exhausted.*)

LUD. There, what do you think of that ? That's our official ceremonial for the reception of visitors of the very highest distinction.

PRINCE (*puzzled*). It's very quaint — very curious indeed. Prettily footed, too. Prettily footed.

LUD. Would you like to see how we say 'good-bye' to visitors of distinction ? That ceremony is also performed with the foot.

PRINCE. Really, this tone — ah, but perhaps you have not completely grasped the situation ?

LUD. Not altogether.

PRINCE. Ah, then I'll give you a lead over. (*Significantly.*) I am the father of the Princess of Monte Carlo. Doesn't that convey any idea to the Grand Ducal mind ?

LUD. (*stolidly*). Nothing definite.

PRINCE (*aside*). H'm — very odd ! Never mind — try again ! (*Aloud.*) This is the daughter of the Prince of Monte Carlo. Do you take ?

LUD. (*still puzzled*). No — not yet. Go on — don't give it up — I daresay it will come presently.

PRINCE. Very odd — never mind — try again. (*With sly significance.*) Twenty years ago ! Little doddle doddle ! *Two* little doddle doddles ! Happy father — hers and yours. Proud mother — yours and hers ! Hah ! *Now* you take ? I see you do ! I see you do !

LUD. Nothing is more annoying than to feel that you're not

equal to the intellectual pressure of the conversation. I wish he'd say something intelligible.

PRINCE. You didn't expect me?

LUD. (*jumping at it*). No, no. I grasp that — thank you very much. (*Shaking hands with him.*) No, I did *not* expect you!

PRINCE. I thought not. But ha! ha! at last I have escaped from my enforced restraint. (*General movement of alarm.*) (*To crowd who are stealing off.*) No, no — you misunderstand me. I mean I've paid my debts!

ALL. Oh! (*They return.*)

PRINCESS (*affectionately*). But, my darling, I'm afraid that even now you don't quite realize who I am! (*Embracing him.*)

BARONESS. Why, you forward little hussy, how dare you? (*Takes her away from* LUDWIG.)

LUD. You mustn't do that, my dear — never in the presence of the Grand Duchess, I beg!

PRINCESS (*weeping*). Oh, papa, he's got a Grand Duchess!

LUD. *A* Grand Duchess! My good girl, I've got three Grand Duchesses!

PRINCESS. Well, I'm sure! Papa, let's go away — this is not a respectable Court.

PRINCE. All these Grand Dukes have their little fancies, my love. This potentate appears to be collecting wives. It's a pretty hobby — I should like to collect a few myself. This (*admiring* BARONESS) is a charming specimen — an antique, I should say — of the early Merovingian period, if I'm not mistaken; and here's another — a Scotch lady, I think (*alluding to* JULIA), and (*alluding to* LISA) a little one thrown in. Two half-quarterns and a makeweight! (*To* LUDWIG.) Have you such a thing as a catalogue of the Museum?

PRINCESS. But I cannot permit Rudolph to keep a museum——

LUD. Rudolph? Get along with you, I'm not Rudolph! Rudolph died yesterday!

PRINCE *and* PRINCESS. What!

LUD. Quite suddenly — of — of — a cardiac affection.

PRINCE *and* PRINCESS. Of a cardiac affection?

LUD. Yes, a pack-of-cardiac affection. He fought a Statutory Duel with me and lost, and I took over all his engagements — including this imperfectly preserved old lady, to whom he has been engaged for the last three weeks.

PRINCESS. Three weeks ! But I've been engaged to him for the last twenty years !

BARONESS, LISA, *and* JULIA. Twenty years !

PRINCE (*aside*). It's all right, my love — they can't get over that. (*Aloud.*) He's yours — take him, and hold him as tight as you can !

PRINCESS. My own ! (*Embracing* LUDWIG.)

LUD. Here's another ! — the fourth in four-and-twenty hours ! Would anybody else like to marry me ? You, ma'am — or you — anybody ! I'm getting used to it !

BARONESS. But let me tell you, ma'am——

JULIA. Why, you impudent little hussy——

LISA. Oh, here's another — here's another ! (*Weeping.*)

PRINCESS. Poor ladies, I'm very sorry for you all; but, you see, I've a prior claim. Come, away we go — there's not a moment to be lost !

CHORUS (*as they dance towards exit*).

> Away to the wedding we'll go
> To summon the charioteers,
> No kind of reluctance we show
> To embark on our married careers —

(*At this moment* RUDOLPH, ERNEST, *and* NOTARY *appear. All kneel in astonishment.*)

RECITATIVE.

RUD., ERN., *and* NOT.

> Forbear ! This may not be !
> Frustrated are your plans !
> With paramount decree
> The Law forbids the banns !

ALL. The Law forbids the banns !

LUD. Not a bit of it ! I've revived the law for another century !

RUD. You didn't revive it ! You couldn't revive it ! You — you are an impostor, sir — a tuppenny rogue, sir ! You — you never were, and in all human probability never will be — Grand Duke of Pfennig Anything !

ALL. What ! ! !

RUD. Never — never, never ! (*Aside.*) Oh, my internal economy !

LUD. That's absurd, you know. I fought the Grand Duke. He drew a King, and I drew an Ace. He perished in inconceivable agonies on the spot. Now, as that's settled, we'll go on with the wedding.

RUD. It — it isn't settled. You — you can't. I — I — (*to* NOTARY). Oh, tell him — tell him ! I can't !

NOT. Well, the fact is, there's been a little mistake here. On reference to the Act that regulates Statutory Duels, I find it is expressly laid down that the Ace shall count invariably as lowest !

ALL. As lowest !

RUD. (*breathlessly*). As lowest — lowest — lowest ! So *you're* the ghoest — ghoest — ghoest ! (*Aside.*) Oh, what *is* the matter with me inside here !

ERN. Well, Julia, as it seems that the law hasn't been revived — and as, consequently, I shall come to life in about three minutes — (*consulting his watch*)——

JULIA. My objection falls to the ground. (*Resignedly.*) Very well !

PRINCESS. And am I to understand that I was on the point of marrying a dead man without knowing it ? (*To* RUDOLPH, *who revives.*) Oh, my love, what a narrow escape I've had !

RUD. Oh — you are the Princess of Monte Carlo, and you've turned up just in time ! Well, you're an attractive little girl, you know, but you're as poor as a rat ! (*They retire up together.*)

LISA. That's all very well, but what is to become of *me* ? (*To* LUDWIG.) If you're a dead man—— (*Clock strikes three.*)

LUD. But I'm not. Time's up — the Act has expired — I've come to life — the parson is still in attendance, and we'll all be married directly.

ALL. Hurrah !

FINALE.

Happy couples, lightly treading,
    Castle chapel will be quite full !
Each shall have a pretty wedding,
    As, of course, is only rightful,
    Though the brides be fair or frightful.

Contradiction little dreading,
 This will be a day delightful —
Each shall have a pretty wedding !
 Such a pretty, pretty wedding !
 Such a pretty wedding !

(*All dance off to get married as the curtain falls.*)

END OF VOLUME ONE

PRINTED BY PURNELL AND SONS, LTD.
PAULTON (SOMERSET) AND LONDON